FEB - - 2012

J GNOV

791.54/3 Jim Henson's The
JIM   storyteller.

$19.95

DATE			

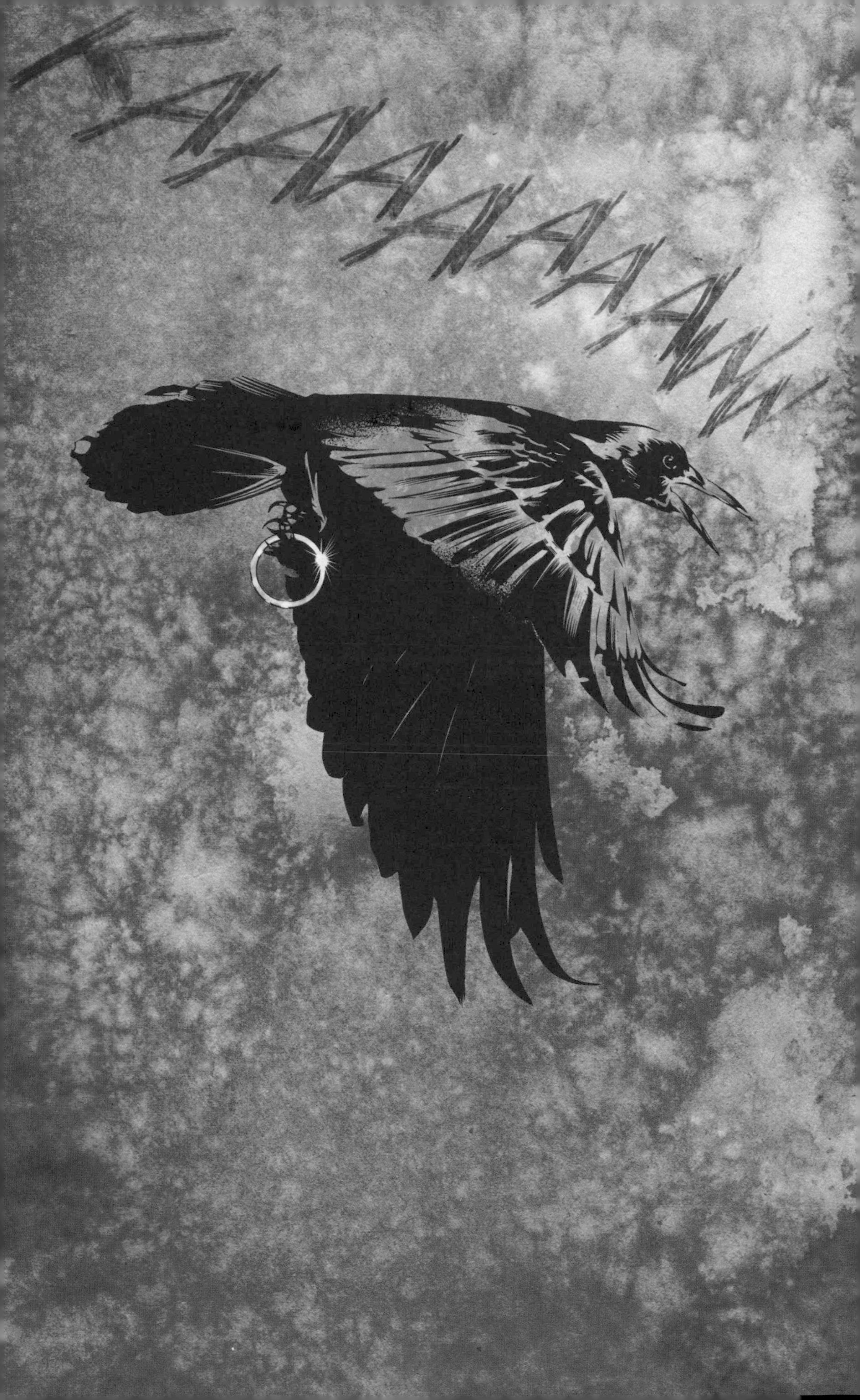
KAAAAAAAWW

When people told
themselves their past
with stories, explained
their present with stories,
foretold the future with
stories, The best place
by the fire was kept for...

Jim Henson's™
THE STORY

TELLER

A fair warning to those
in possession of this tome,
through purchase or
barter, gift or theft...

My stories are old. Some as old as mankind. Some even older. These are tales witnessed by me, or shouted at me, or whispered to me. And now I am telling them to you. And though they be fantastic, and astounding, and astonishing, though they contain amazing events you would not for one moment believe to have actually happened...you would do well to learn lessons from them, one and all.

For therein lies my warning, dear reader: There is truth in fiction. Myths spring from the real and actual, and to the real and actual they inform.
So turn the page, dearies, and marvel at magic, mysteries, cranes and kings. But heed each myth's moral, lest you become the star of your own tragic story...

The Storyteller

The Stories

To Be Told

The Witch Baby - Pg 84

Based on the unproduced *Storyteller* teleplay written by Anthony Minghella, Susan Kodieck, Anne Mountfield

Adapted by Nate Cosby, Roman Cliquet, Adam Street

Rus Wooton • *Designer, Letterer (Select Stories)*
Nate Cosby • *Editor*
Scott Newman • *Production Manager*

Patrick Scherberger, Mike Maihack • *Cover Artists*
Additional illustrations by Dennis Calero, Mitch Gerads, Janet K. Lee, Mike Maihack & David Petersen

Special thanks to Brian Henson, Lisa Henson, Jim Formanek, Nicole Goldman, Karen Falk, Maryanne Pittman, Melissa Segal, Hillary Howell, Jill Peterson, Jennifer Nicholas, Justin Hilden, Mel Caylo, the entire Jim Henson Company team.

PJ Bickett • *CEO*
Mark Smylie • *CCO*
Mike Kennedy • *Publisher*
Stephen Christy • *Editor-in-Chief*

ARCHAIA
NEW STORIES. NEW WORLDS.

Jim Henson
THE JIM HENSON COMPANY

Published by **Archaia**

Archaia Entertainment LLC
1680 Vine Street, Suite 1010
Los Angeles, California, 90028, USA
www.archaia.com

THE STORYTELLER VOLUME ONE. November 2011. FIRST PRINTING

10 9 8 7 6 5 4 3 2 1

ISBN: 1-936393-24-7
ISBN 13: 978-1-936393-24-4

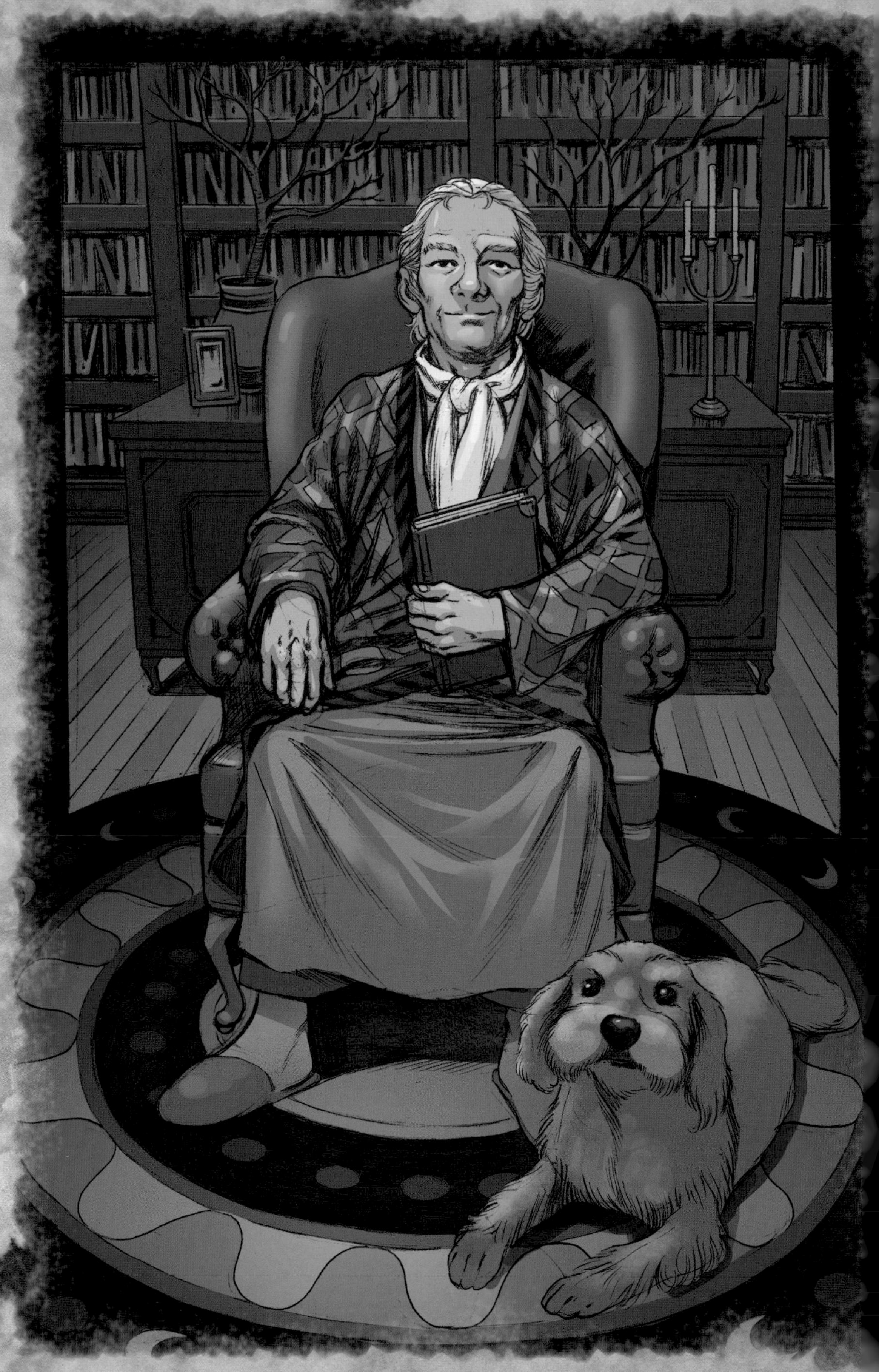

Art by Roman Oliquet & Adam Street

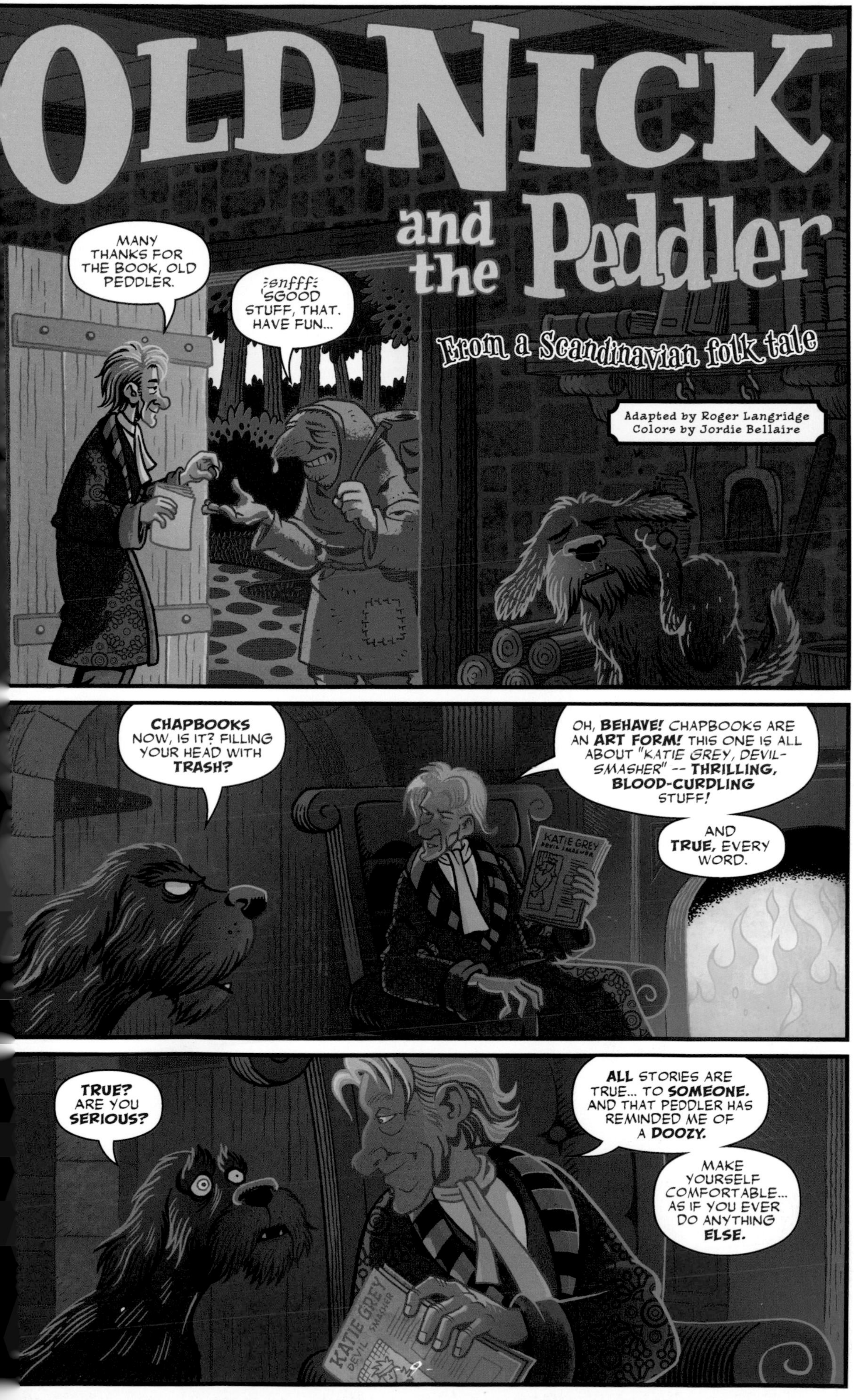
OLD NICK and the Peddler
From a Scandinavian folk tale
Adapted by Roger Langridge
Colors by Jordie Bellaire
MANY THANKS FOR THE BOOK, OLD PEDDLER.
≈snfff≈ 'SGOOD STUFF, THAT. HAVE FUN...
CHAPBOOKS NOW, IS IT? FILLING YOUR HEAD WITH TRASH?
OH, BEHAVE! CHAPBOOKS ARE AN ART FORM! THIS ONE IS ALL ABOUT "KATIE GREY, DEVIL-SMASHER" -- THRILLING, BLOOD-CURDLING STUFF!
AND TRUE, EVERY WORD.
KATIE GREY DEVIL SMASHER
TRUE? ARE YOU SERIOUS?
ALL STORIES ARE TRUE... TO SOMEONE. AND THAT PEDDLER HAS REMINDED ME OF A DOOZY.
MAKE YOURSELF COMFORTABLE... AS IF YOU EVER DO ANYTHING ELSE.
KATIE GREY DEVIL SMASHER

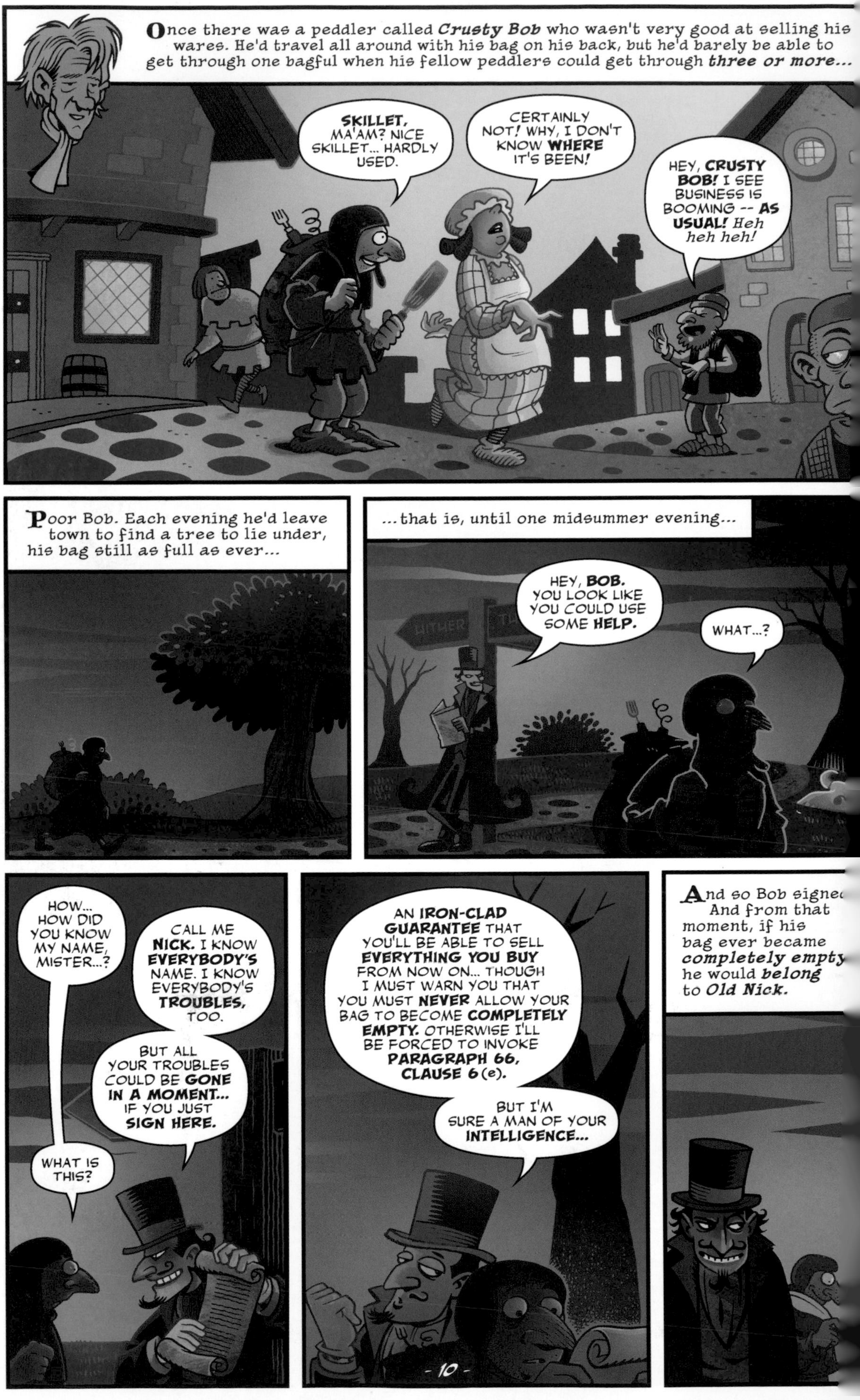
Once there was a peddler called Crusty Bob who wasn't very good at selling his wares. He'd travel all around with his bag on his back, but he'd barely be able to get through one bagful when his fellow peddlers could get through three or more...
SKILLET, MA'AM? NICE SKILLET... HARDLY USED.
CERTAINLY NOT! WHY, I DON'T KNOW WHERE IT'S BEEN!
HEY, CRUSTY BOB! I SEE BUSINESS IS BOOMING -- AS USUAL! Heh heh heh!
Poor Bob. Each evening he'd leave town to find a tree to lie under, his bag still as full as ever...
...that is, until one midsummer evening...
HEY, BOB. YOU LOOK LIKE YOU COULD USE SOME HELP.
WHAT...?
HOW... HOW DID YOU KNOW MY NAME, MISTER...?
CALL ME NICK. I KNOW EVERYBODY'S NAME. I KNOW EVERYBODY'S TROUBLES, TOO.
BUT ALL YOUR TROUBLES COULD BE GONE IN A MOMENT... IF YOU JUST SIGN HERE.
WHAT IS THIS?
AN IRON-CLAD GUARANTEE THAT YOU'LL BE ABLE TO SELL EVERYTHING YOU BUY FROM NOW ON... THOUGH I MUST WARN YOU THAT YOU MUST NEVER ALLOW YOUR BAG TO BECOME COMPLETELY EMPTY. OTHERWISE I'LL BE FORCED TO INVOKE PARAGRAPH 66, CLAUSE 6(e).
BUT I'M SURE A MAN OF YOUR INTELLIGENCE...
And so Bob signe And from that moment, if his bag ever became completely empt he would belong to Old Nick.

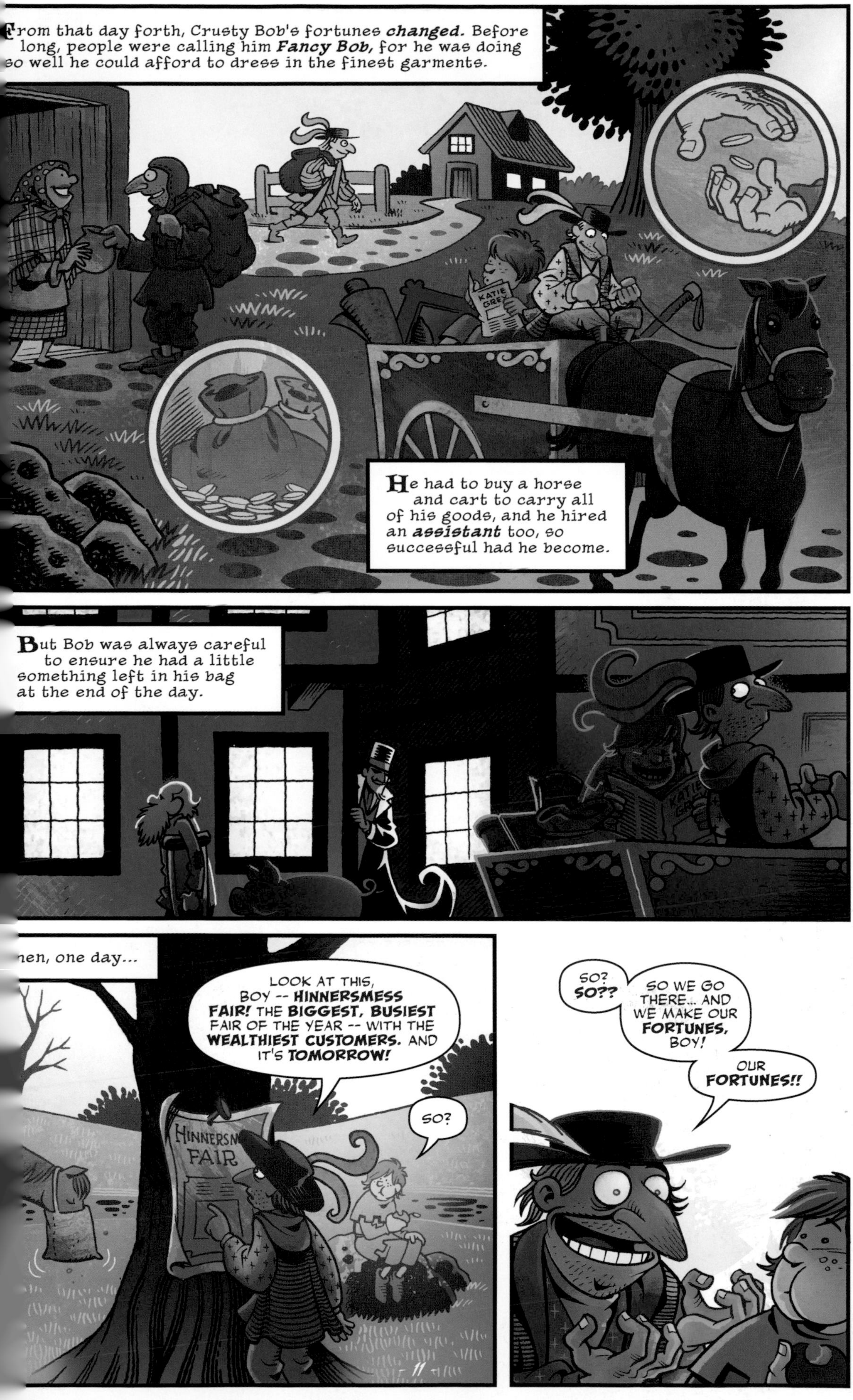
From that day forth, Crusty Bob's fortunes *changed.* Before long, people were calling him *Fancy Bob,* for he was doing so well he could afford to dress in the finest garments.
KATIE GREY
He had to buy a horse and cart to carry all of his goods, and he hired an *assistant* too, so successful had he become.
But Bob was always careful to ensure he had a little something left in his bag at the end of the day.
KATIE GREY
hen, one day...
LOOK AT THIS, BOY -- **HINNERSMESS FAIR!** THE **BIGGEST, BUSIEST** FAIR OF THE YEAR -- WITH THE **WEALTHIEST CUSTOMERS.** AND IT'S **TOMORROW!**
HINNERSM FAIR
SO?
SO? **SO??**
SO WE GO THERE... AND WE MAKE OUR **FORTUNES,** BOY!
OUR **FORTUNES!!**

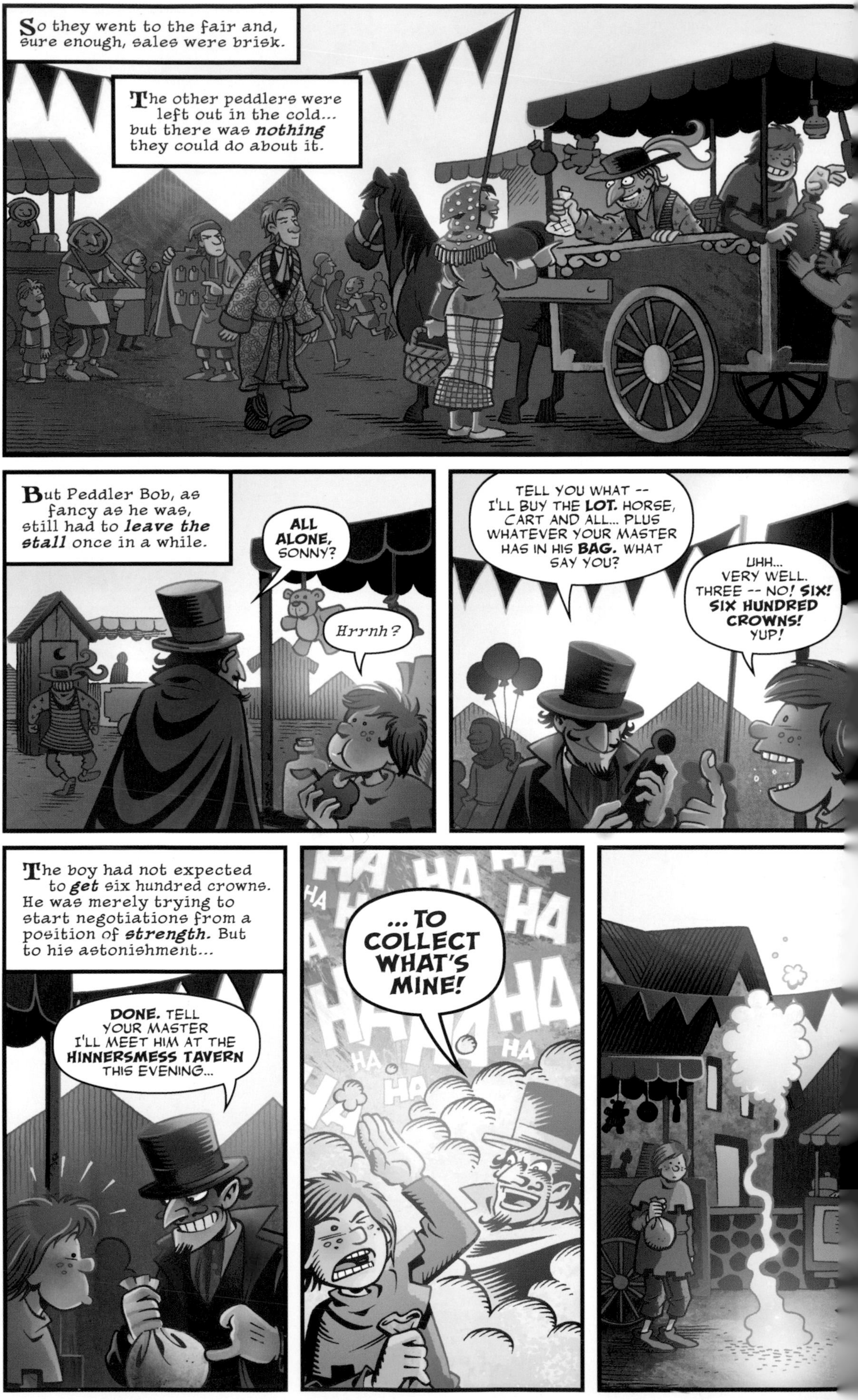
So they went to the fair and, sure enough, sales were brisk.
The other peddlers were left out in the cold... but there was *nothing* they could do about it.
But Peddler Bob, as fancy as he was, still had to *leave the stall* once in a while.
ALL ALONE, SONNY?
Hrrnh?
TELL YOU WHAT -- I'LL BUY THE LOT. HORSE, CART AND ALL... PLUS WHATEVER YOUR MASTER HAS IN HIS BAG. WHAT SAY YOU?
UHH... VERY WELL. THREE -- NO! SIX! SIX HUNDRED CROWNS! YUP!
The boy had not expected to *get* six hundred crowns. He was merely trying to start negotiations from a position of *strength.* But to his astonishment...
DONE. TELL YOUR MASTER I'LL MEET HIM AT THE HINNERSMESS TAVERN THIS EVENING...
HA HA HA HA HA HA HA HA HA HA HA HA
... TO COLLECT WHAT'S MINE!

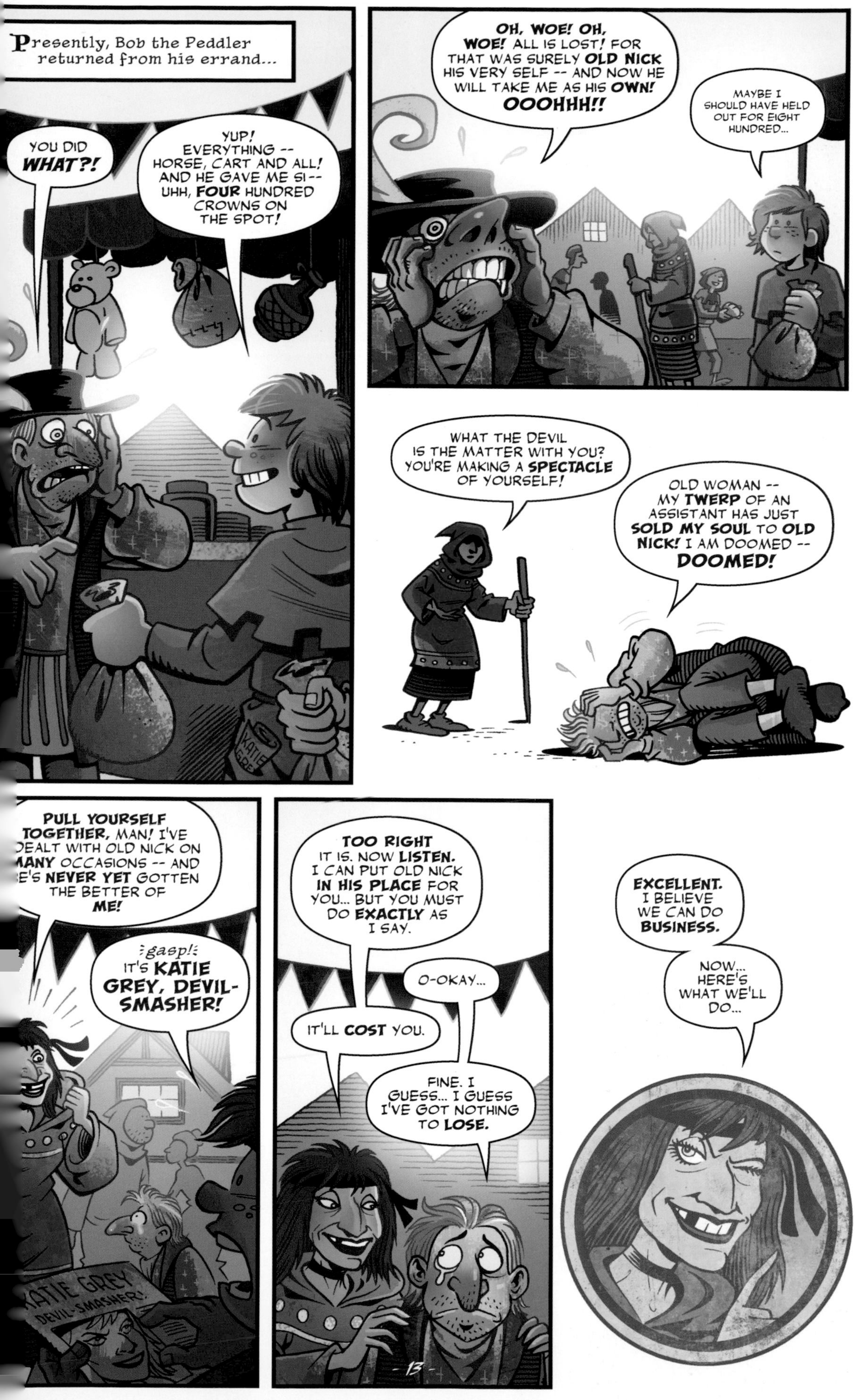

Presently, Bob the Peddler returned from his errand...
YOU DID WHAT?!
YUP! EVERYTHING -- HORSE, CART AND ALL! AND HE GAVE ME SI-- UHH, FOUR HUNDRED CROWNS ON THE SPOT!
KATIE GREY
OH, WOE! OH, WOE! ALL IS LOST! FOR THAT WAS SURELY OLD NICK HIS VERY SELF -- AND NOW HE WILL TAKE ME AS HIS OWN! OOOHHH!!
MAYBE I SHOULD HAVE HELD OUT FOR EIGHT HUNDRED...
WHAT THE DEVIL IS THE MATTER WITH YOU? YOU'RE MAKING A SPECTACLE OF YOURSELF!
OLD WOMAN -- MY TWERP OF AN ASSISTANT HAS JUST SOLD MY SOUL TO OLD NICK! I AM DOOMED -- DOOMED!
PULL YOURSELF TOGETHER, MAN! I'VE DEALT WITH OLD NICK ON MANY OCCASIONS -- AND E'S NEVER YET GOTTEN THE BETTER OF ME!
gasp! IT'S KATIE GREY, DEVIL-SMASHER!
KATIE GREY DEVIL-SMASHER!
TOO RIGHT IT IS. NOW LISTEN. I CAN PUT OLD NICK IN HIS PLACE FOR YOU... BUT YOU MUST DO EXACTLY AS I SAY.
O-OKAY...
IT'LL COST YOU.
FINE. I GUESS... I GUESS I'VE GOT NOTHING TO LOSE.
EXCELLENT. I BELIEVE WE CAN DO BUSINESS.
NOW... HERE'S WHAT WE'LL DO...

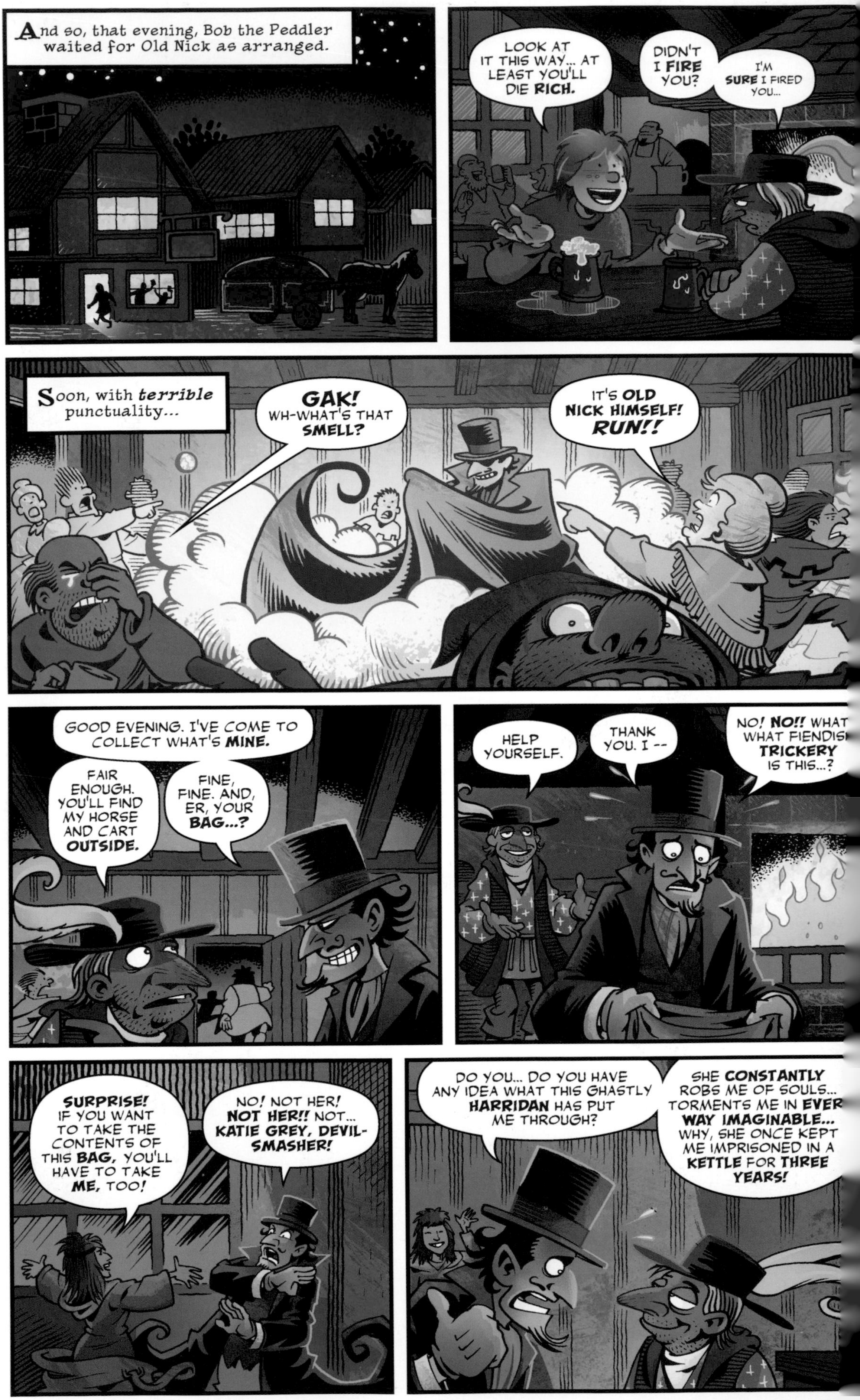
And so, that evening, Bob the Peddler waited for Old Nick as arranged.
LOOK AT IT THIS WAY... AT LEAST YOU'LL DIE RICH.
DIDN'T I FIRE YOU?
I'M SURE I FIRED YOU...
Soon, with terrible punctuality...
GAK! WH-WHAT'S THAT SMELL?
IT'S OLD NICK HIMSELF! RUN!!
GOOD EVENING. I'VE COME TO COLLECT WHAT'S MINE.
FAIR ENOUGH. YOU'LL FIND MY HORSE AND CART OUTSIDE.
FINE, FINE. AND, ER, YOUR BAG...?
HELP YOURSELF.
THANK YOU. I --
NO! NO!! WHAT WHAT FIENDISH TRICKERY IS THIS...?
SURPRISE! IF YOU WANT TO TAKE THE CONTENTS OF THIS BAG, YOU'LL HAVE TO TAKE ME, TOO!
NO! NOT HER! NOT HER!! NOT... KATIE GREY, DEVIL-SMASHER!
DO YOU... DO YOU HAVE ANY IDEA WHAT THIS GHASTLY HARRIDAN HAS PUT ME THROUGH?
SHE CONSTANTLY ROBS ME OF SOULS... TORMENTS ME IN EVERY WAY IMAGINABLE... WHY, SHE ONCE KEPT ME IMPRISONED IN A KETTLE FOR THREE YEARS!

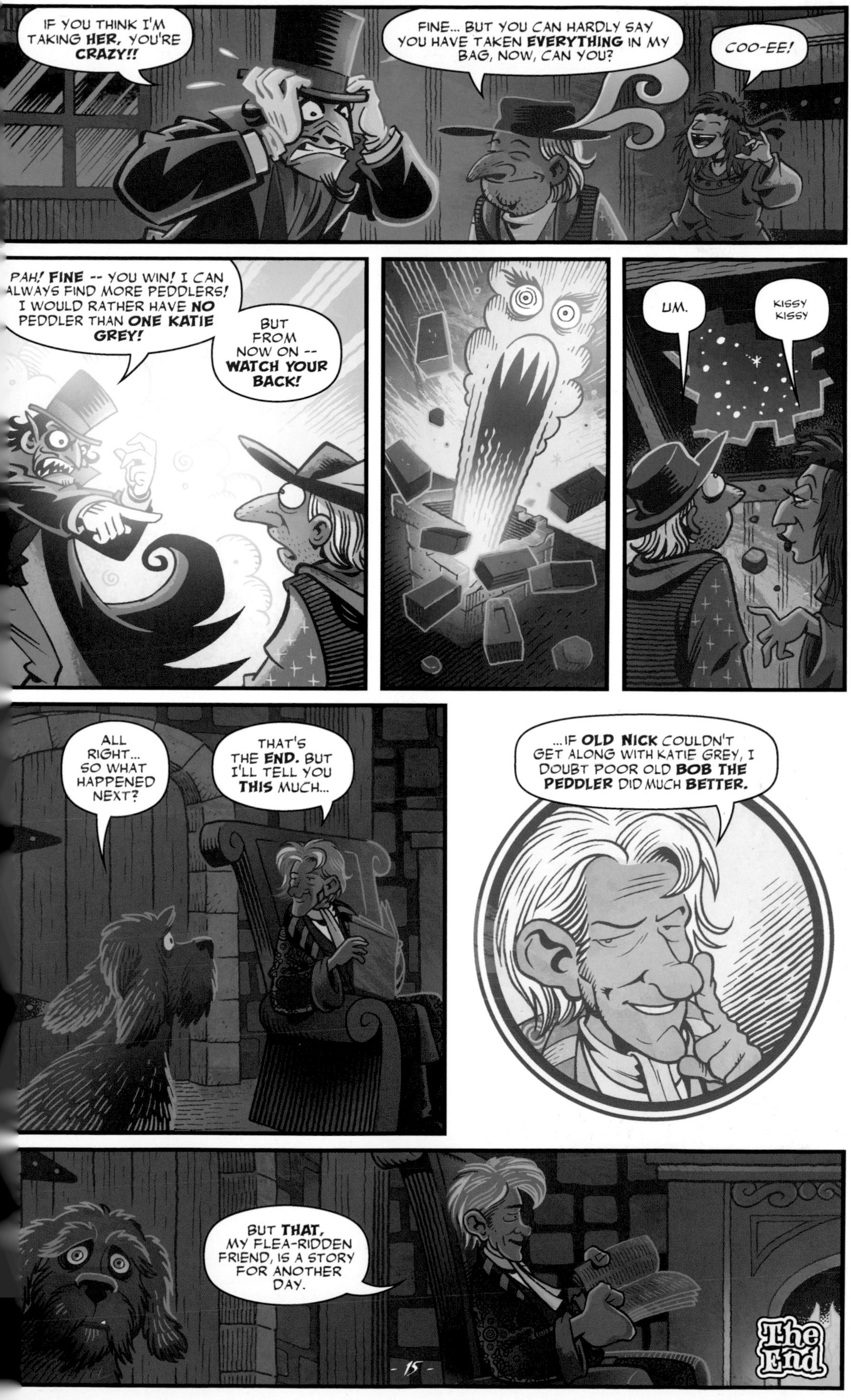
IF YOU THINK I'M TAKING HER, YOU'RE CRAZY!!
FINE... BUT YOU CAN HARDLY SAY YOU HAVE TAKEN EVERYTHING IN MY BAG, NOW, CAN YOU?
COO-EE!
PAH! FINE -- YOU WIN! I CAN ALWAYS FIND MORE PEDDLERS! I WOULD RATHER HAVE NO PEDDLER THAN ONE KATIE GREY!
BUT FROM NOW ON -- WATCH YOUR BACK!
UM.
KISSY KISSY
ALL RIGHT... SO WHAT HAPPENED NEXT?
THAT'S THE END. BUT I'LL TELL YOU THIS MUCH...
...IF OLD NICK COULDN'T GET ALONG WITH KATIE GREY, I DOUBT POOR OLD BOB THE PEDDLER DID MUCH BETTER.
BUT THAT, MY FLEA-RIDDEN FRIEND, IS A STORY FOR ANOTHER DAY.
The End

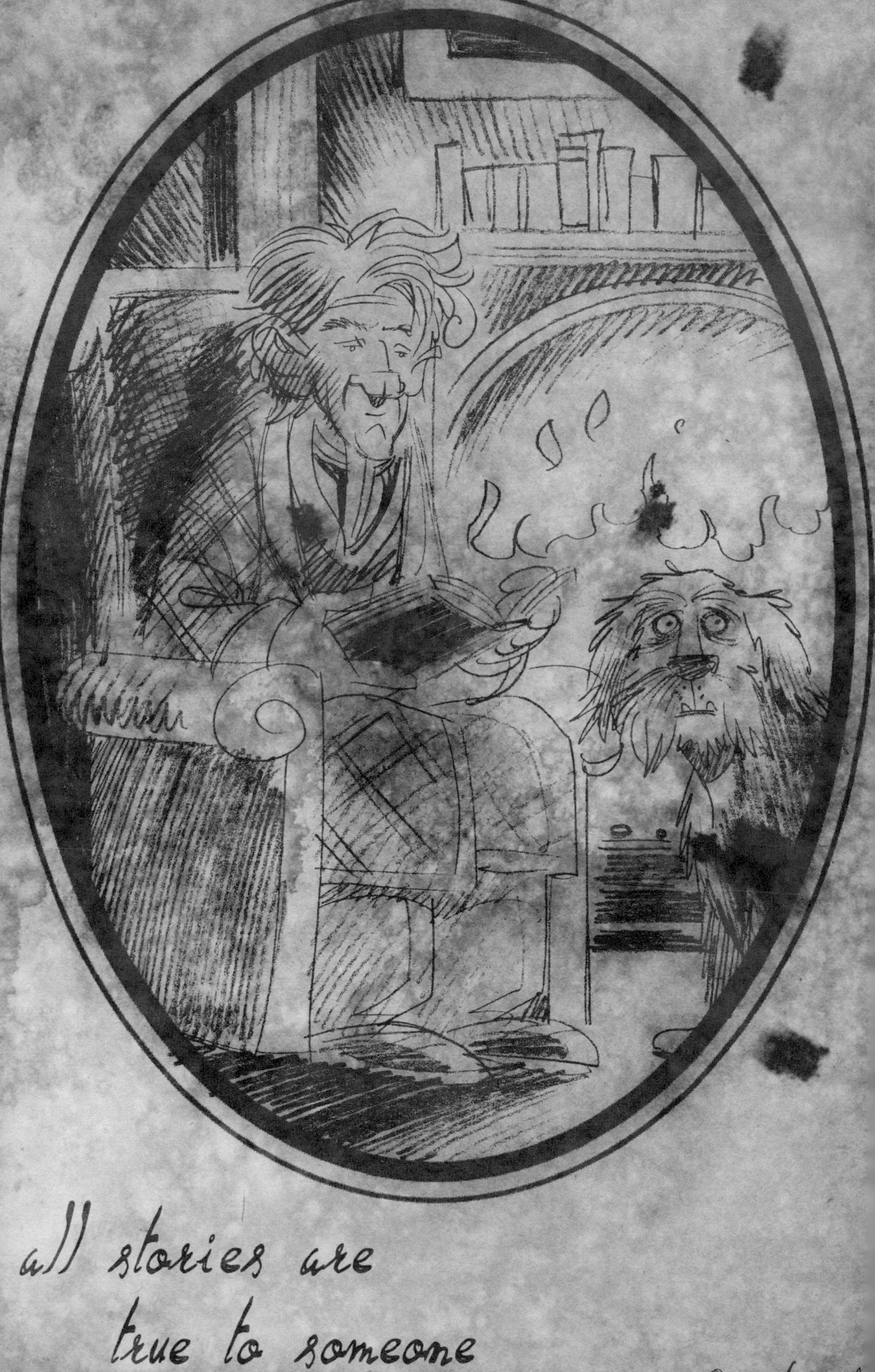

all stories are
true to someone

Art by Roger Langridge

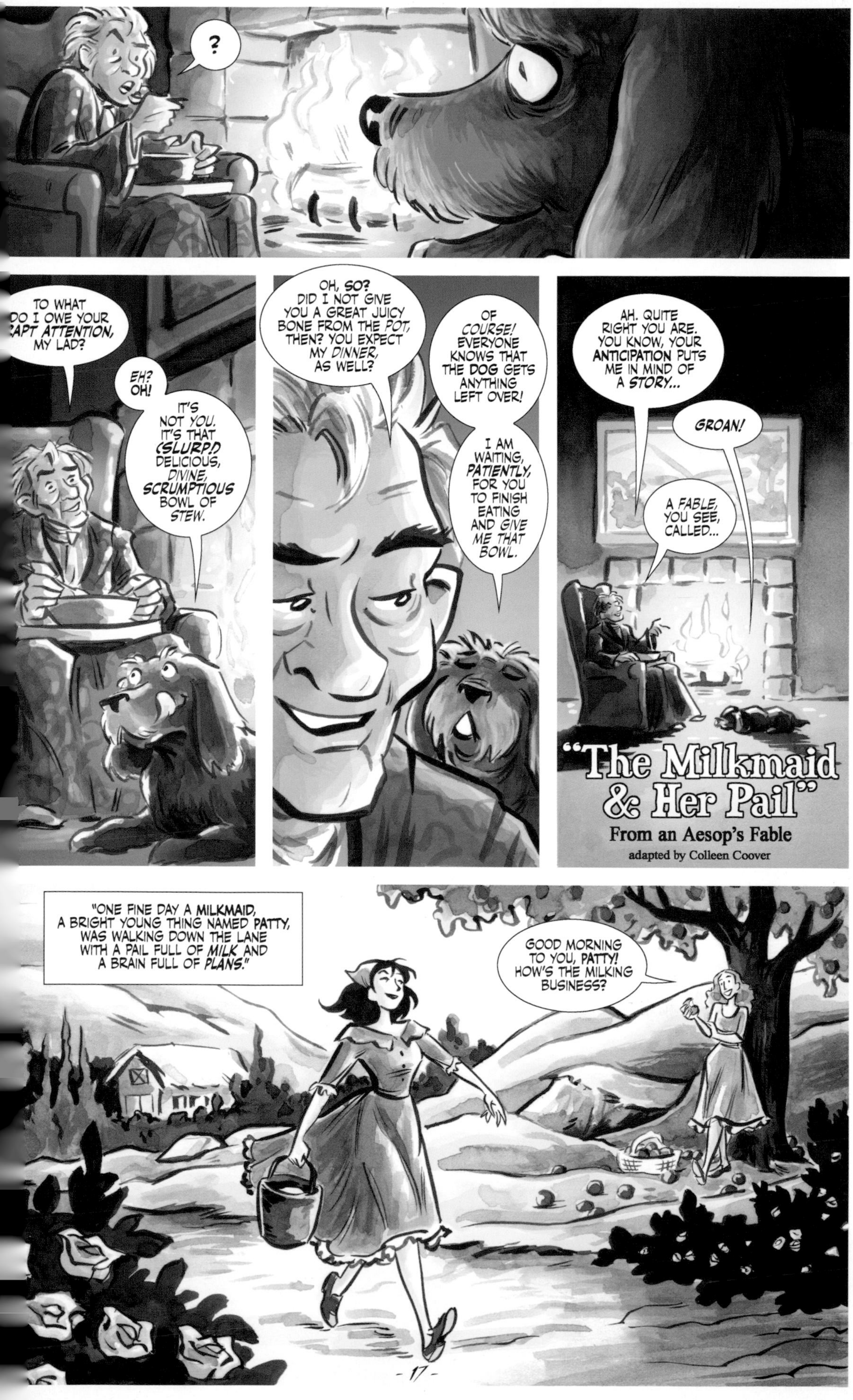
?
TO WHAT DO I OWE YOUR RAPT ATTENTION, MY LAD?
EH? OH!
IT'S NOT YOU. IT'S THAT (SLURP!) DELICIOUS, DIVINE, SCRUMPTIOUS BOWL OF STEW.
OH, SO? DID I NOT GIVE YOU A GREAT JUICY BONE FROM THE POT, THEN? YOU EXPECT MY DINNER, AS WELL?
OF COURSE! EVERYONE KNOWS THAT THE DOG GETS ANYTHING LEFT OVER!
I AM WAITING, PATIENTLY, FOR YOU TO FINISH EATING AND GIVE ME THAT BOWL.
AH. QUITE RIGHT YOU ARE. YOU KNOW, YOUR ANTICIPATION PUTS ME IN MIND OF A STORY...
GROAN!
A FABLE, YOU SEE, CALLED...
"The Milkmaid & Her Pail"
From an Aesop's Fable
adapted by Colleen Coover
"ONE FINE DAY A MILKMAID, A BRIGHT YOUNG THING NAMED PATTY, WAS WALKING DOWN THE LANE WITH A PAIL FULL OF MILK AND A BRAIN FULL OF PLANS."
GOOD MORNING TO YOU, PATTY! HOW'S THE MILKING BUSINESS?

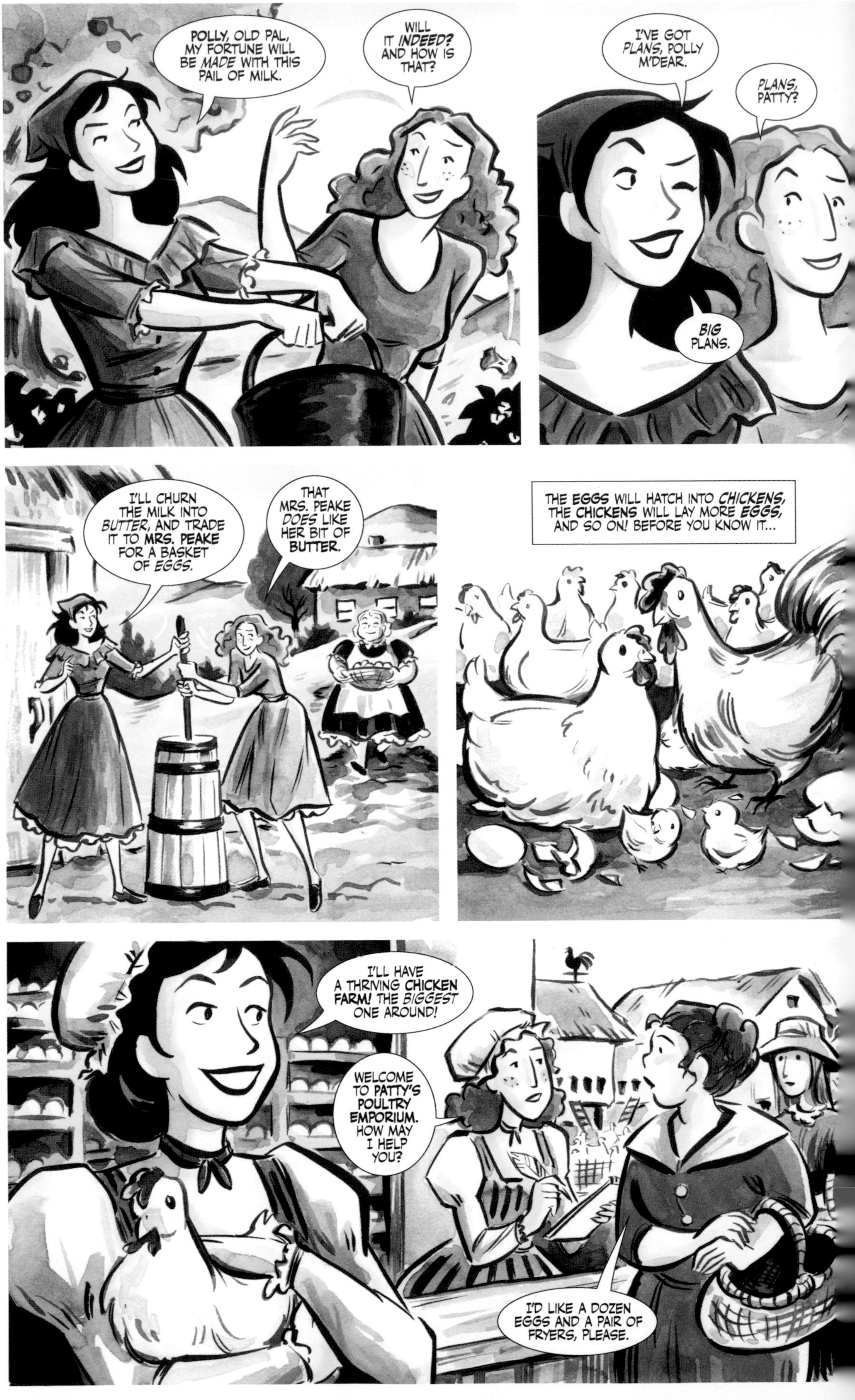
POLLY, OLD PAL, MY FORTUNE WILL BE MADE WITH THIS PAIL OF MILK.
WILL IT INDEED? AND HOW IS THAT?
I'VE GOT PLANS, POLLY M'DEAR.
PLANS, PATTY?
BIG PLANS.
I'LL CHURN THE MILK INTO BUTTER, AND TRADE IT TO MRS. PEAKE FOR A BASKET OF EGGS.
THAT MRS. PEAKE DOES LIKE HER BIT OF BUTTER.
THE EGGS WILL HATCH INTO CHICKENS, THE CHICKENS WILL LAY MORE EGGS, AND SO ON! BEFORE YOU KNOW IT...
I'LL HAVE A THRIVING CHICKEN FARM! THE BIGGEST ONE AROUND!
WELCOME TO PATTY'S POULTRY EMPORIUM. HOW MAY I HELP YOU?
I'D LIKE A DOZEN EGGS AND A PAIR OF FRYERS, PLEASE.

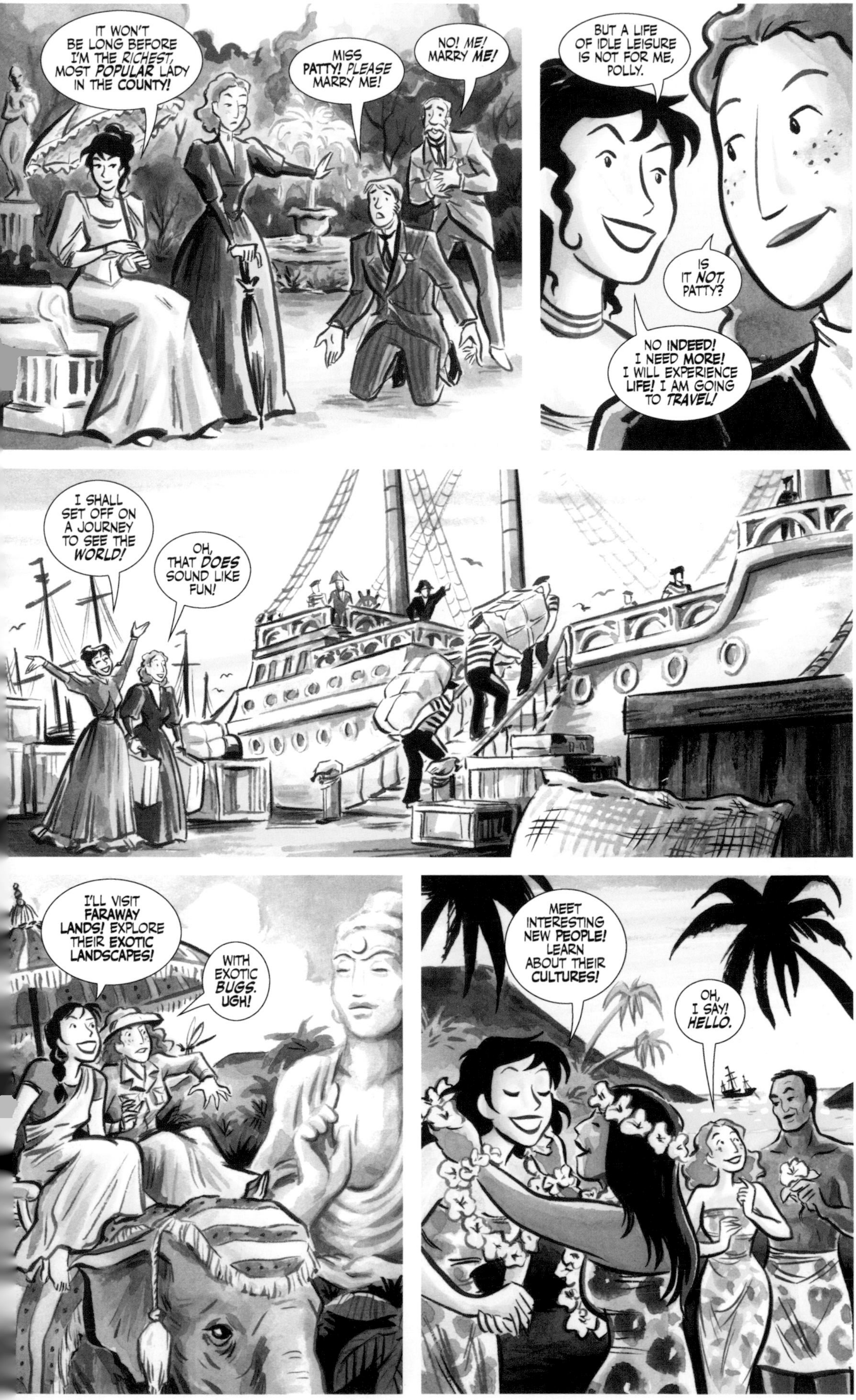
IT WON'T BE LONG BEFORE I'M THE *RICHEST*, MOST **POPULAR** LADY IN THE **COUNTY!**
MISS **PATTY!** *PLEASE* MARRY ME!
NO! *ME!* MARRY ***ME!***
BUT A LIFE OF IDLE LEISURE IS NOT FOR ME, POLLY.
IS IT ***NOT,*** PATTY?
NO **INDEED!** I NEED **MORE!** I WILL EXPERIENCE **LIFE!** I AM GOING TO ***TRAVEL!***
I SHALL SET OFF ON A JOURNEY TO SEE THE ***WORLD!***
OH, THAT ***DOES*** SOUND LIKE FUN!
I'LL VISIT **FARAWAY LANDS!** EXPLORE THEIR **EXOTIC LANDSCAPES!**
WITH EXOTIC ***BUGS.*** **UGH!**
MEET INTERESTING NEW **PEOPLE!** LEARN ABOUT THEIR **CULTURES!**
OH, I SAY! ***HELLO.***

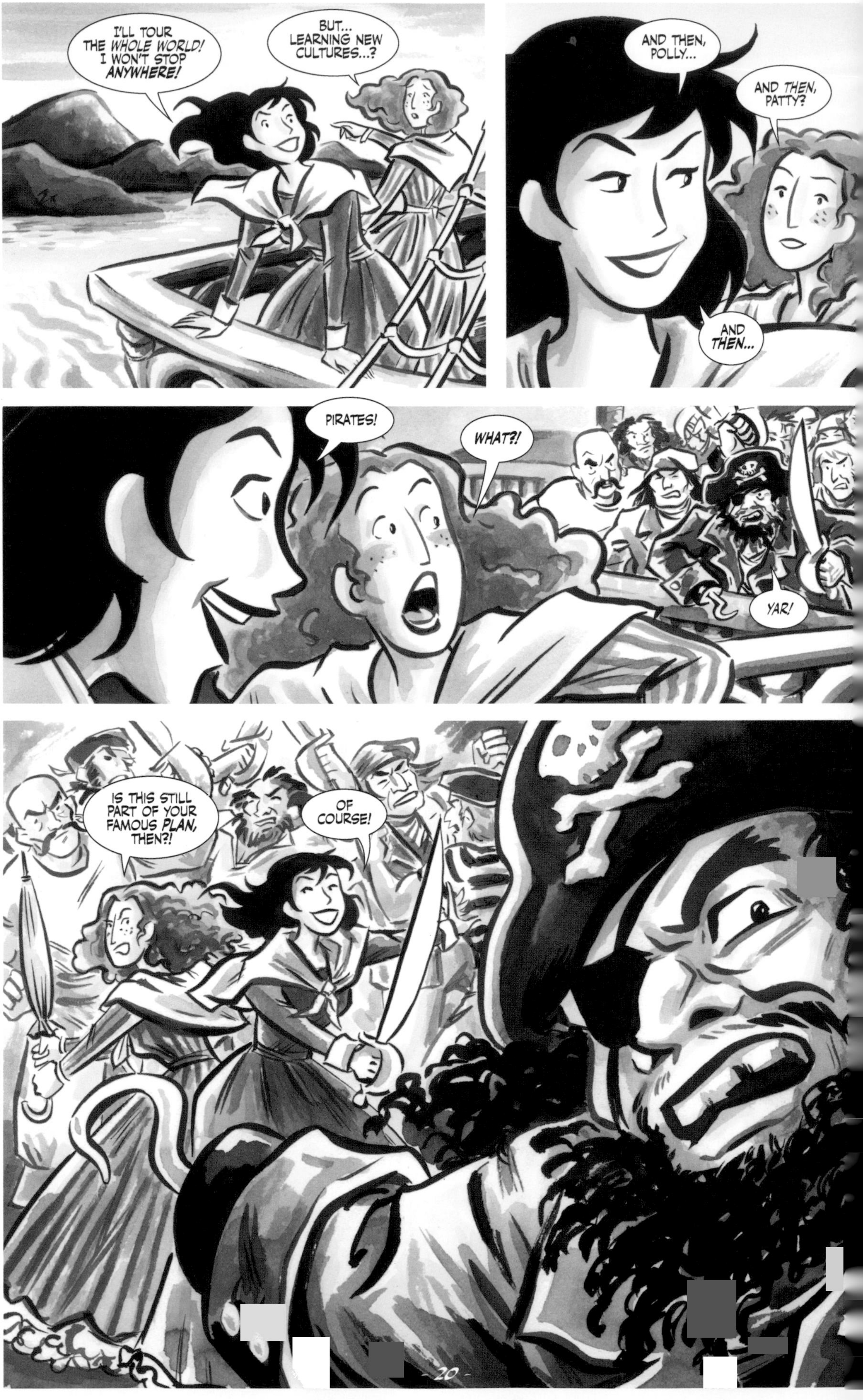
I'LL TOUR THE *WHOLE WORLD!* I WON'T STOP ***ANYWHERE!***
BUT... LEARNING NEW CULTURES...?
AND THEN, POLLY...
AND *THEN,* PATTY?
AND ***THEN...***
PIRATES!
WHAT?!
YAR!
IS THIS STILL PART OF YOUR FAMOUS *PLAN,* THEN?!
OF COURSE!

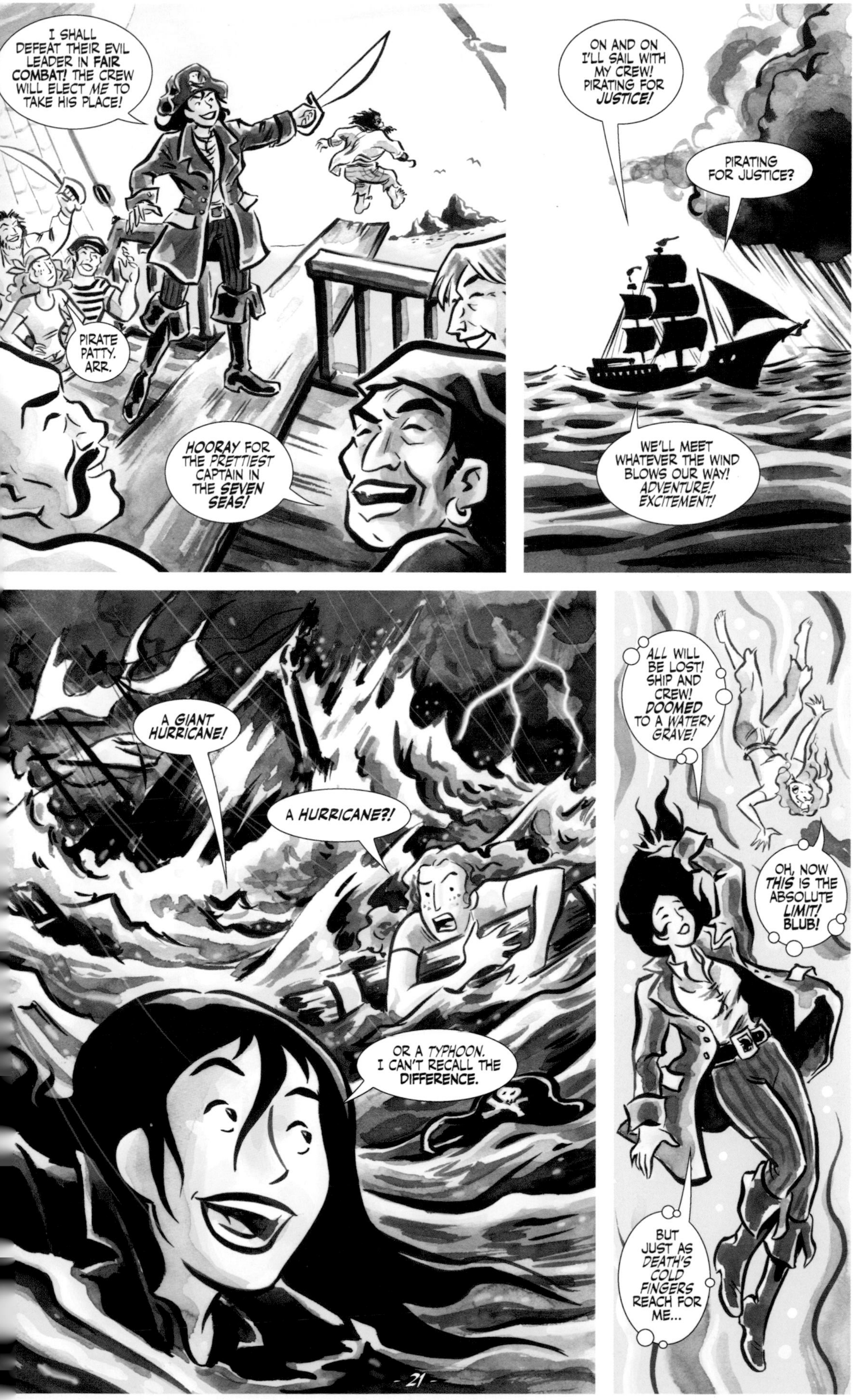
I SHALL DEFEAT THEIR EVIL LEADER IN **FAIR COMBAT!** THE CREW WILL ELECT *ME* TO TAKE HIS PLACE!
PIRATE PATTY. ARR.
HOORAY FOR THE *PRETTIEST* CAPTAIN IN THE ***SEVEN SEAS!***
ON AND ON I'LL SAIL WITH MY CREW! PIRATING FOR ***JUSTICE!***
PIRATING FOR JUSTICE?
WE'LL MEET WHATEVER THE WIND BLOWS OUR WAY! *ADVENTURE! EXCITEMENT!*
A *GIANT* ***HURRICANE!***
A ***HURRICANE?!***
OR A *TYPHOON.* I CAN'T RECALL THE **DIFFERENCE.**
ALL WILL BE LOST! SHIP AND CREW! ***DOOMED*** TO A *WATERY GRAVE!*
OH, NOW ***THIS*** IS THE ABSOLUTE ***LIMIT!*** BLUB!
BUT JUST AS *DEATH'S COLD FINGERS* REACH FOR ME...

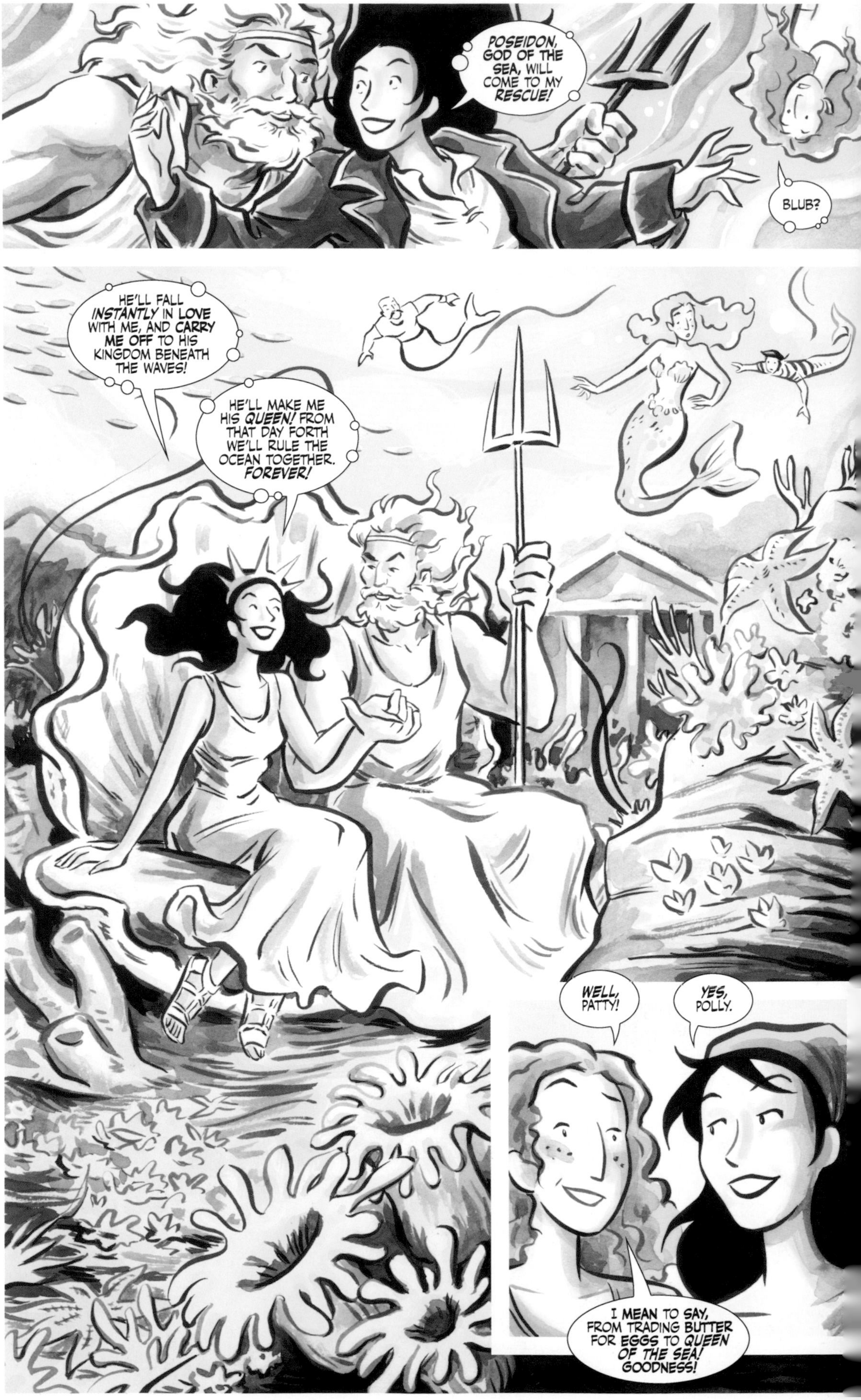
POSEIDON, GOD OF THE SEA, WILL COME TO MY RESCUE!
BLUB?
HE'LL FALL INSTANTLY IN LOVE WITH ME, AND CARRY ME OFF TO HIS KINGDOM BENEATH THE WAVES!
HE'LL MAKE ME HIS QUEEN! FROM THAT DAY FORTH WE'LL RULE THE OCEAN TOGETHER. FOREVER!
WELL, PATTY!
YES, POLLY.
I MEAN TO SAY, FROM TRADING BUTTER FOR EGGS TO QUEEN OF THE SEA! GOODNESS!

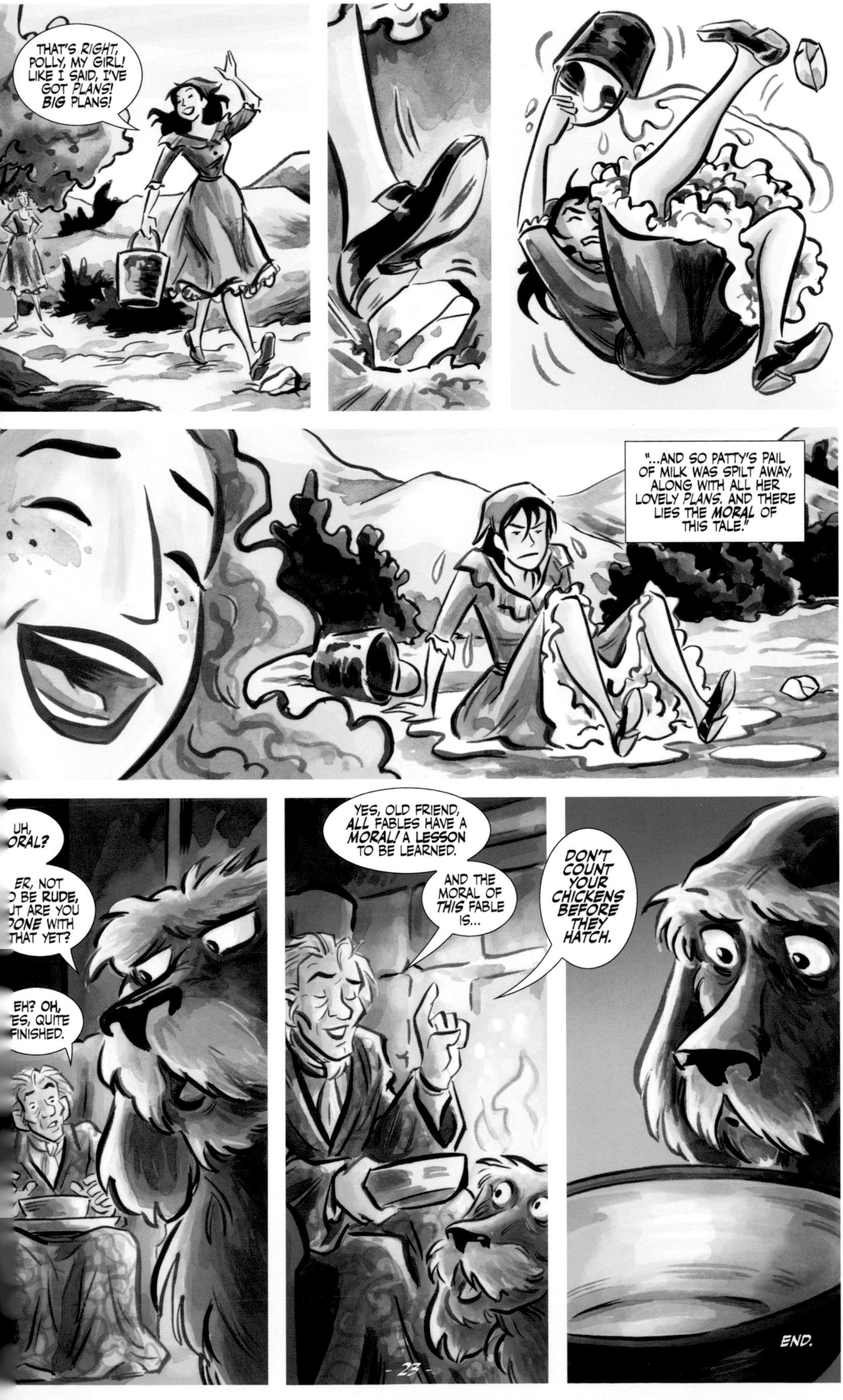
THAT'S *RIGHT*, POLLY, MY GIRL! LIKE I SAID, I'VE GOT *PLANS*! *BIG* PLANS!
"...AND SO PATTY'S PAIL OF MILK WAS SPILT AWAY, ALONG WITH ALL HER LOVELY *PLANS*. AND THERE LIES THE *MORAL* OF THIS TALE."
UH, ORAL?
ER, NOT O BE RUDE, UT ARE YOU ONE WITH THAT YET?
EH? OH, ES, QUITE FINISHED.
YES, OLD FRIEND, ***ALL*** FABLES HAVE A ***MORAL!*** A LESSON TO BE LEARNED.
AND THE MORAL OF *THIS* FABLE IS...
DON'T COUNT YOUR CHICKENS BEFORE THEY HATCH.
END.

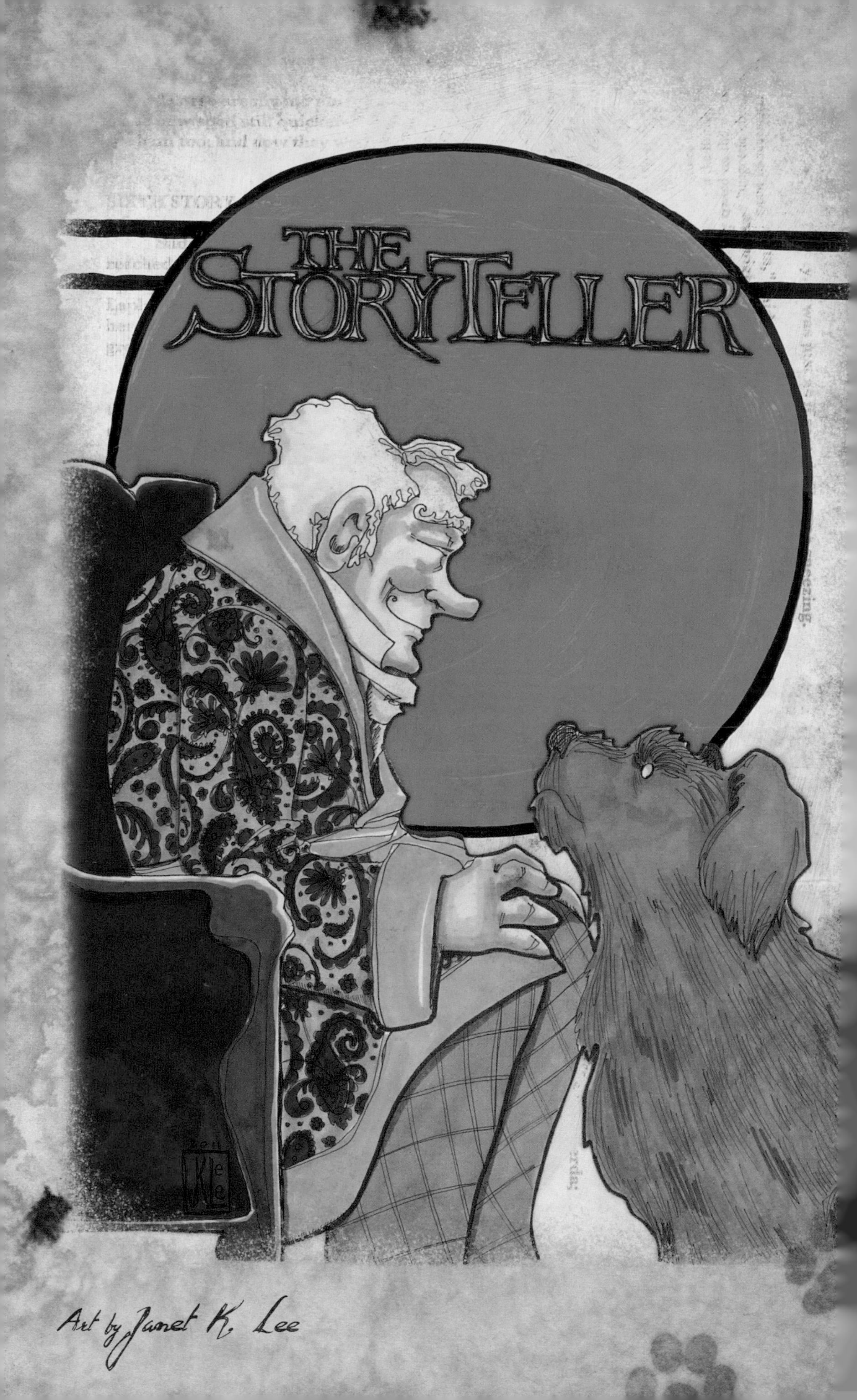
THE STORYTELLER

Art by Janet K. Lee

An Agreement Between Friends

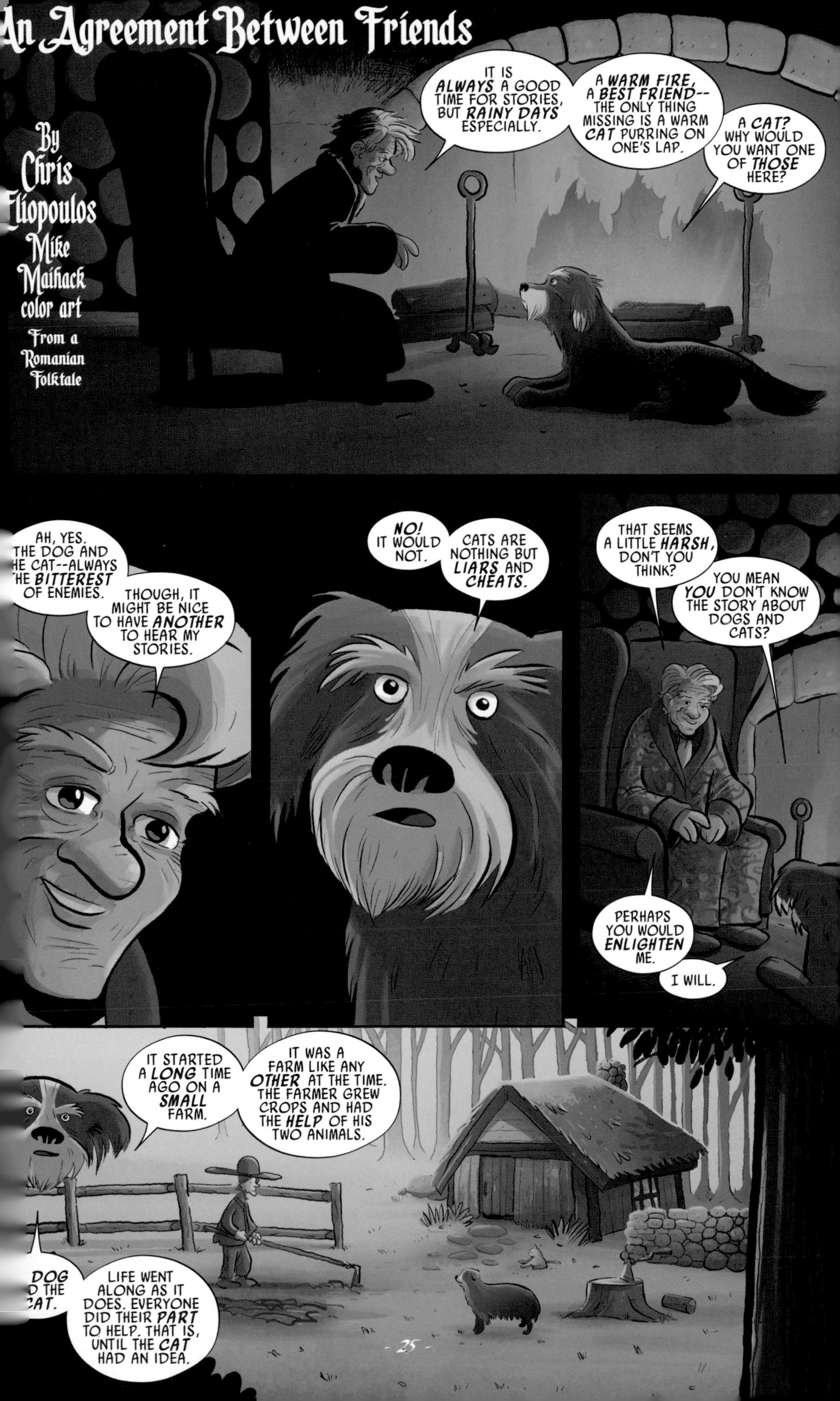

By Chris Eliopoulos
Mike Maihack color art
From a Romanian Folktale
IT IS ALWAYS A GOOD TIME FOR STORIES, BUT RAINY DAYS' ESPECIALLY.
A WARM FIRE, A BEST FRIEND-- THE ONLY THING MISSING IS A WARM CAT PURRING ON ONE'S LAP.
A CAT? WHY WOULD YOU WANT ONE OF THOSE HERE?
AH, YES. THE DOG AND HE CAT--ALWAYS HE BITTEREST OF ENEMIES.
THOUGH, IT MIGHT BE NICE TO HAVE ANOTHER TO HEAR MY STORIES.
NO! IT WOULD NOT.
CATS ARE NOTHING BUT LIARS AND CHEATS.
THAT SEEMS A LITTLE HARSH, DON'T YOU THINK?
YOU MEAN YOU DON'T KNOW THE STORY ABOUT DOGS AND CATS?
PERHAPS YOU WOULD ENLIGHTEN ME.
I WILL.
IT STARTED A LONG TIME AGO ON A SMALL FARM.
IT WAS A FARM LIKE ANY OTHER AT THE TIME. THE FARMER GREW CROPS AND HAD THE HELP OF HIS TWO ANIMALS.
DOG D THE CAT.
LIFE WENT ALONG AS IT DOES. EVERYONE DID THEIR PART TO HELP. THAT IS, UNTIL THE CAT HAD AN IDEA.

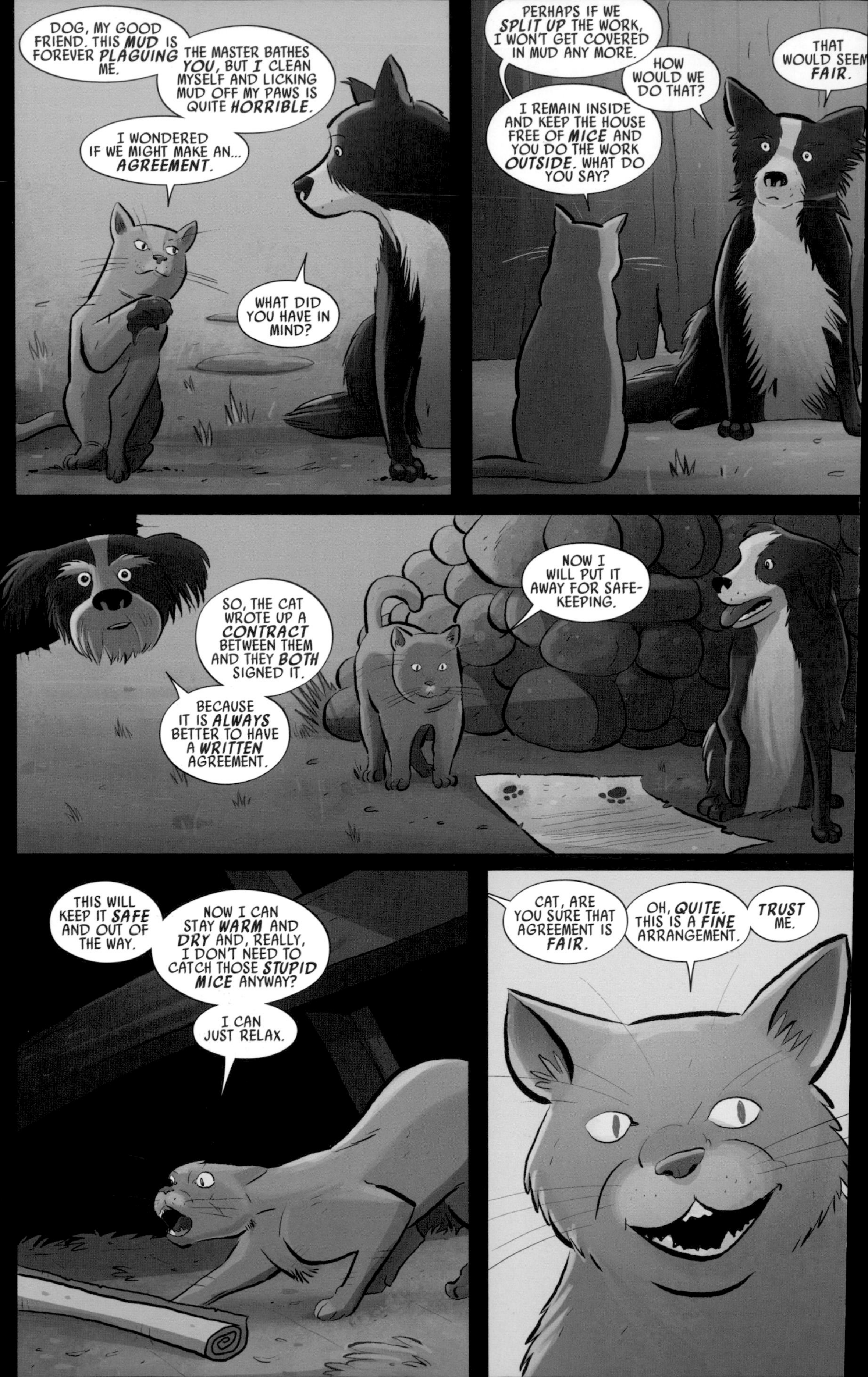

DOG, MY GOOD FRIEND. THIS MUD IS FOREVER PLAGUING ME.
THE MASTER BATHES YOU, BUT I CLEAN MYSELF AND LICKING MUD OFF MY PAWS IS QUITE HORRIBLE.
I WONDERED IF WE MIGHT MAKE AN... AGREEMENT.
WHAT DID YOU HAVE IN MIND?
PERHAPS IF WE SPLIT UP THE WORK, I WON'T GET COVERED IN MUD ANY MORE.
HOW WOULD WE DO THAT?
I REMAIN INSIDE AND KEEP THE HOUSE FREE OF MICE AND YOU DO THE WORK OUTSIDE. WHAT DO YOU SAY?
THAT WOULD SEEM FAIR.
SO, THE CAT WROTE UP A CONTRACT BETWEEN THEM AND THEY BOTH SIGNED IT.
BECAUSE IT IS ALWAYS BETTER TO HAVE A WRITTEN AGREEMENT.
NOW I WILL PUT IT AWAY FOR SAFE-KEEPING.
THIS WILL KEEP IT SAFE AND OUT OF THE WAY.
NOW I CAN STAY WARM AND DRY AND, REALLY, I DON'T NEED TO CATCH THOSE STUPID MICE ANYWAY?
I CAN JUST RELAX.
CAT, ARE YOU SURE THAT AGREEMENT IS FAIR.
OH, QUITE. THIS IS A FINE ARRANGEMENT.
TRUST ME.

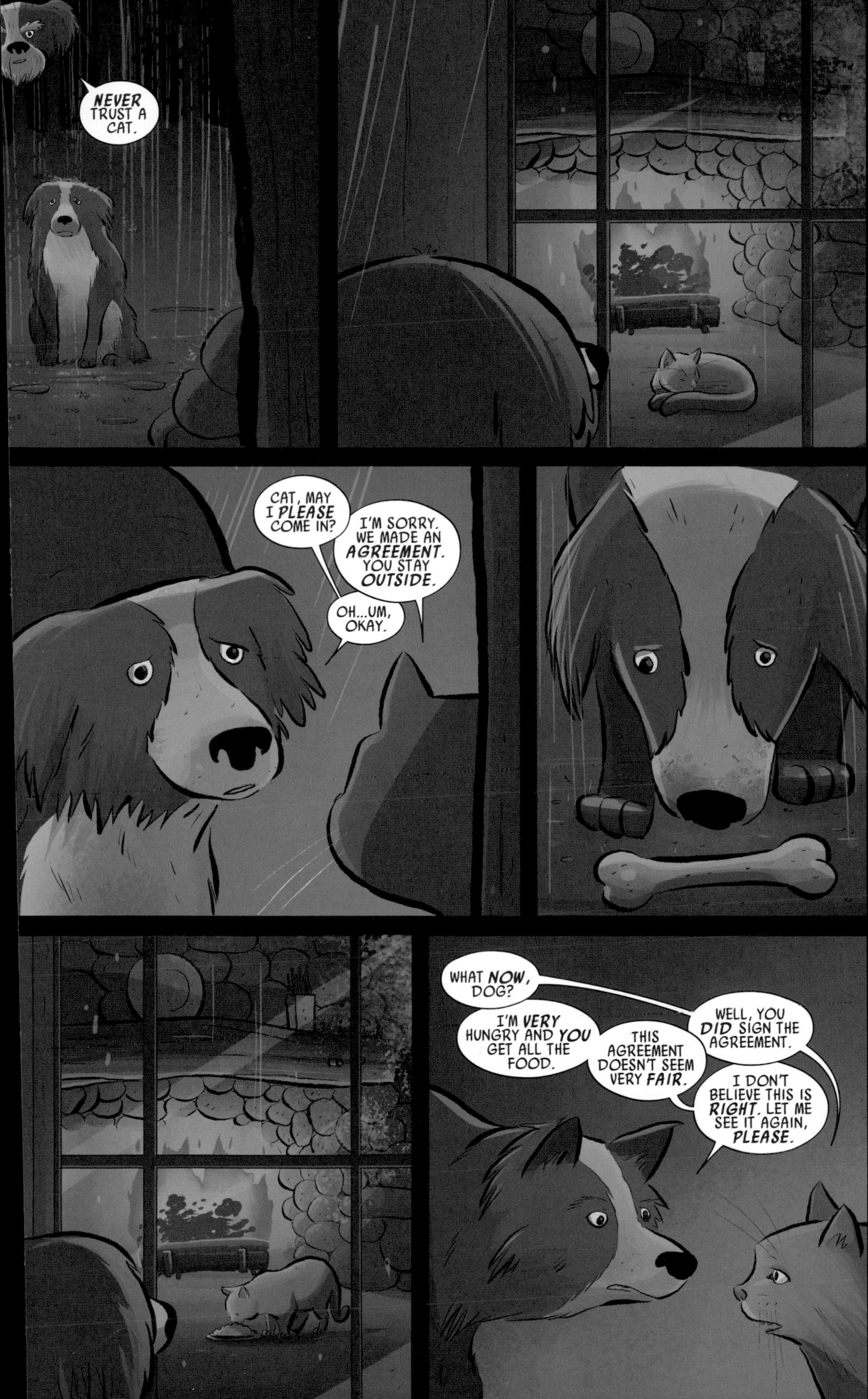
NEVER TRUST A CAT.
CAT, MAY I PLEASE COME IN?
I'M SORRY. WE MADE AN AGREEMENT. YOU STAY OUTSIDE.
OH...UM, OKAY.
WHAT NOW, DOG?
I'M VERY HUNGRY AND YOU GET ALL THE FOOD.
WELL, YOU DID SIGN THE AGREEMENT.
THIS AGREEMENT DOESN'T SEEM VERY FAIR.
I DON'T BELIEVE THIS IS RIGHT. LET ME SEE IT AGAIN, PLEASE.

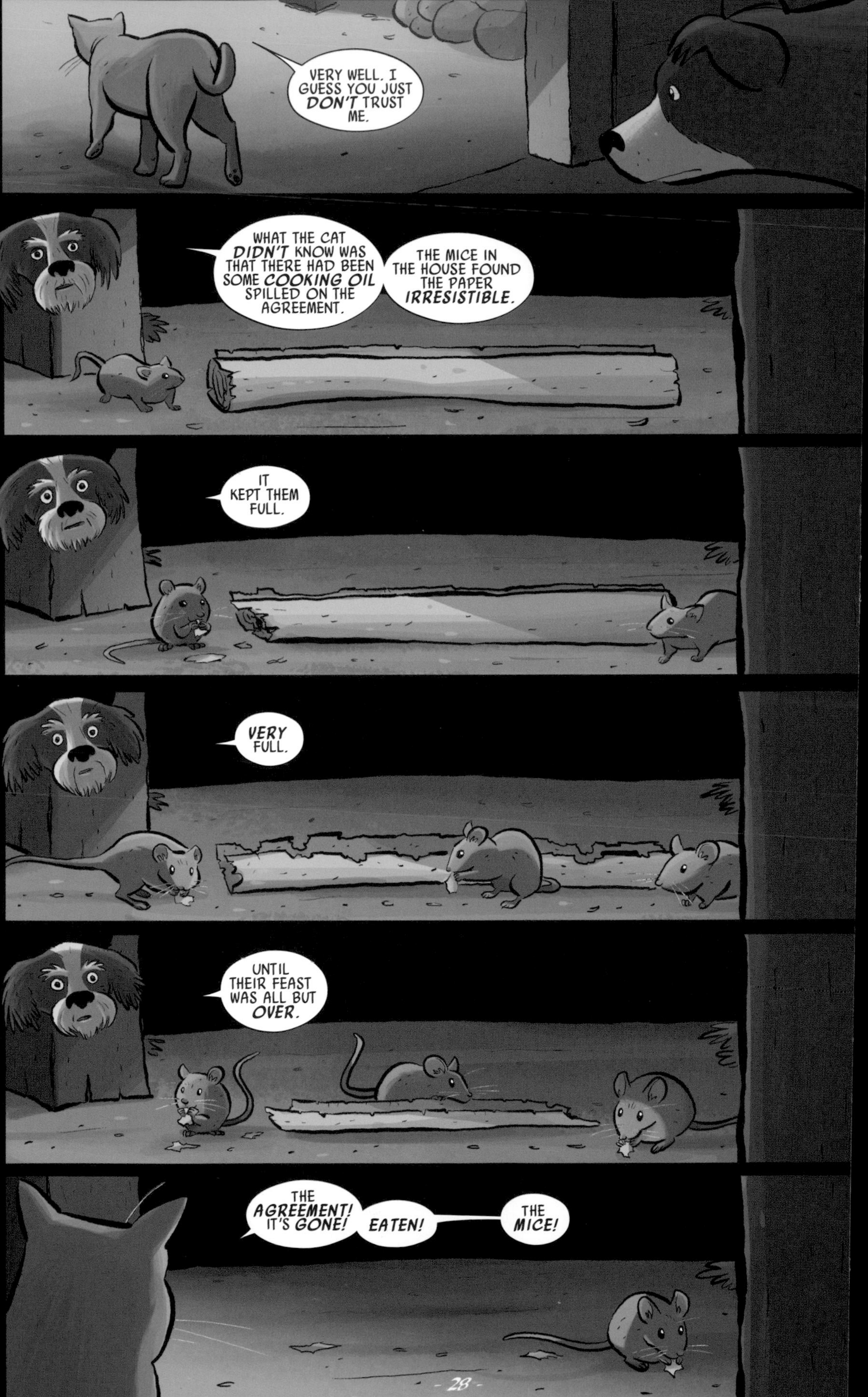
VERY WELL. I GUESS YOU JUST DON'T TRUST ME.
WHAT THE CAT DIDN'T KNOW WAS THAT THERE HAD BEEN SOME COOKING OIL SPILLED ON THE AGREEMENT.
THE MICE IN THE HOUSE FOUND THE PAPER IRRESISTIBLE.
IT KEPT THEM FULL.
VERY FULL.
UNTIL THEIR FEAST WAS ALL BUT OVER.
THE AGREEMENT! IT'S GONE!
EATEN!
THE MICE!

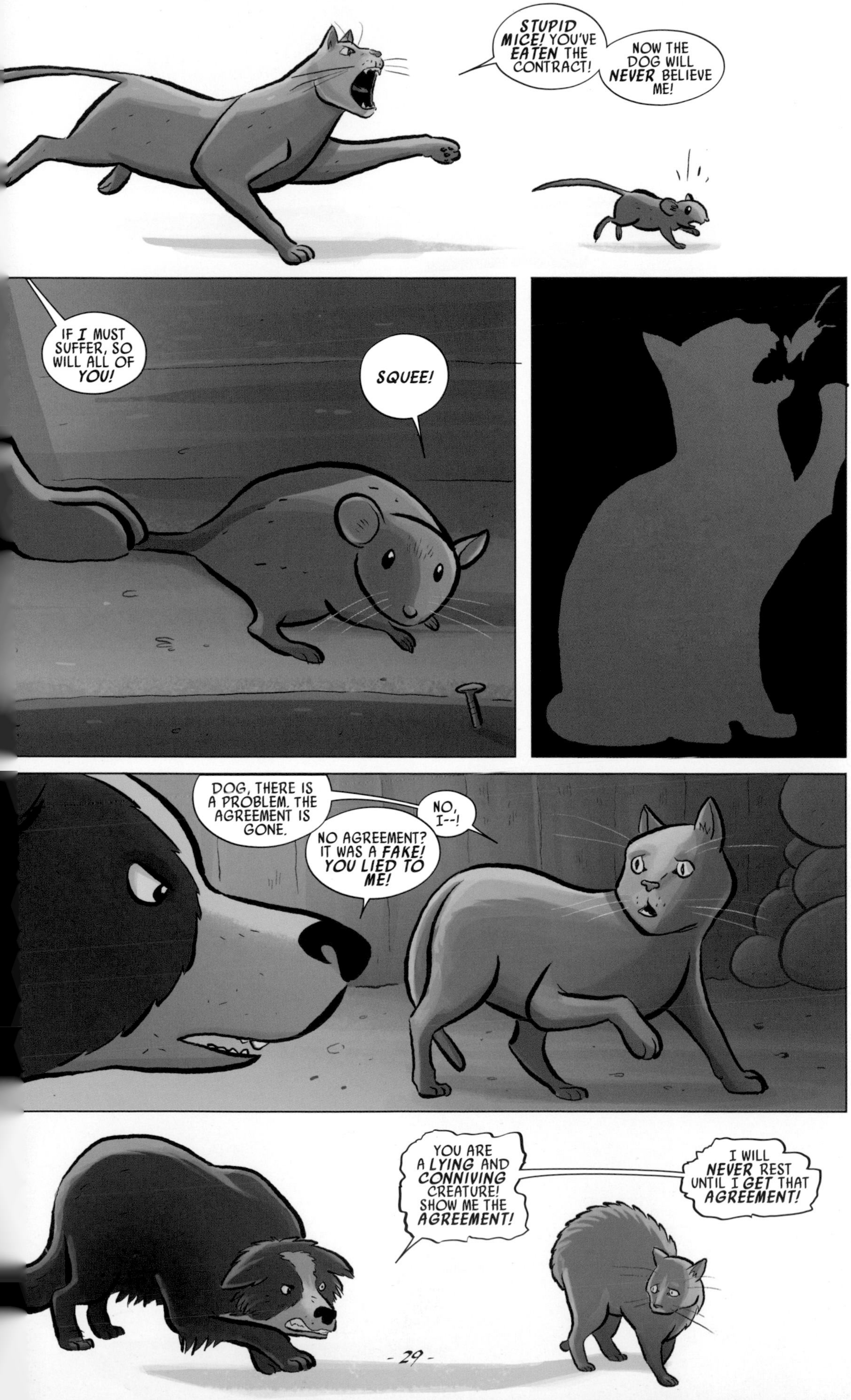
STUPID MICE! YOU'VE EATEN THE CONTRACT!
NOW THE DOG WILL NEVER BELIEVE ME!
IF I MUST SUFFER, SO WILL ALL OF YOU!
SQUEE!
DOG, THERE IS A PROBLEM. THE AGREEMENT IS GONE.
NO AGREEMENT? IT WAS A FAKE! YOU LIED TO ME!
NO, I--!
YOU ARE A LYING AND CONNIVING CREATURE! SHOW ME THE AGREEMENT!
I WILL NEVER REST UNTIL I GET THAT AGREEMENT!

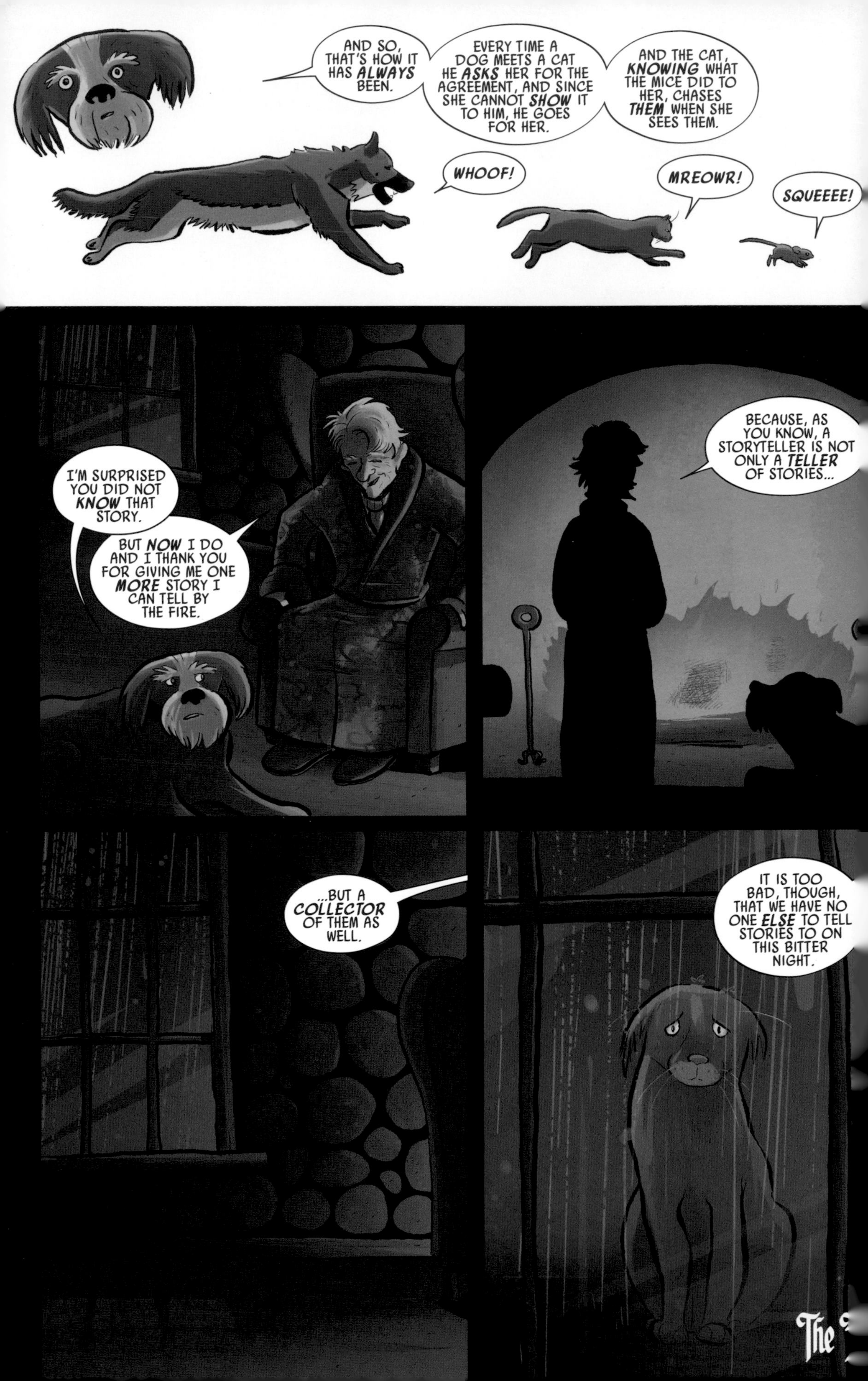
AND SO, THAT'S HOW IT HAS ALWAYS BEEN.
EVERY TIME A DOG MEETS A CAT HE ASKS HER FOR THE AGREEMENT, AND SINCE SHE CANNOT SHOW IT TO HIM, HE GOES FOR HER.
AND THE CAT, KNOWING WHAT THE MICE DID TO HER, CHASES THEM WHEN SHE SEES THEM.
WHOOF!
MREOWR!
SQUEEEE!
I'M SURPRISED YOU DID NOT KNOW THAT STORY.
BUT NOW I DO AND I THANK YOU FOR GIVING ME ONE MORE STORY I CAN TELL BY THE FIRE.
BECAUSE, AS YOU KNOW, A STORYTELLER IS NOT ONLY A TELLER OF STORIES...
...BUT A COLLECTOR OF THEM AS WELL.
IT IS TOO BAD, THOUGH, THAT WE HAVE NO ONE ELSE TO TELL STORIES TO ON THIS BITTER NIGHT.

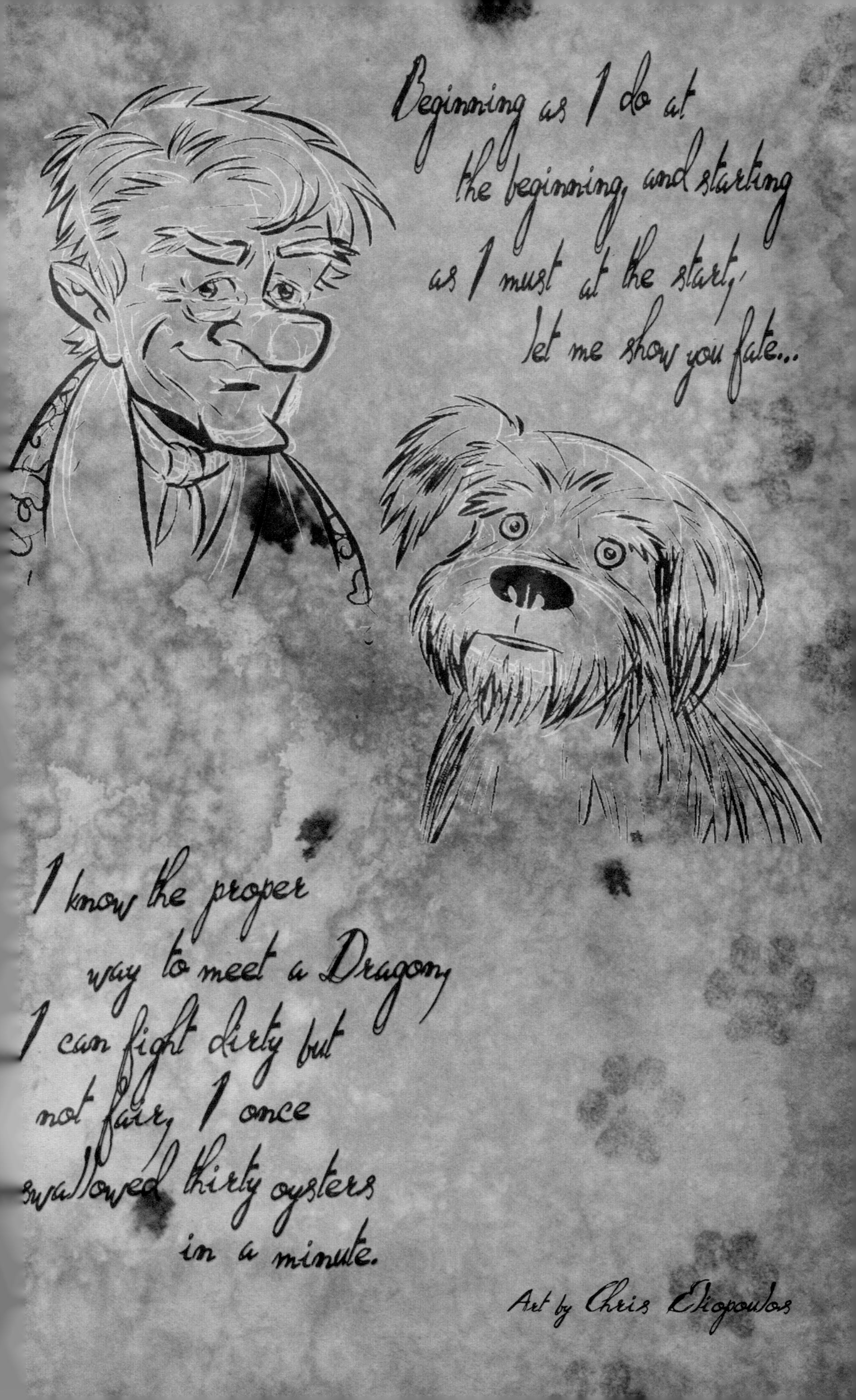
Beginning as I do at the beginning, and starting as I must at the start, let me show you fate...
I know the proper way to meet a Dragon, I can fight dirty but not fair, I once swallowed thirty oysters in a minute.
Art by Chris Eliopoulos

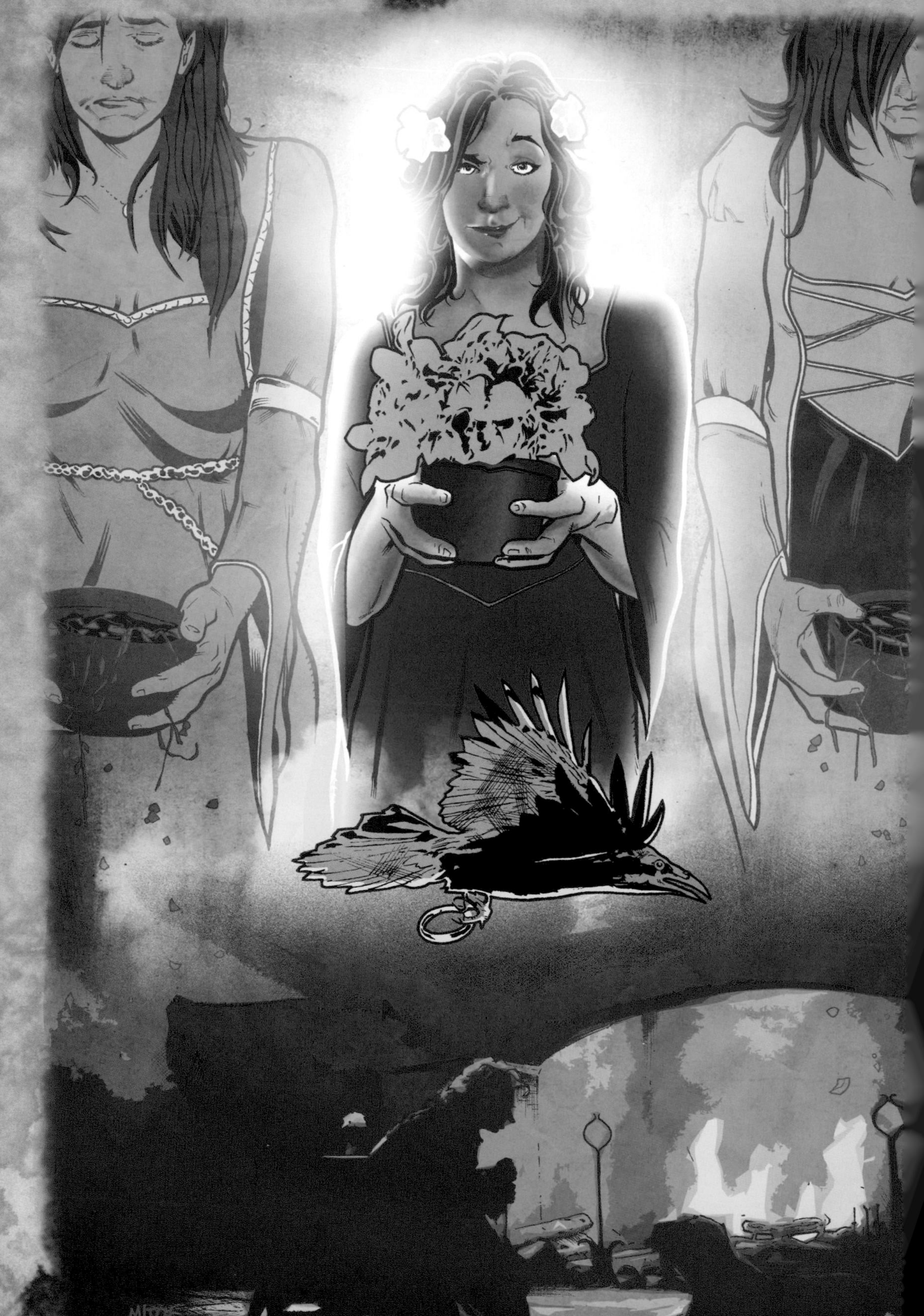
MITCH

Art by Mitch Gerads

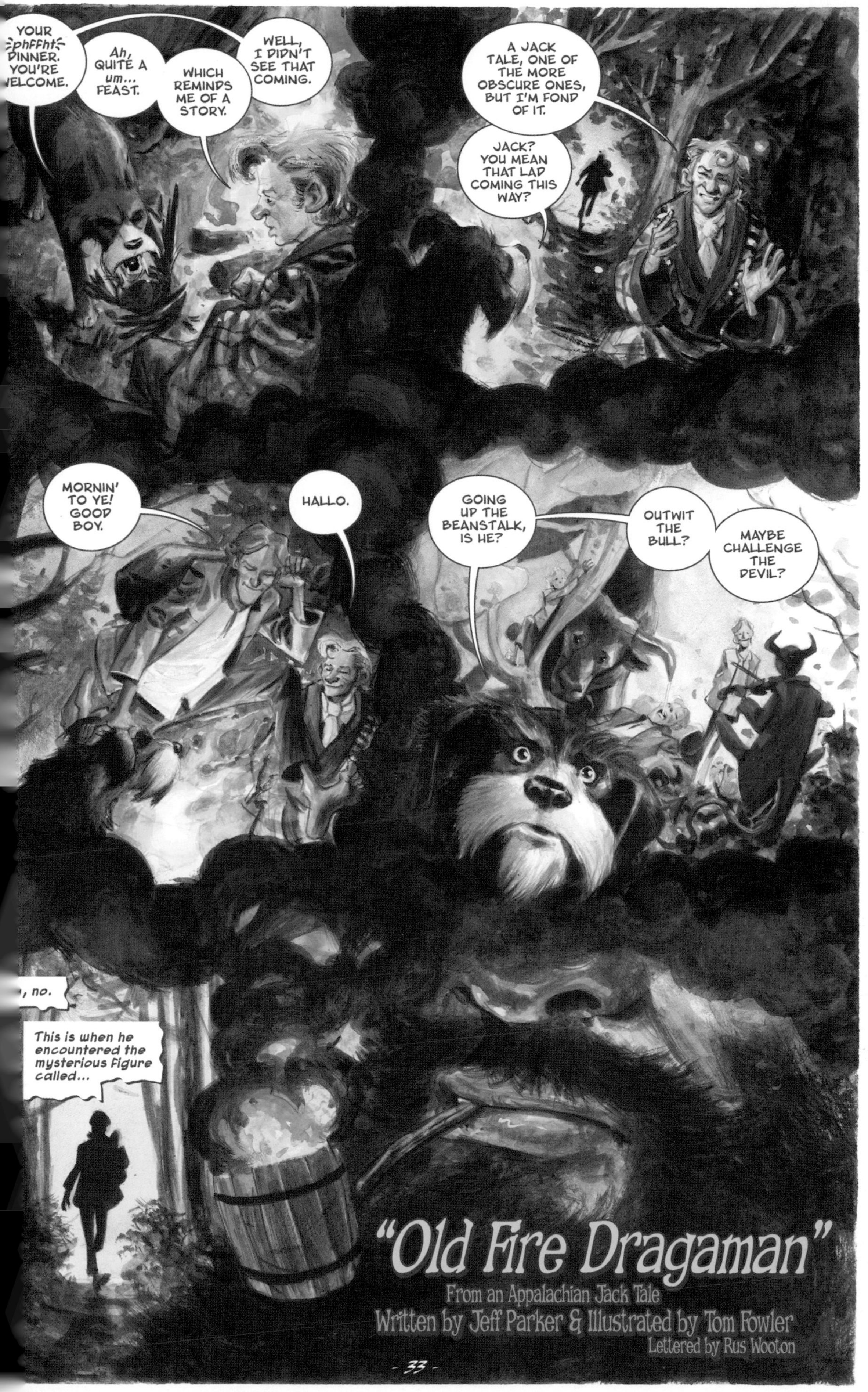

YOUR phffht DINNER. YOU'RE WELCOME.
Ah, QUITE A um... FEAST.
WHICH REMINDS ME OF A STORY.
WELL, I DIDN'T SEE THAT COMING.
A JACK TALE, ONE OF THE MORE OBSCURE ONES, BUT I'M FOND OF IT.
JACK? YOU MEAN THAT LAD COMING THIS WAY?
MORNIN' TO YE! GOOD BOY.
HALLO.
GOING UP THE BEANSTALK, IS HE?
OUTWIT THE BULL?
MAYBE CHALLENGE THE DEVIL?
, no.
This is when he encountered the mysterious figure called...
"Old Fire Dragaman"
From an Appalachian Jack Tale
Written by Jeff Parker & Illustrated by Tom Fowler
Lettered by Rus Wooton

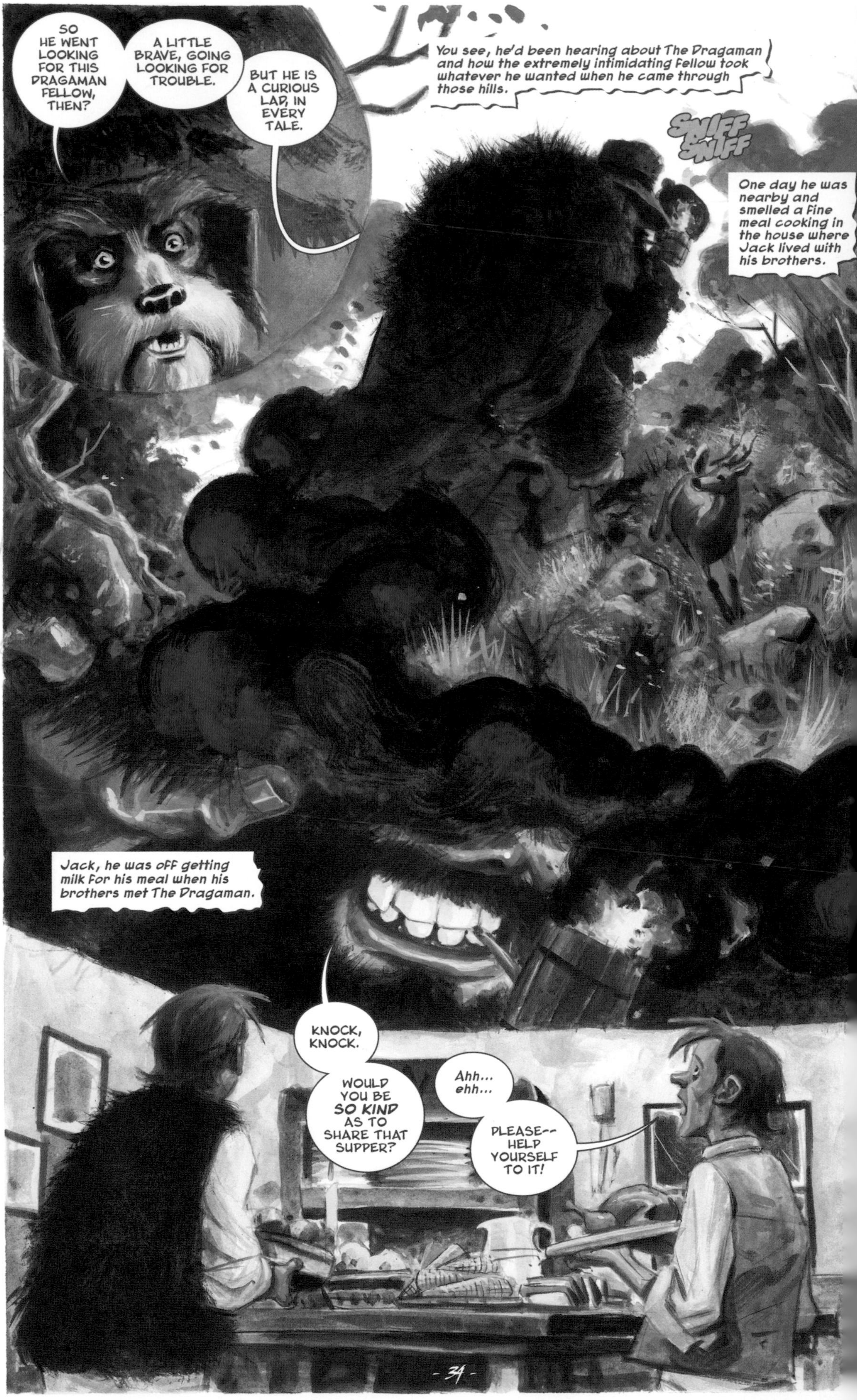
SO HE WENT LOOKING FOR THIS DRAGAMAN FELLOW, THEN?
A LITTLE BRAVE, GOING LOOKING FOR TROUBLE.
BUT HE IS A CURIOUS LAD, IN EVERY TALE.
You see, he'd been hearing about The Dragaman and how the extremely intimidating fellow took whatever he wanted when he came through those hills.
SNIFF SNIFF
One day he was nearby and smelled a fine meal cooking in the house where Jack lived with his brothers.
Jack, he was off getting milk for his meal when his brothers met The Dragaman.
KNOCK, KNOCK.
WOULD YOU BE SO KIND AS TO SHARE THAT SUPPER?
Ahh... ehh...
PLEASE-- HELP YOURSELF TO IT!

The lads had saved up for a feast, but it was gone in less than no time.
CHOMP
GLUR
CRUNCH
GLUK
When Jack returned, he could barely believe the story his older kinfolk told.
WHERE'S OUR FEAST?
THE OLD FIRE DRAGAMAN ET IT ALL!
AND YOU HEROES JUST LET HIM?
YOU'RE FULL OF BIG TALK NOW, JACK-- BUT WAIT 'TIL YOU FACE THE MAN!
YOU'LL LOSE YOUR NERVE AND YOUR HEART! THEY'LL END UP IN HIS STOMACH, TOO!
COWARDS Y' ARE! WITH A GOOD HICKORY I'LL LEARN HIM ABOUT TAKING OUR THINGS!
THEN I'LL DRAG HIM THROUGH THE HILLS AS AN EXAMPLE!
So boastful Jack started out to find the thieving giant. His hungry belly spoke louder than his brothers' words of warning!

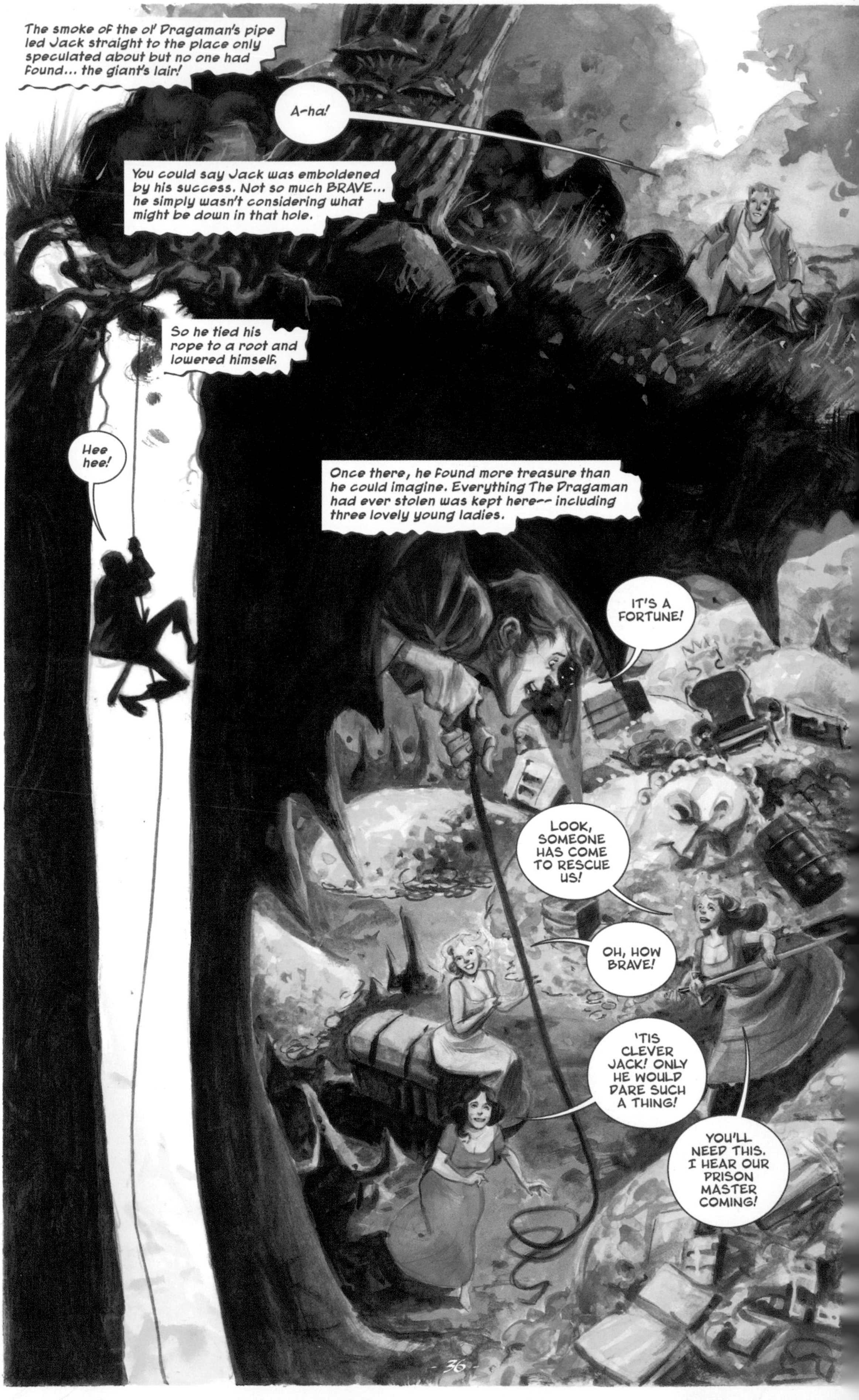
The smoke of the ol' Dragaman's pipe led Jack straight to the place only speculated about but no one had found... the giant's lair!
A-ha!
You could say Jack was emboldened by his success. Not so much BRAVE... he simply wasn't considering what might be down in that hole.
So he tied his rope to a root and lowered himself.
Hee hee!
Once there, he found more treasure than he could imagine. Everything The Dragaman had ever stolen was kept here-- including three lovely young ladies.
IT'S A FORTUNE!
LOOK, SOMEONE HAS COME TO RESCUE US!
OH, HOW BRAVE!
'TIS CLEVER JACK! ONLY HE WOULD DARE SUCH A THING!
YOU'LL NEED THIS. I HEAR OUR PRISON MASTER COMING!

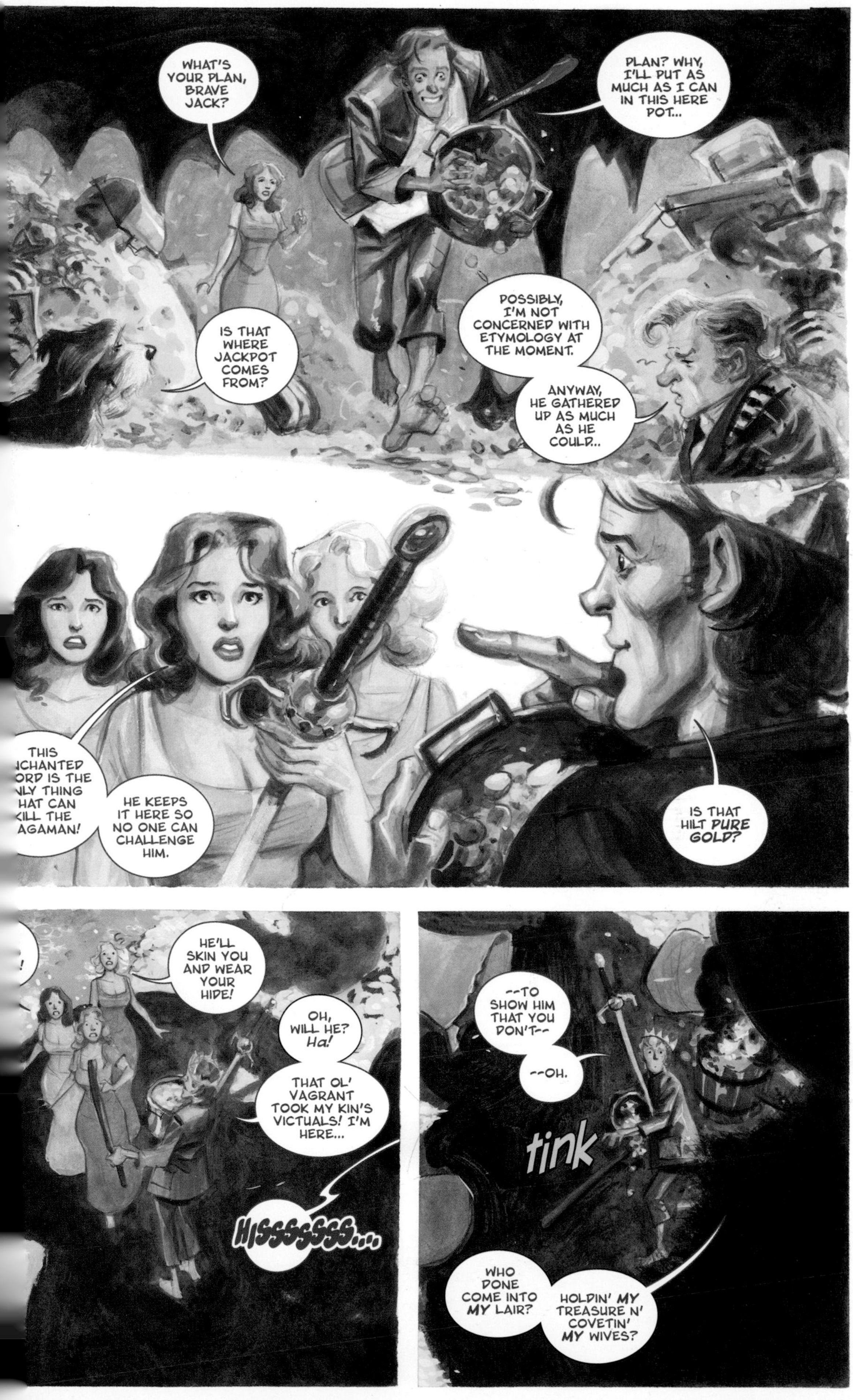

WHAT'S YOUR PLAN, BRAVE JACK?
PLAN? WHY, I'LL PUT AS MUCH AS I CAN IN THIS HERE POT...
IS THAT WHERE JACKPOT COMES FROM?
POSSIBLY, I'M NOT CONCERNED WITH ETYMOLOGY AT THE MOMENT.
ANYWAY, HE GATHERED UP AS MUCH AS HE COULD...
THIS NCHANTED ORD IS THE NLY THING HAT CAN KILL THE AGAMAN!
HE KEEPS IT HERE SO NO ONE CAN CHALLENGE HIM.
IS THAT HILT *PURE GOLD?*
HE'LL SKIN YOU AND WEAR YOUR HIDE!
OH, WILL HE? *Ha!*
THAT OL' VAGRANT TOOK MY KIN'S VICTUALS! I'M HERE...
HISSSSSSS...
--TO SHOW HIM THAT YOU DON'T--
--OH.
tink
WHO DONE COME INTO *MY* LAIR?
HOLDIN' *MY* TREASURE N' COVETIN' *MY* WIVES?

WHO WOULD STROLL INTO A DRAGON'S LAIR?
I... JUST WANTED TO ASK HOW YOU ENJOYED OUR FEAST.
RUN, RUN!!!
SAVE US!
So now Jack knew why the big man was always bellowing smoke as he saw the true nature of what he was up against.
In fairness to anyone paying attention, it was right there in his name.

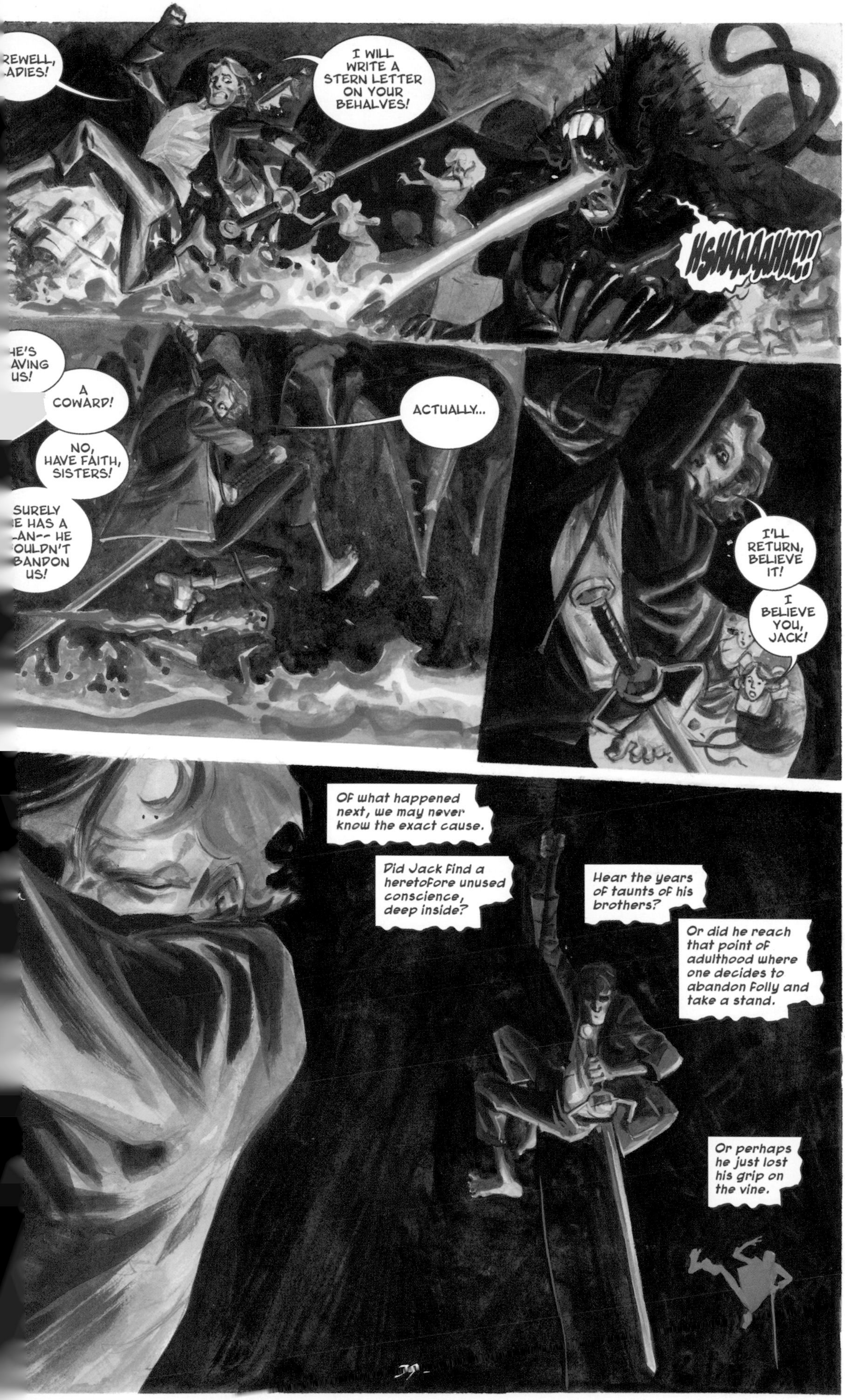

REWELL, ADIES!
I WILL WRITE A STERN LETTER ON YOUR BEHALVES!
HSHAAAAAHH!!!
HE'S AVING US!
A COWARD!
ACTUALLY...
NO, HAVE FAITH, SISTERS!
SURELY E HAS A LAN-- HE OULDN'T BANDON US!
I'LL RETURN, BELIEVE IT!
I BELIEVE YOU, JACK!
Of what happened next, we may never know the exact cause.
Did Jack find a heretofore unused conscience, deep inside?
Hear the years of taunts of his brothers?
Or did he reach that point of adulthood where one decides to abandon folly and take a stand.
Or perhaps he just lost his grip on the vine.

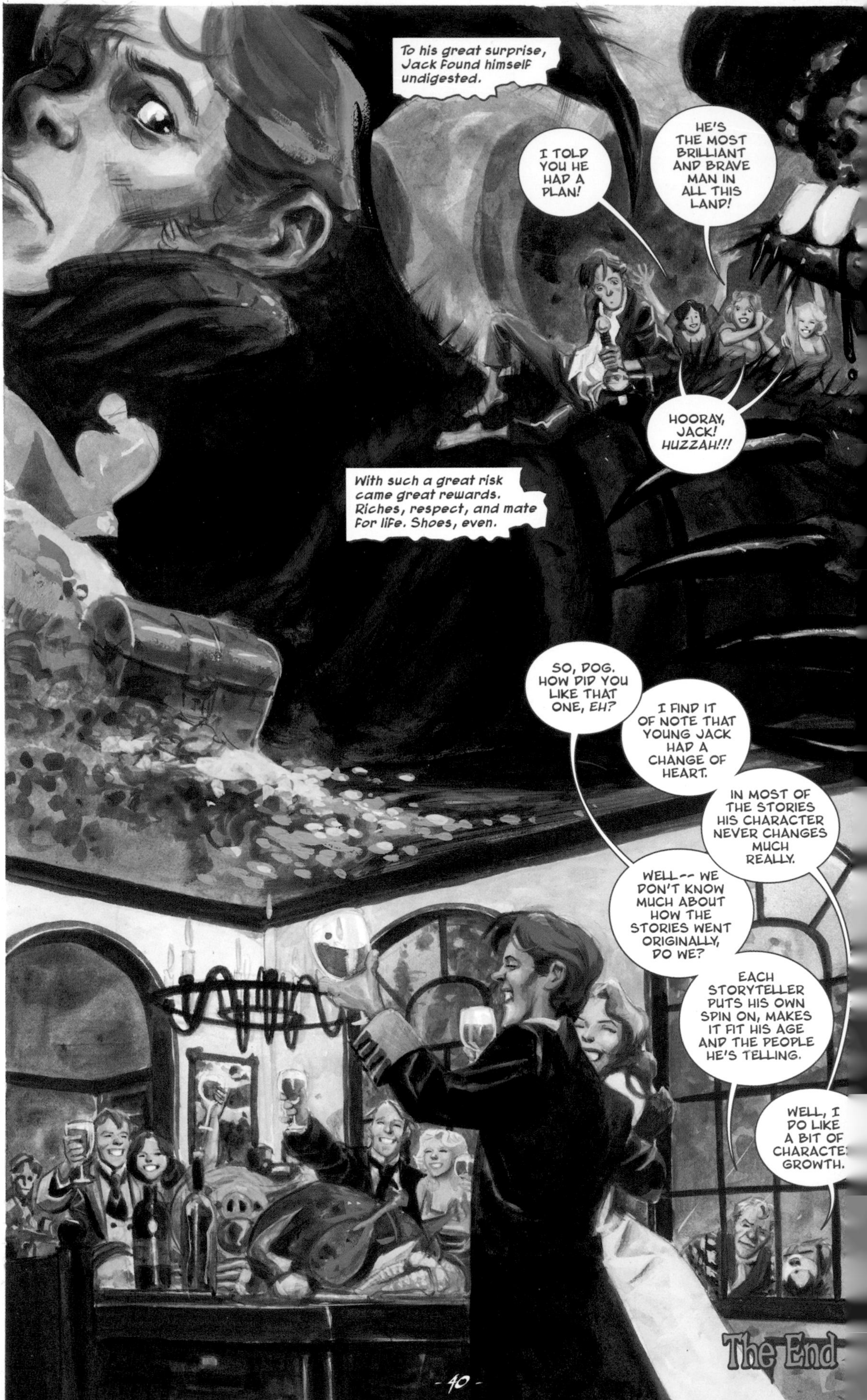
To his great surprise, Jack found himself undigested.
I TOLD YOU HE HAD A PLAN!
HE'S THE MOST BRILLIANT AND BRAVE MAN IN ALL THIS LAND!
HOORAY, JACK! HUZZAH!!!
With such a great risk came great rewards. Riches, respect, and mate for life. Shoes, even.
SO, DOG. HOW DID YOU LIKE THAT ONE, EH?
I FIND IT OF NOTE THAT YOUNG JACK HAD A CHANGE OF HEART.
IN MOST OF THE STORIES HIS CHARACTER NEVER CHANGES MUCH REALLY.
WELL-- WE DON'T KNOW MUCH ABOUT HOW THE STORIES WENT ORIGINALLY, DO WE?
EACH STORYTELLER PUTS HIS OWN SPIN ON, MAKES IT FIT HIS AGE AND THE PEOPLE HE'S TELLING.
WELL, I DO LIKE A BIT OF CHARACTER GROWTH.
The End

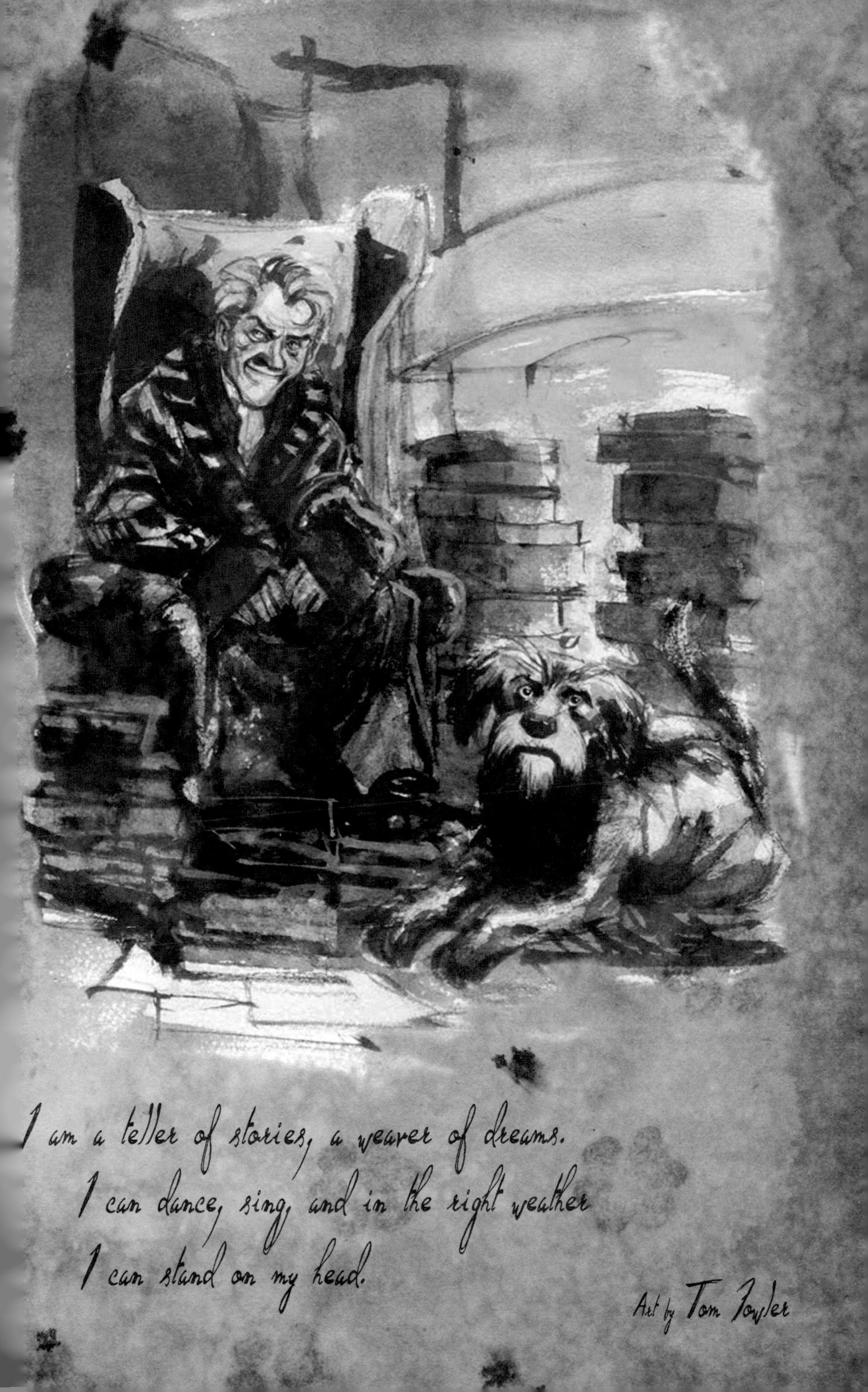

I am a teller of stories, a weaver of dreams.
I can dance, sing, and in the right weather
I can stand on my head.

Art by Tom Fowler

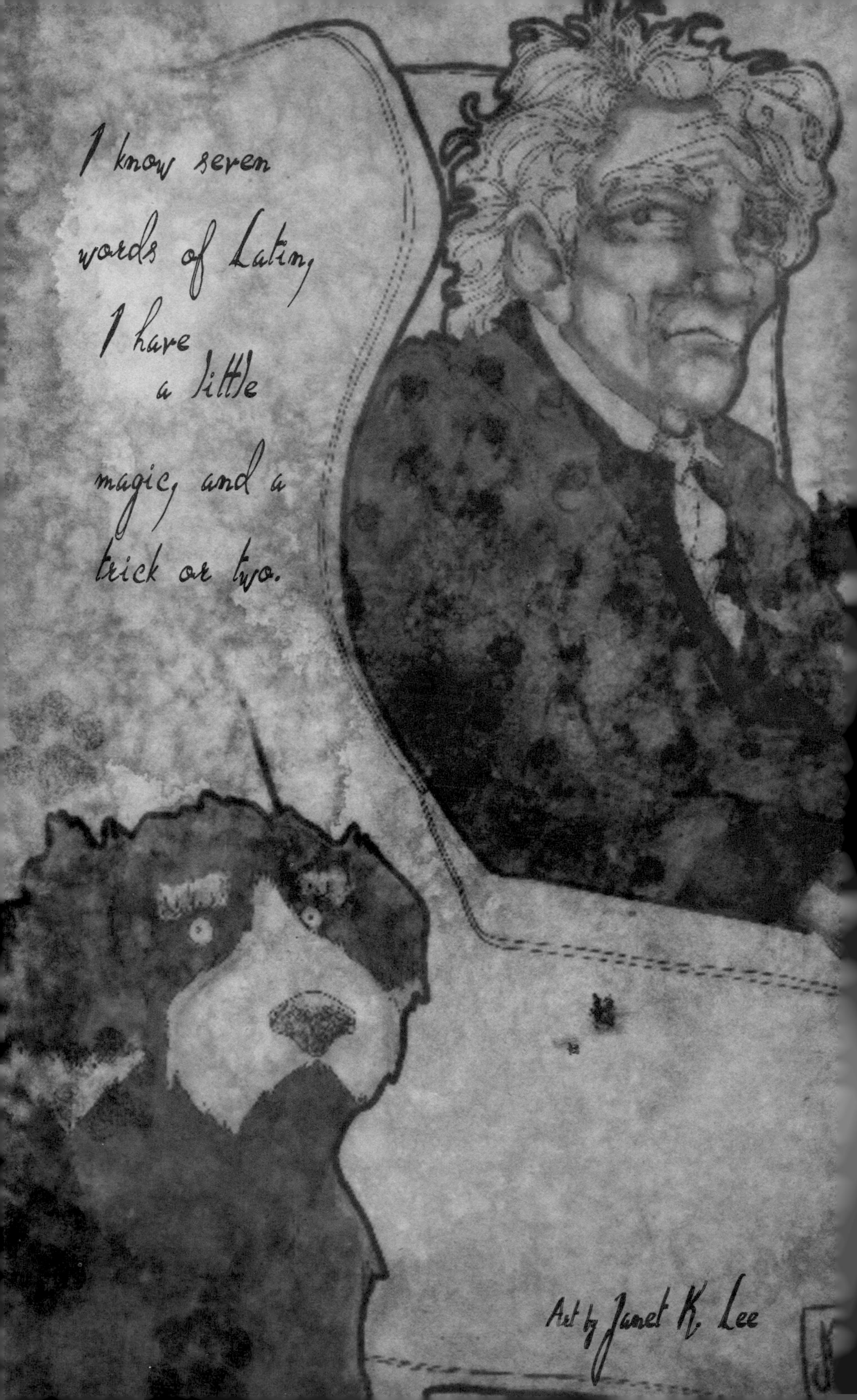
I know seven words of Latin, I have a little magic, and a trick or two.
Art by Janet K. Lee

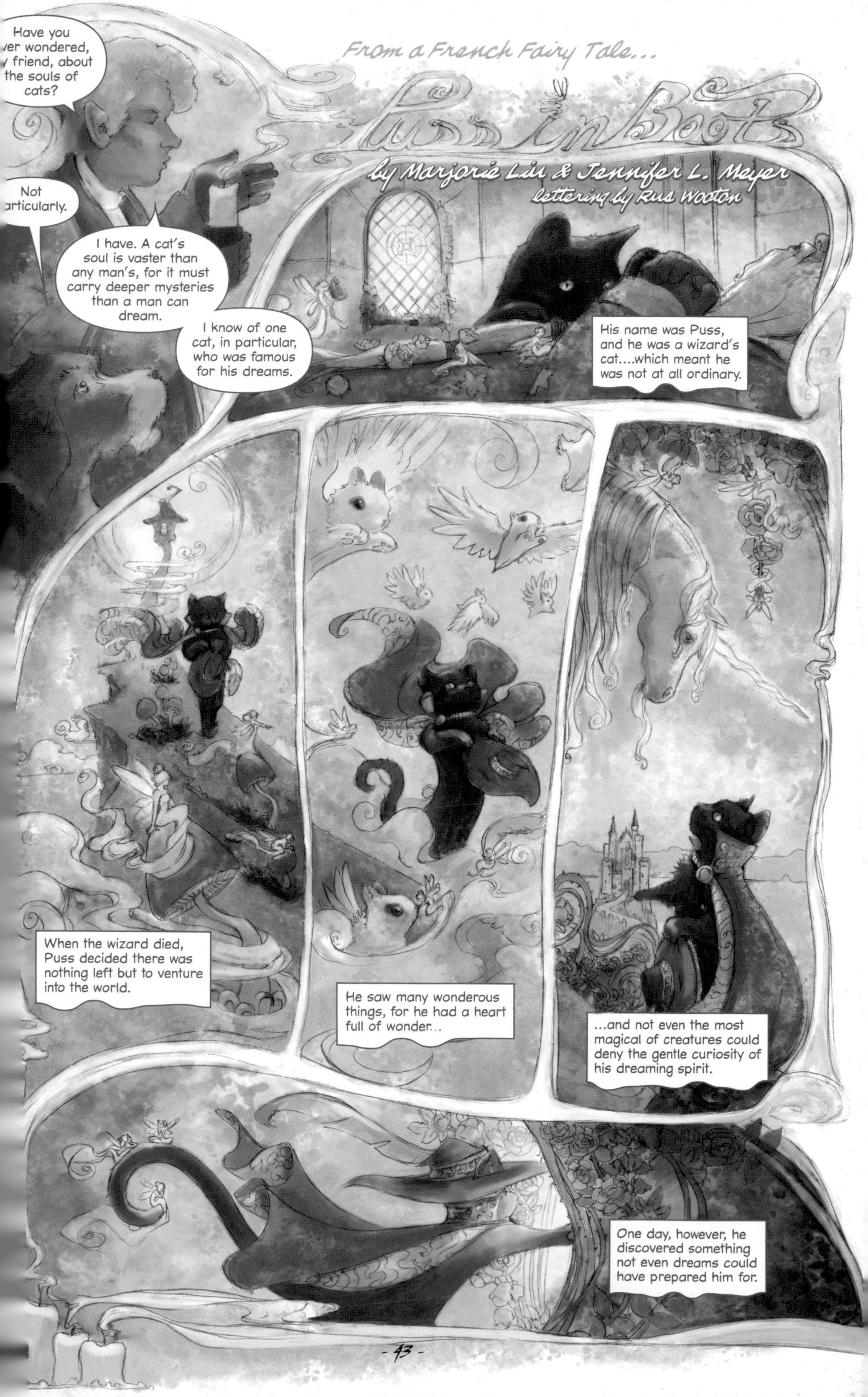

From a French Fairy Tale...
Puss in Boots
by Marjorie Liu & Jennifer L. Meyer
lettering by Rus Wooton
Have you ver wondered, y friend, about the souls of cats?
Not articularly.
I have. A cat's soul is vaster than any man's, for it must carry deeper mysteries than a man can dream.
I know of one cat, in particular, who was famous for his dreams.
His name was Puss, and he was a wizard's cat....which meant he was not at all ordinary.
When the wizard died, Puss decided there was nothing left but to venture into the world.
He saw many wonderous things, for he had a heart full of wonder...
...and not even the most magical of creatures could deny the gentle curiosity of his dreaming spirit.
One day, however, he discovered something not even dreams could have prepared him for.

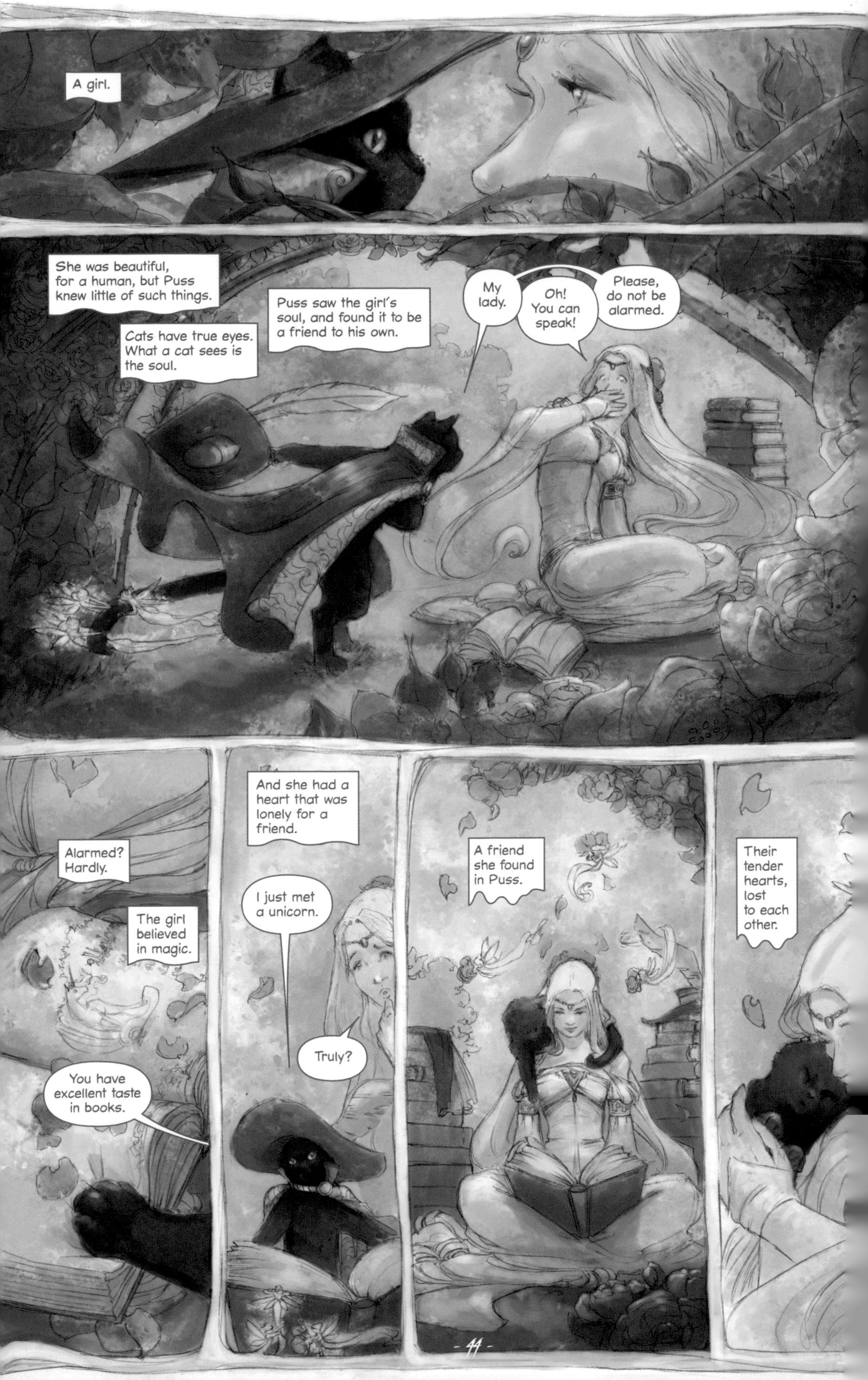
A girl.
She was beautiful, for a human, but Puss knew little of such things.
Cats have true eyes. What a cat sees is the soul.
Puss saw the girl's soul, and found it to be a friend to his own.
My lady.
Oh! You can speak!
Please, do not be alarmed.
Alarmed? Hardly.
The girl believed in magic.
You have excellent taste in books.
And she had a heart that was lonely for a friend.
I just met a unicorn.
Truly?
A friend she found in Puss.
Their tender hearts, lost to each other.

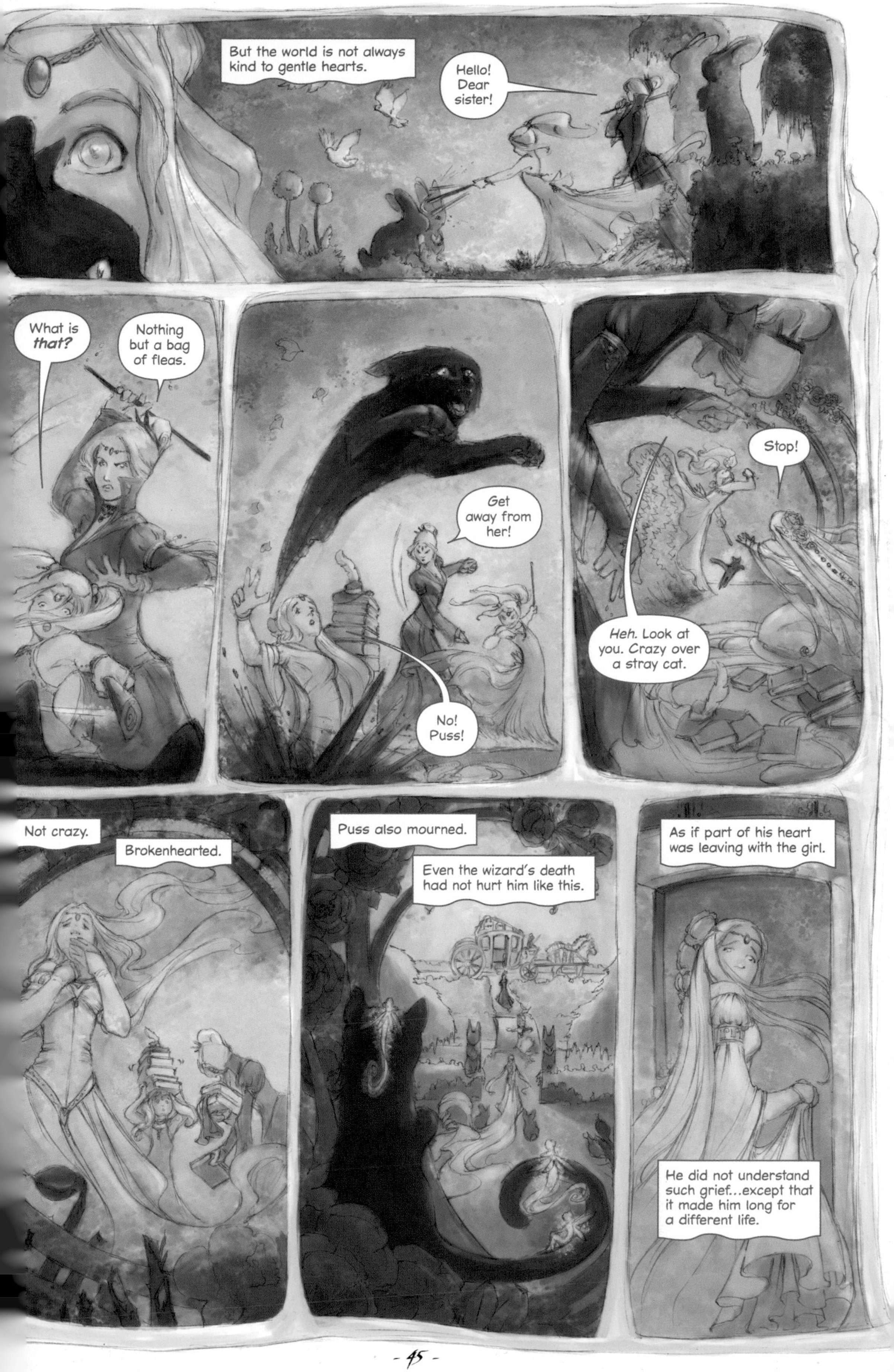
But the world is not always kind to gentle hearts.
Hello! Dear sister!
What is *that?*
Nothing but a bag of fleas.
Get away from her!
No! Puss!
Stop!
Heh. Look at you. Crazy over a stray cat.
Not crazy.
Brokenhearted.
Puss also mourned.
Even the wizard's death had not hurt him like this.
As if part of his heart was leaving with the girl.
He did not understand such grief...except that it made him long for a different life.

And so he asked the fairies to turn him into a man.

A man who could not be chased off by sticks or loud voices.

A man who might mean something to a girl.

The fairies begged him to make another wish. There was nothing wrong with being a cat.

But he was adamant.

So they spun their light...

...and tangled him in their magic...

...and turned Puss into a man.

They presente him a pair of boots, as a gi

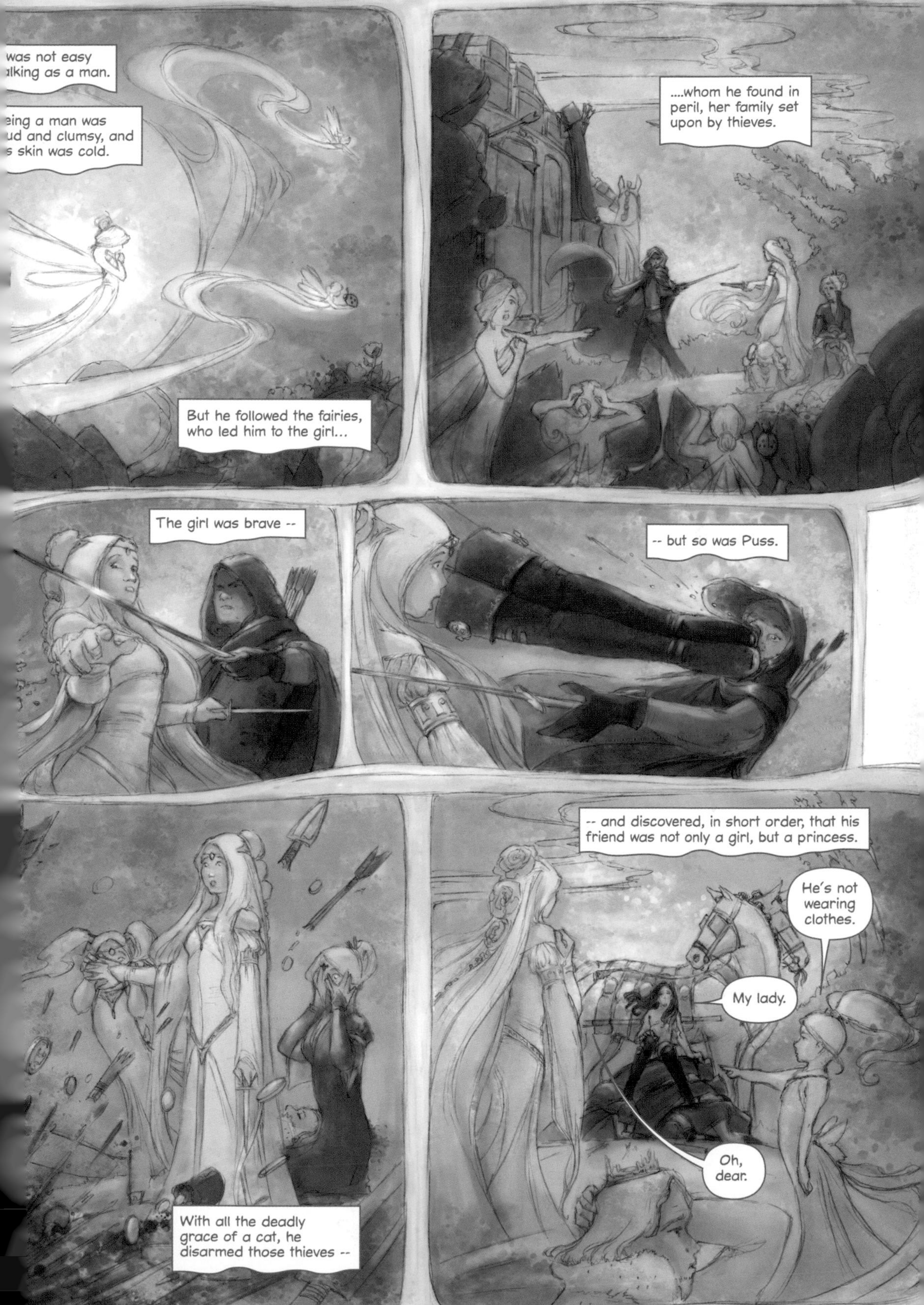
was not easy
alking as a man.
eing a man was
ud and clumsy, and
s skin was cold.
But he followed the fairies,
who led him to the girl...
....whom he found in
peril, her family set
upon by thieves.
The girl was brave --
-- but so was Puss.
With all the deadly
grace of a cat, he
disarmed those thieves --
-- and discovered, in short order, that his
friend was not only a girl, but a princess.
He's not
wearing
clothes.
My lady.
Oh,
dear.

The grateful king gave Puss clothing, and allowed him to ride in the carriage with his family.

Together again, the bond between Puss and the girl fell into place. And with it, something even deeper.

You have excellent taste in books.

You should know...I met a unicorn once.

You...you did?

Pffft.

Don't encourage her, hero.

Our sister is to be married. No time for reading then. Her future husband doesn't like books.

We're here!

To a prince she had never met, but who was powerful and rich.

Married?

None of whi mattered to princess. St did not love

- 48 -

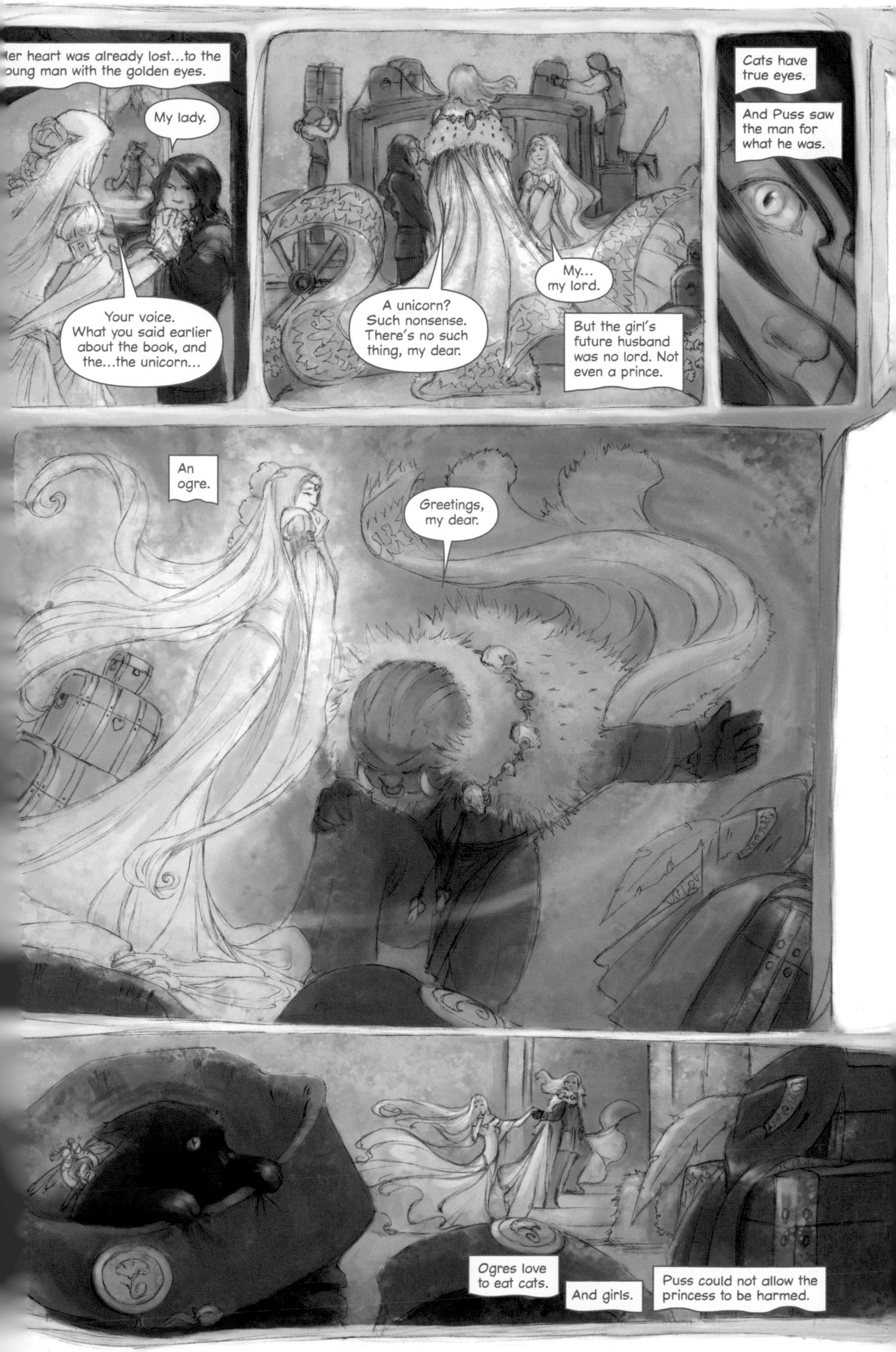

ler heart was already lost...to the oung man with the golden eyes.
My lady.
Your voice. What you said earlier about the book, and the...the unicorn...
A unicorn? Such nonsense. There's no such thing, my dear.
My... my lord.
But the girl's future husband was no lord. Not even a prince.
Cats have true eyes.
And Puss saw the man for what he was.
An ogre.
Greetings, my dear.
Ogres love to eat cats.
And girls.
Puss could not allow the princess to be harmed.

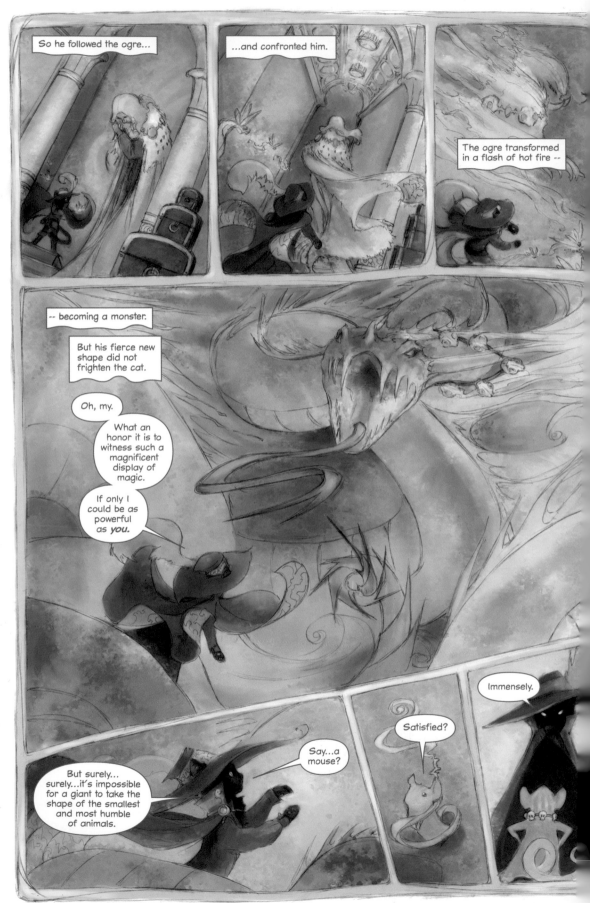

So he followed the ogre...

...and confronted him.

The ogre transformed in a flash of hot fire --

-- becoming a monster.

But his fierce new shape did not frighten the cat.

Oh, my.

What an honor it is to witness such a magnificent display of magic.

If only I could be as powerful as *you.*

But surely... surely...it's impossible for a giant to take the shape of the smallest and most humble of animals.

Say...a mouse?

Satisfied?

Immensely.

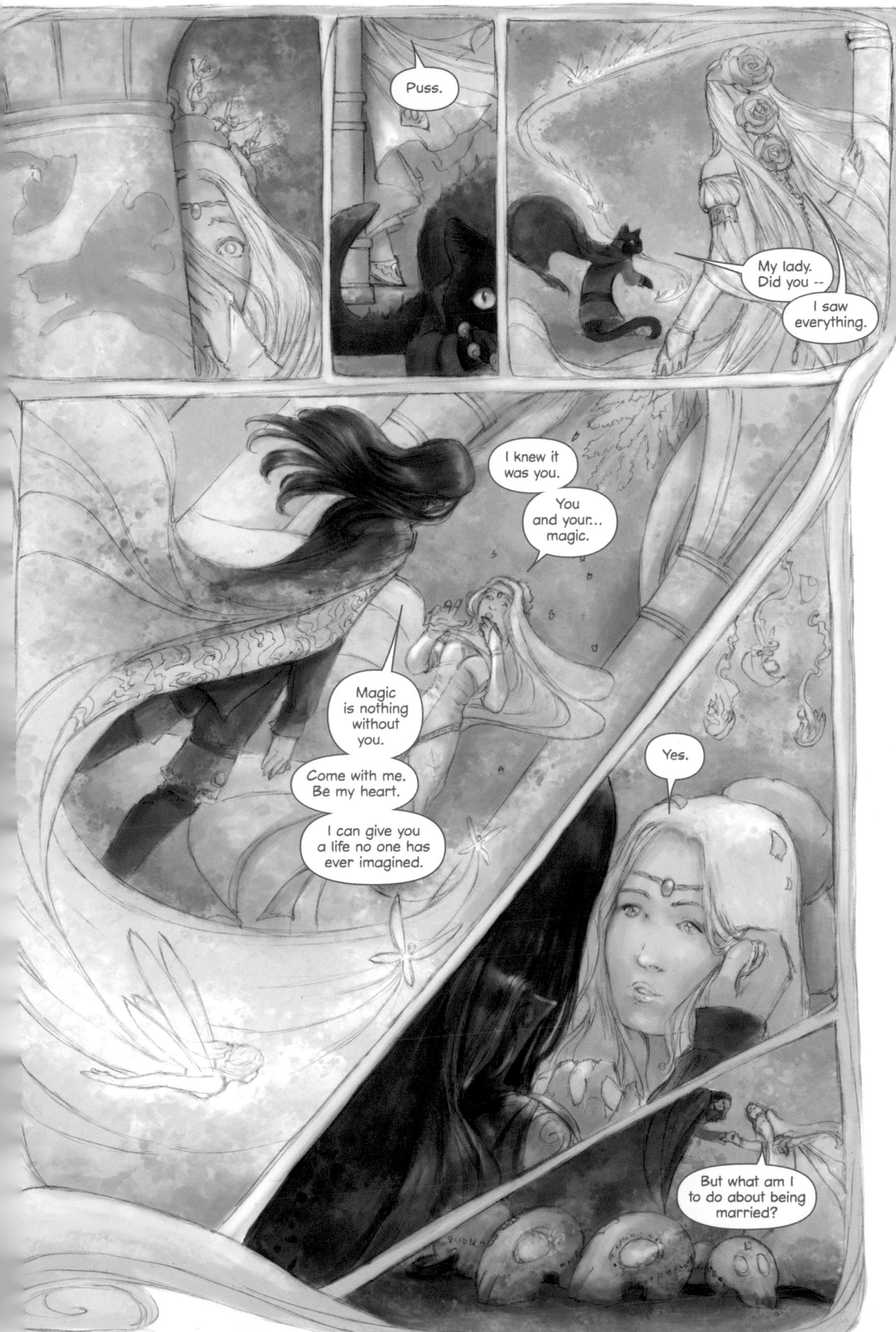

Puss.
My lady. Did you --
I saw everything.
I knew it was you.
You and your... magic.
Magic is nothing without you.
Come with me. Be my heart.
I can give you a life no one has ever imagined.
Yes.
But what am I to do about being married?

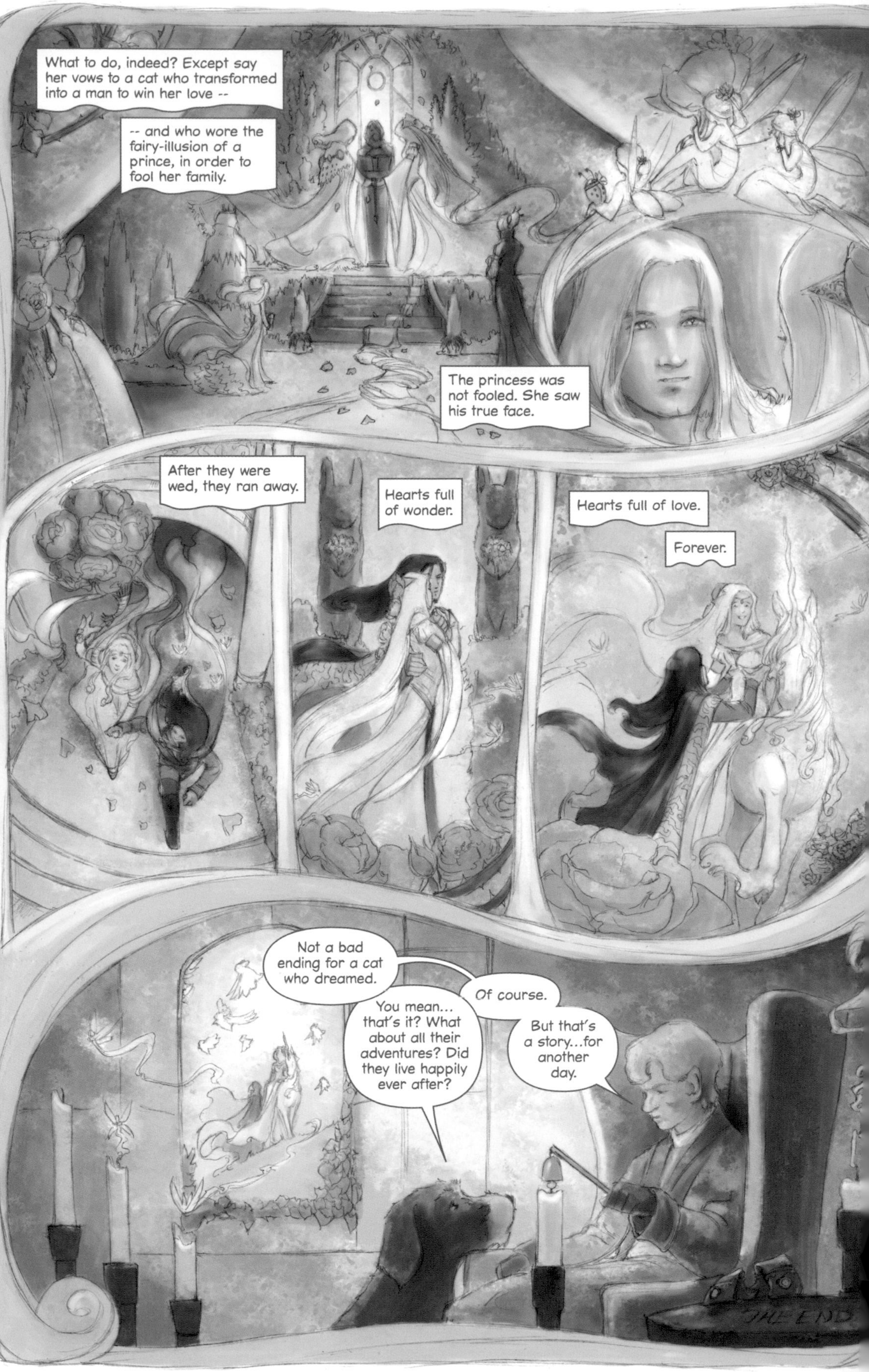
What to do, indeed? Except say her vows to a cat who transformed into a man to win her love --
-- and who wore the fairy-illusion of a prince, in order to fool her family.
The princess was not fooled. She saw his true face.
After they were wed, they ran away.
Hearts full of wonder.
Hearts full of love.
Forever.
Not a bad ending for a cat who dreamed.
Of course.
You mean... that's it? What about all their adventures? Did they live happily ever after?
But that's a story...for another day.
THE END

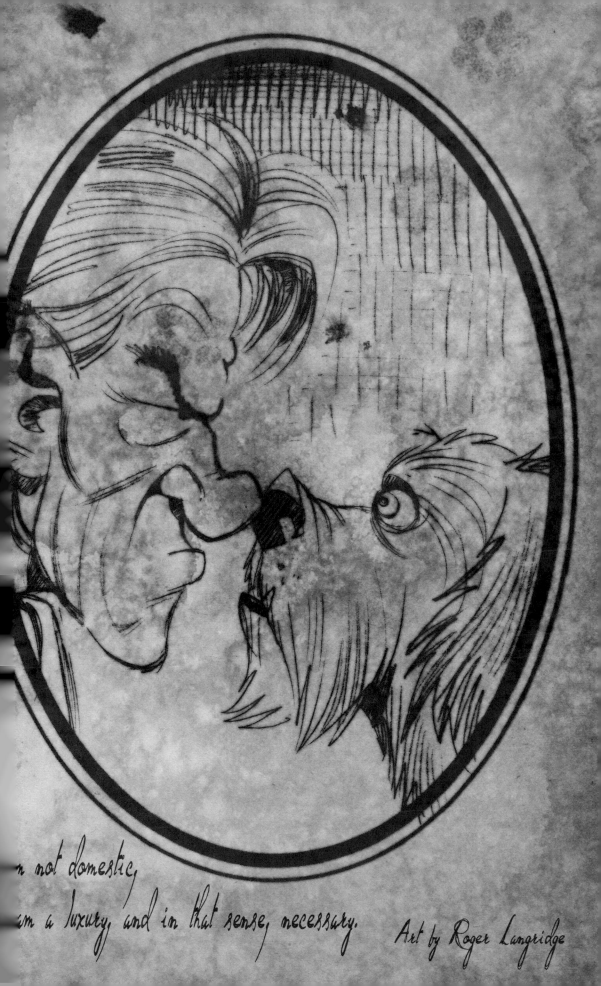

n not domestic,

m a luxury, and in that sense, necessary.

Art by Roger Langridge

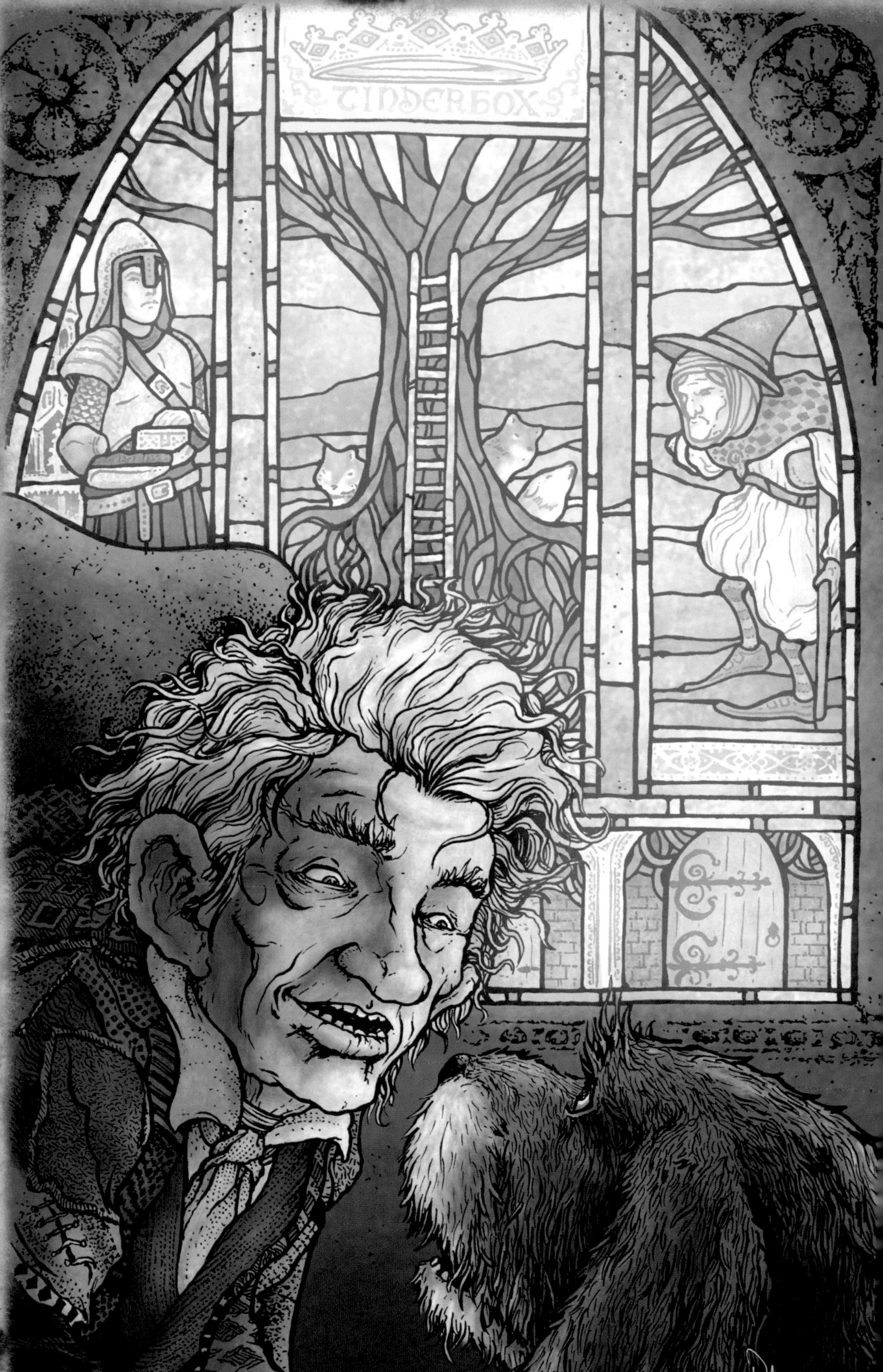
TINDERBOX
Petersen

Art by David Petersen

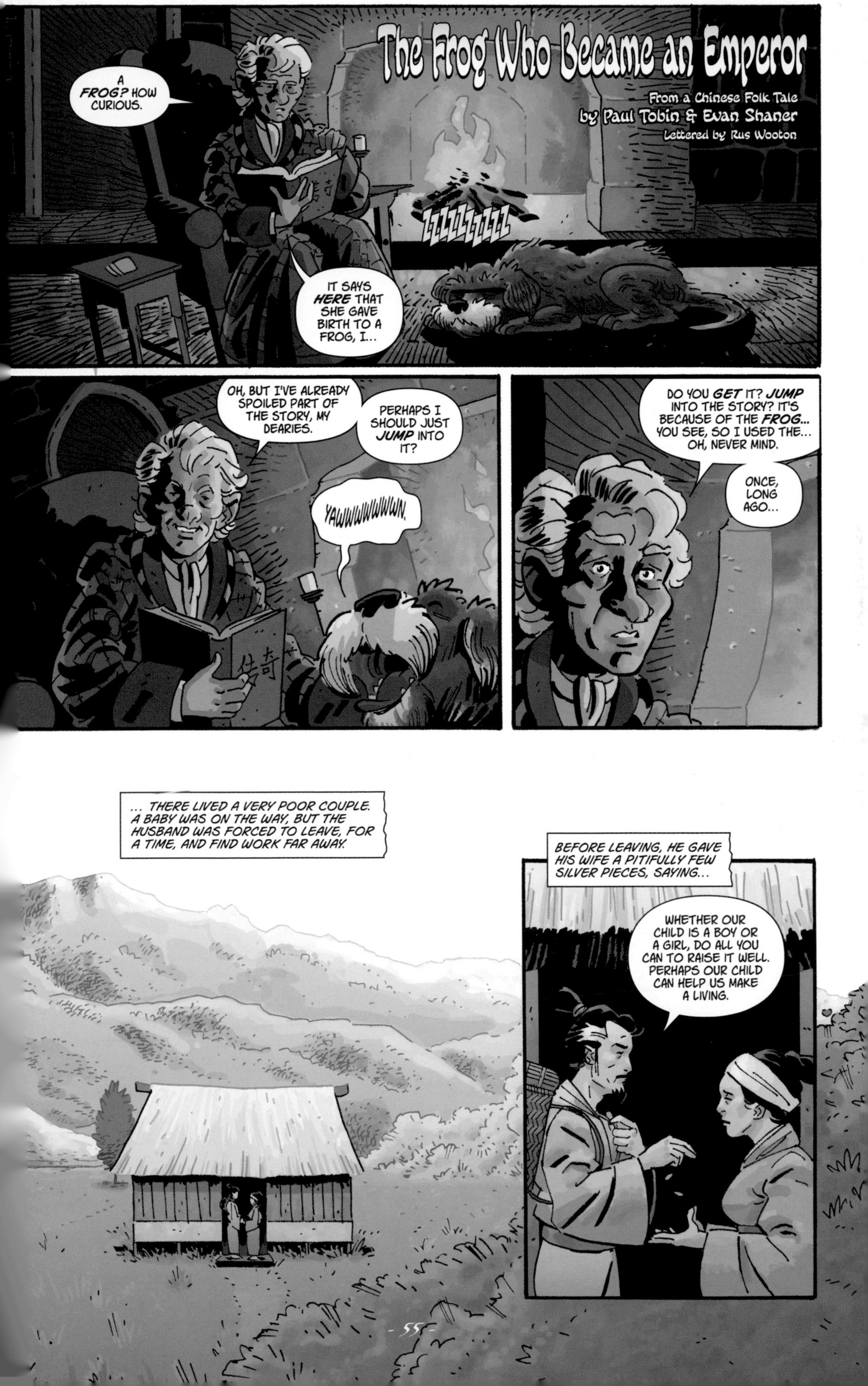
The Frog Who Became an Emperor
From a Chinese Folk Tale
by Paul Tobin & Evan Shaner
Lettered by Rus Wooton
A FROG? HOW CURIOUS.
IT SAYS HERE THAT SHE GAVE BIRTH TO A FROG, I...
ZZZZZZZZZZ
OH, BUT I'VE ALREADY SPOILED PART OF THE STORY, MY DEARIES.
PERHAPS I SHOULD JUST JUMP INTO IT?
YAWWWWWWWN.
DO YOU GET IT? JUMP INTO THE STORY? IT'S BECAUSE OF THE FROG... YOU SEE, SO I USED THE... OH, NEVER MIND.
ONCE, LONG AGO...
... THERE LIVED A VERY POOR COUPLE. A BABY WAS ON THE WAY, BUT THE HUSBAND WAS FORCED TO LEAVE, FOR A TIME, AND FIND WORK FAR AWAY.
BEFORE LEAVING, HE GAVE HIS WIFE A PITIFULLY FEW SILVER PIECES, SAYING...
WHETHER OUR CHILD IS A BOY OR A GIRL, DO ALL YOU CAN TO RAISE IT WELL. PERHAPS OUR CHILD CAN HELP US MAKE A LIVING.

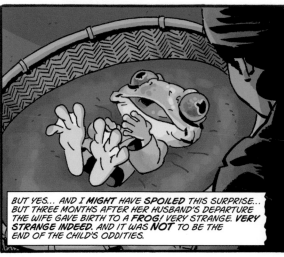

FOR, WITHIN A FEW MONTHS THE FROG-CHILD HAD GROWN QUITE LARGE, AND ONE DAY EVEN *SPOKE*, SAYING...

MOTHER... FATHER WILL BE COMING BACK TONIGHT.

BUT YES... AND *I* MIGHT HAVE *SPOILED* THIS SURPRISE... BUT THREE MONTHS AFTER HER HUSBAND'S DEPARTURE THE WIFE GAVE BIRTH TO A *FROG!* VERY STRANGE. *VERY STRANGE INDEED.* AND IT WAS *NOT* TO BE THE END OF THE CHILD'S ODDITIES.

AND SURE ENOUGH, THE HUSBAND DID COME HOME THAT VERY NIGHT.

MY LOVE!

DAD!

THE FATHER, TO BE SURE, MUST HAVE HAD SOME *QUESTIONS.*

THE THING ABOUT HIS SON BEING A *FROG* I'M GUESSING.

OKAY... FIRST OF ALL... YOU'RE A *FROG.* SECOND OF ALL... HOW DID YOU KNOW I WAS COMING HOME TONIGHT?

AS TO ME BEING A FROG... WHY, *YES...* THAT'S *OBVIOUS.*

THE ANSWER TO YOUR QUESTION IS *EQUALLY* OBVIOUS. IT IS BECAUSE I KNOW *EVERYTHING* UNDER HEAVEN.

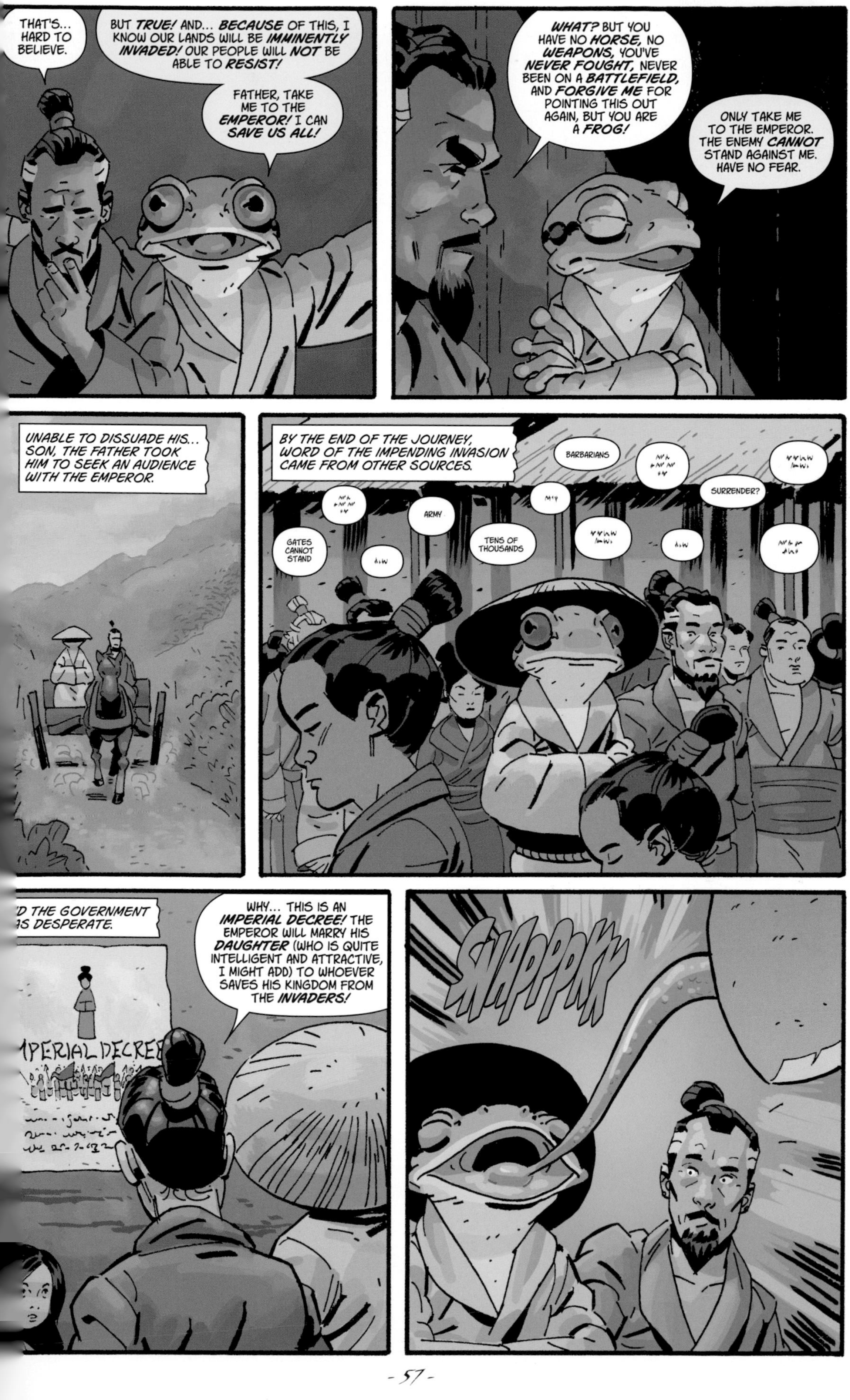
THAT'S... HARD TO BELIEVE.
BUT TRUE! AND... BECAUSE OF THIS, I KNOW OUR LANDS WILL BE IMMINENTLY INVADED! OUR PEOPLE WILL NOT BE ABLE TO RESIST!
FATHER, TAKE ME TO THE EMPEROR! I CAN SAVE US ALL!
WHAT? BUT YOU HAVE NO HORSE, NO WEAPONS, YOU'VE NEVER FOUGHT, NEVER BEEN ON A BATTLEFIELD, AND FORGIVE ME FOR POINTING THIS OUT AGAIN, BUT YOU ARE A FROG!
ONLY TAKE ME TO THE EMPEROR. THE ENEMY CANNOT STAND AGAINST ME. HAVE NO FEAR.
UNABLE TO DISSUADE HIS... SON, THE FATHER TOOK HIM TO SEEK AN AUDIENCE WITH THE EMPEROR.
BY THE END OF THE JOURNEY, WORD OF THE IMPENDING INVASION CAME FROM OTHER SOURCES.
BARBARIANS
SURRENDER?
ARMY
GATES CANNOT STAND
TENS OF THOUSANDS
D THE GOVERNMENT AS DESPERATE.
WHY... THIS IS AN IMPERIAL DECREE! THE EMPEROR WILL MARRY HIS DAUGHTER (WHO IS QUITE INTELLIGENT AND ATTRACTIVE, I MIGHT ADD) TO WHOEVER SAVES HIS KINGDOM FROM THE INVADERS!
PERIAL DECREE
SHAPPKK

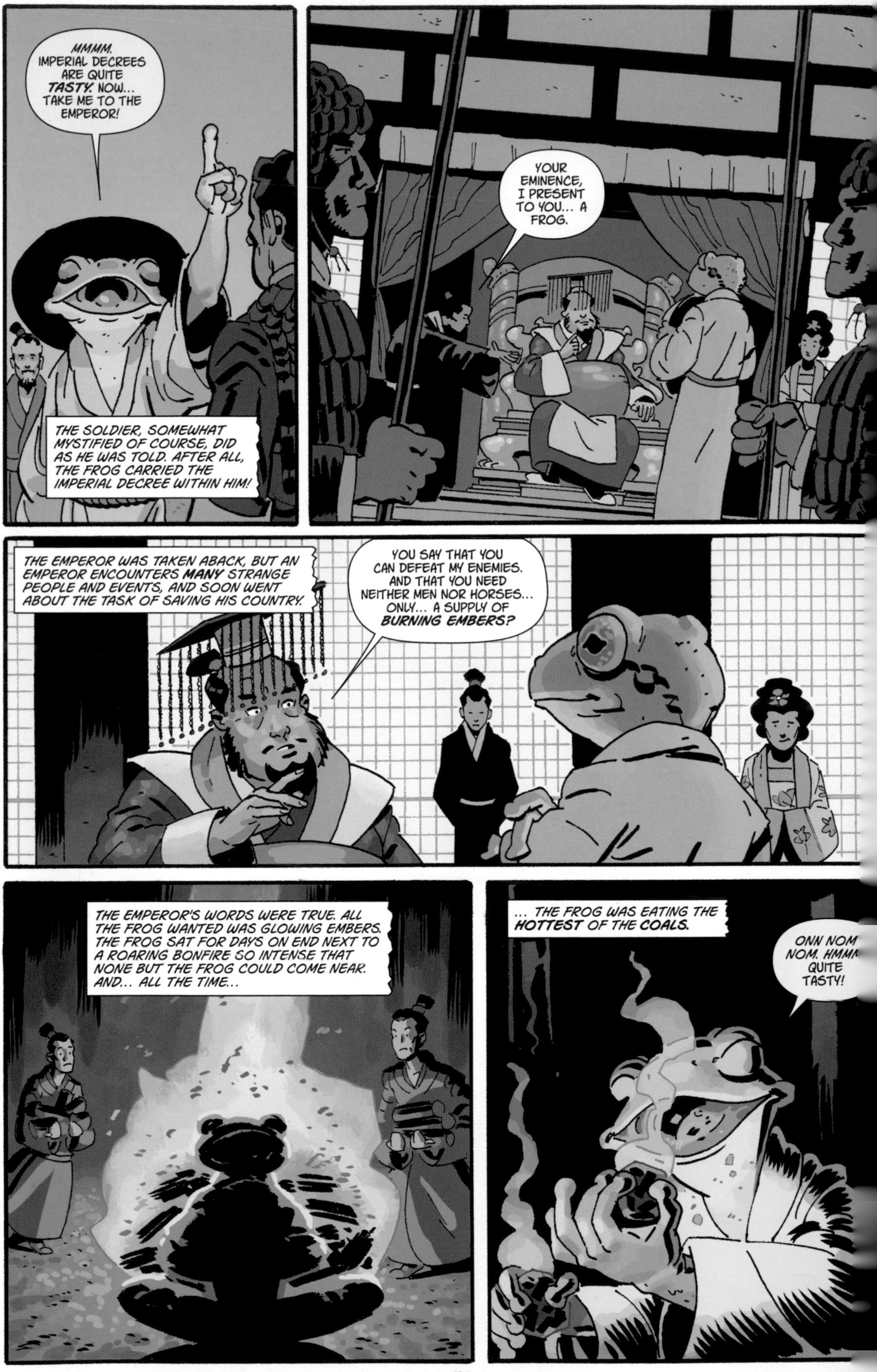
MMMM. IMPERIAL DECREES ARE QUITE TASTY. NOW... TAKE ME TO THE EMPEROR!
THE SOLDIER, SOMEWHAT MYSTIFIED OF COURSE, DID AS HE WAS TOLD. AFTER ALL, THE FROG CARRIED THE IMPERIAL DECREE WITHIN HIM!
YOUR EMINENCE, I PRESENT TO YOU... A FROG.
THE EMPEROR WAS TAKEN ABACK, BUT AN EMPEROR ENCOUNTERS MANY STRANGE PEOPLE AND EVENTS, AND SOON WENT ABOUT THE TASK OF SAVING HIS COUNTRY.
YOU SAY THAT YOU CAN DEFEAT MY ENEMIES. AND THAT YOU NEED NEITHER MEN NOR HORSES... ONLY... A SUPPLY OF BURNING EMBERS?
THE EMPEROR'S WORDS WERE TRUE. ALL THE FROG WANTED WAS GLOWING EMBERS. THE FROG SAT FOR DAYS ON END NEXT TO A ROARING BONFIRE SO INTENSE THAT NONE BUT THE FROG COULD COME NEAR. AND... ALL THE TIME...
... THE FROG WAS EATING THE HOTTEST OF THE COALS.
ONN NOM NOM. HMMM QUITE TASTY!

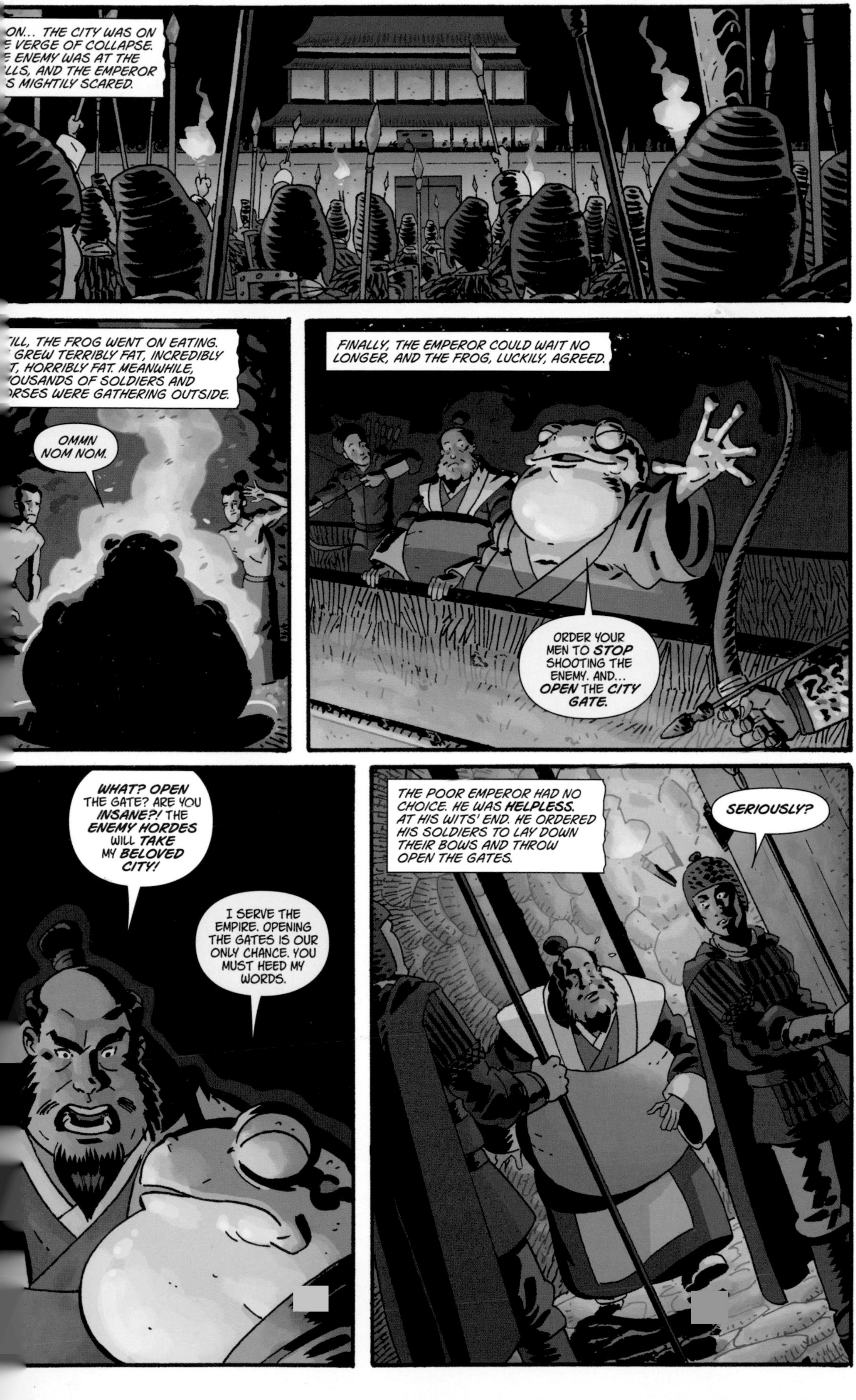

ON... THE CITY WAS ON
E VERGE OF COLLAPSE.
E ENEMY WAS AT THE
LLS, AND THE EMPEROR
S MIGHTILY SCARED.
ILL, THE FROG WENT ON EATING.
GREW TERRIBLY FAT, INCREDIBLY
T, HORRIBLY FAT. MEANWHILE,
OUSANDS OF SOLDIERS AND
RSES WERE GATHERING OUTSIDE.
OMMN NOM NOM.
FINALLY, THE EMPEROR COULD WAIT NO LONGER, AND THE FROG, LUCKILY, AGREED.
ORDER YOUR MEN TO STOP SHOOTING THE ENEMY. AND... OPEN THE CITY GATE.
WHAT? OPEN THE GATE? ARE YOU INSANE?! THE ENEMY HORDES WILL TAKE MY BELOVED CITY!
I SERVE THE EMPIRE. OPENING THE GATES IS OUR ONLY CHANCE. YOU MUST HEED MY WORDS.
THE POOR EMPEROR HAD NO CHOICE. HE WAS HELPLESS. AT HIS WITS' END. HE ORDERED HIS SOLDIERS TO LAY DOWN THEIR BOWS AND THROW OPEN THE GATES.
SERIOUSLY?

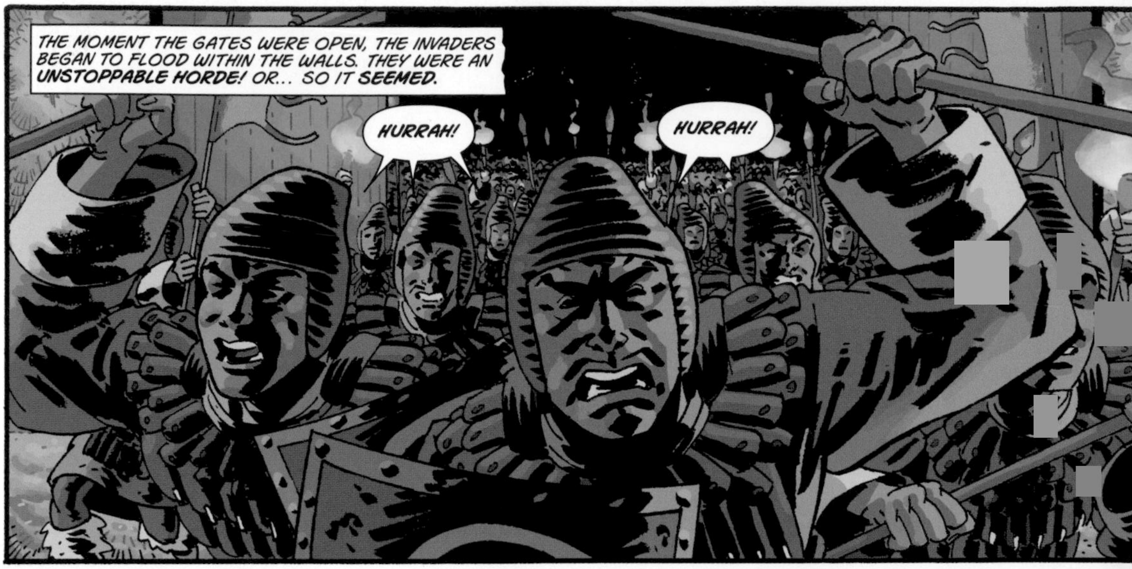
THE MOMENT THE GATES WERE OPEN, THE INVADERS BEGAN TO FLOOD WITHIN THE WALLS. THEY WERE AN UNSTOPPABLE HORDE! OR... SO IT SEEMED.
HURRAH!
HURRAH!

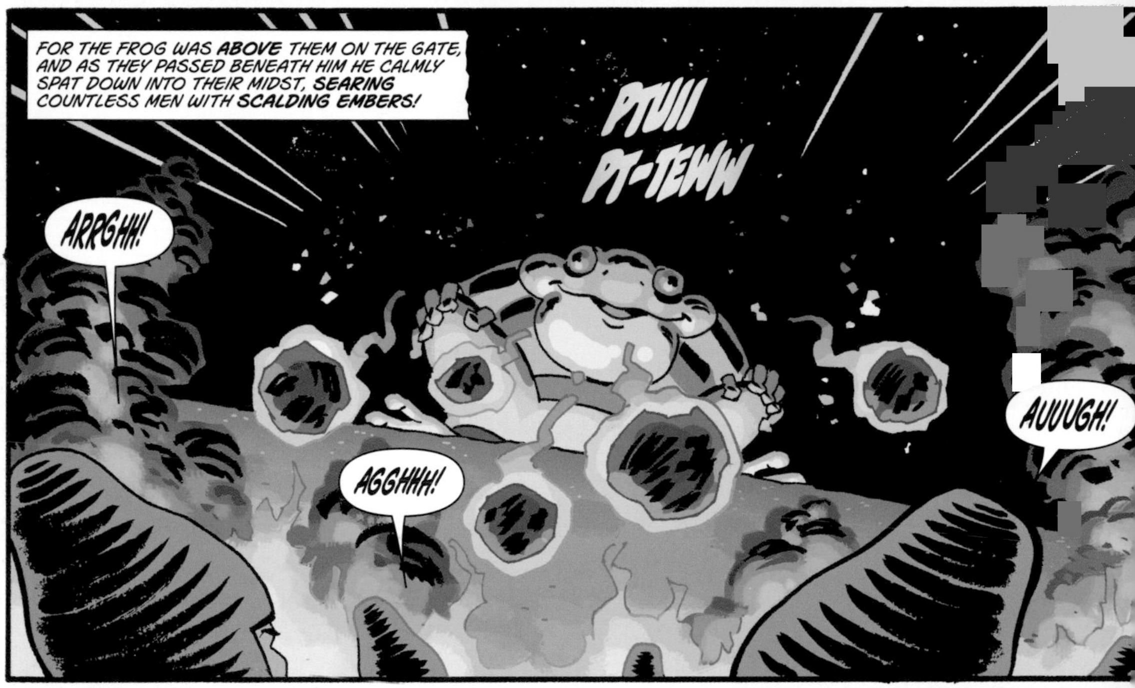
FOR THE FROG WAS ABOVE THEM ON THE GATE, AND AS THEY PASSED BENEATH HIM HE CALMLY SPAT DOWN INTO THEIR MIDST, SEARING COUNTLESS MEN WITH SCALDING EMBERS!
PTUII
PT-TEWW
ARRGHH!
AGGHHH!
AUUUGH!

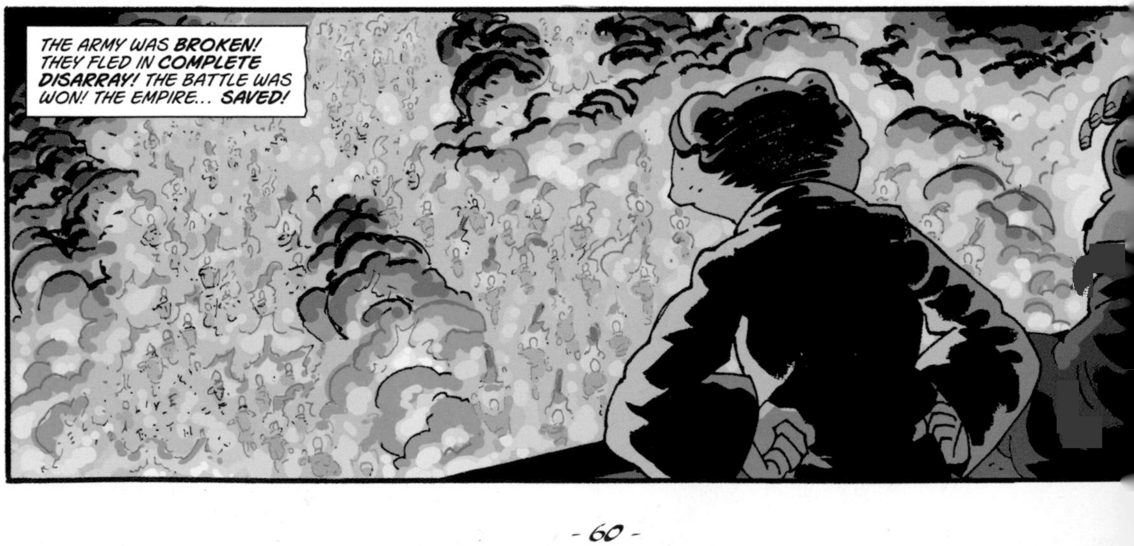
THE ARMY WAS BROKEN! THEY FLED IN COMPLETE DISARRAY! THE BATTLE WAS WON! THE EMPIRE... SAVED!

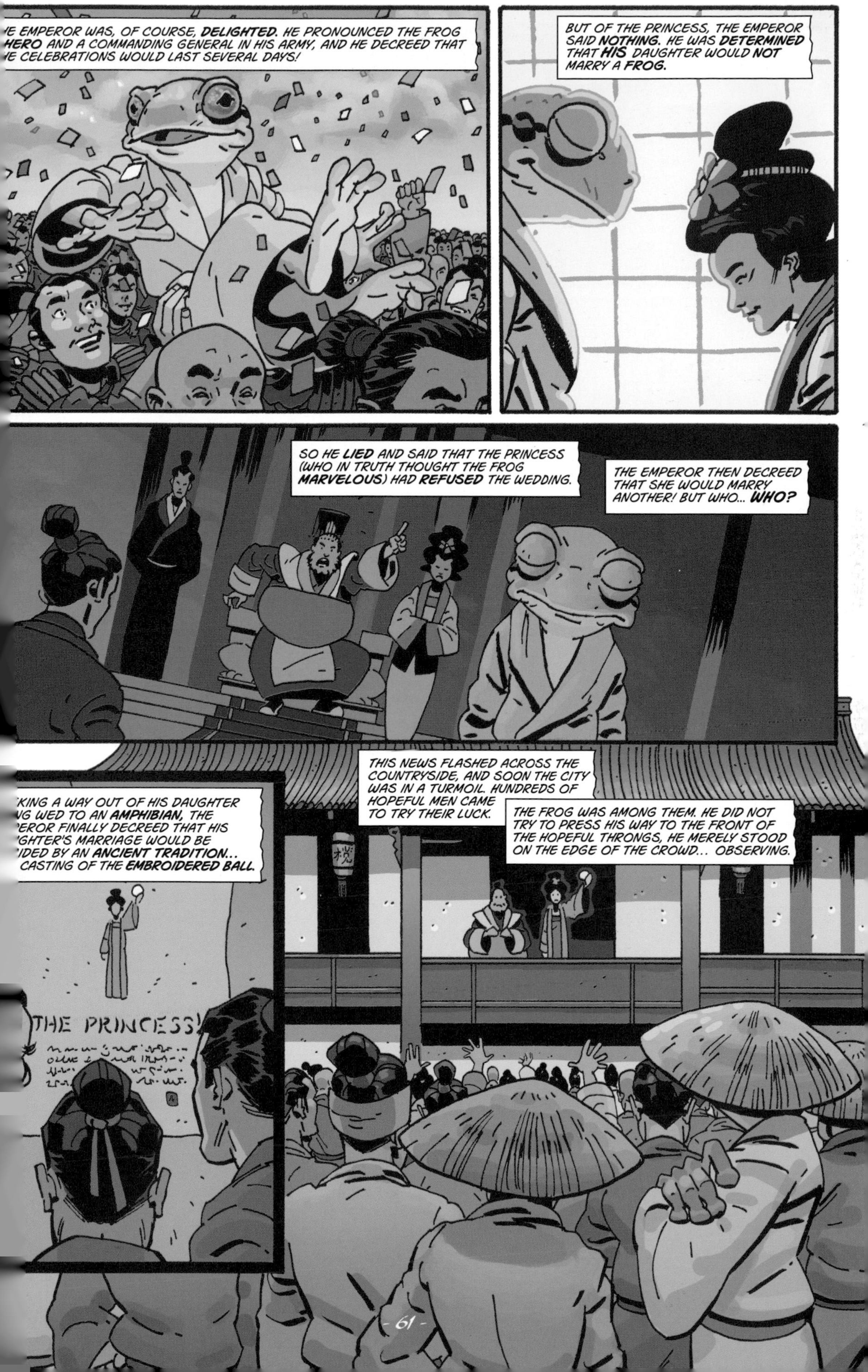
E EMPEROR WAS, OF COURSE, DELIGHTED. HE PRONOUNCED THE FROG
HERO AND A COMMANDING GENERAL IN HIS ARMY, AND HE DECREED THAT
E CELEBRATIONS WOULD LAST SEVERAL DAYS!
BUT OF THE PRINCESS, THE EMPEROR SAID NOTHING. HE WAS DETERMINED THAT HIS DAUGHTER WOULD NOT MARRY A FROG.
SO HE LIED AND SAID THAT THE PRINCESS (WHO IN TRUTH THOUGHT THE FROG MARVELOUS) HAD REFUSED THE WEDDING.
THE EMPEROR THEN DECREED THAT SHE WOULD MARRY ANOTHER! BUT WHO... WHO?
KING A WAY OUT OF HIS DAUGHTER
NG WED TO AN AMPHIBIAN, THE
PEROR FINALLY DECREED THAT HIS
GHTER'S MARRIAGE WOULD BE
IDED BY AN ANCIENT TRADITION...
CASTING OF THE EMBROIDERED BALL.
THIS NEWS FLASHED ACROSS THE COUNTRYSIDE, AND SOON THE CITY WAS IN A TURMOIL. HUNDREDS OF HOPEFUL MEN CAME TO TRY THEIR LUCK.
THE FROG WAS AMONG THEM. HE DID NOT TRY TO PRESS HIS WAY TO THE FRONT OF THE HOPEFUL THRONGS, HE MERELY STOOD ON THE EDGE OF THE CROWD... OBSERVING.
THE PRINCESS!

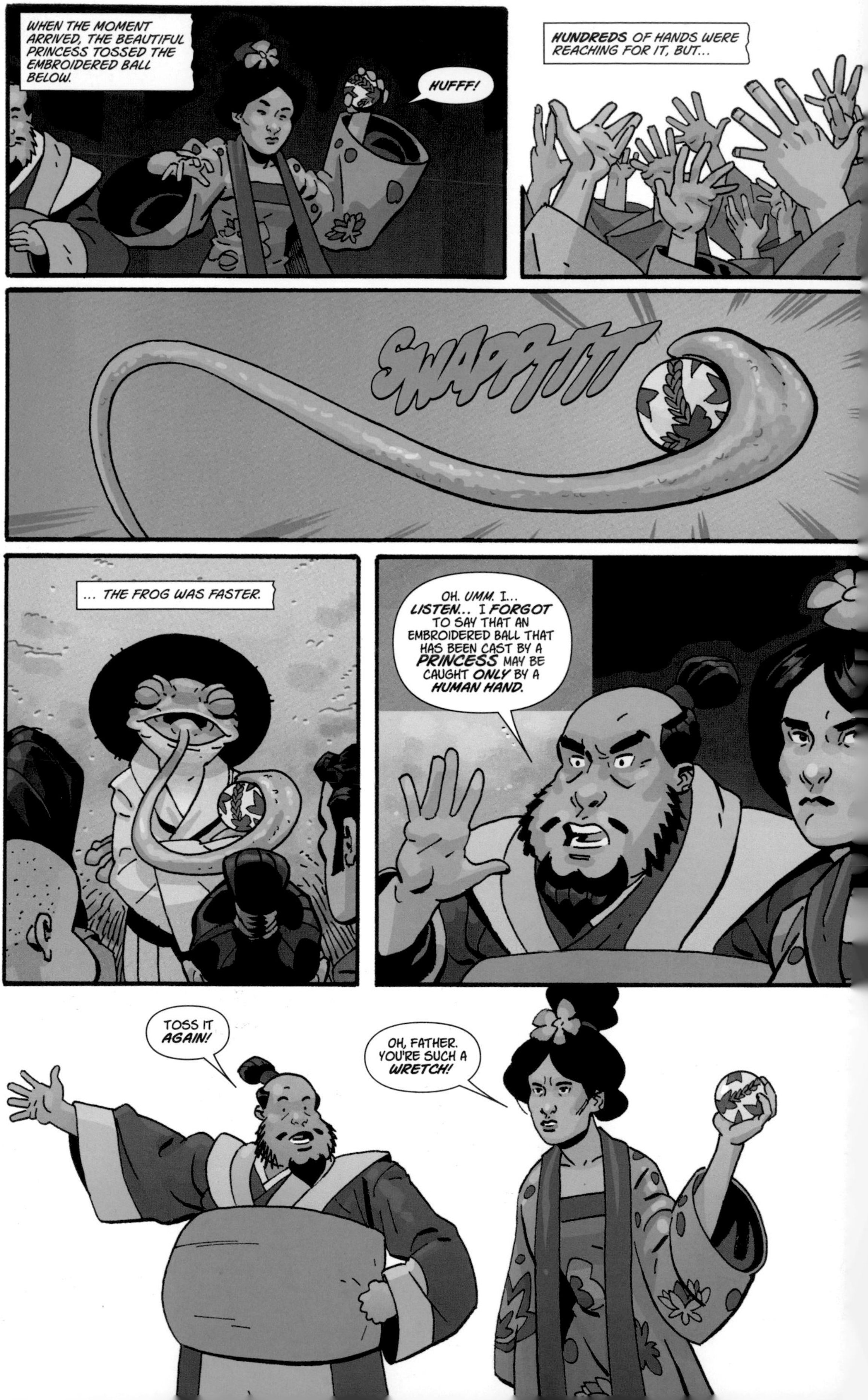
WHEN THE MOMENT ARRIVED, THE BEAUTIFUL PRINCESS TOSSED THE EMBROIDERED BALL BELOW.
HUFFF!
HUNDREDS OF HANDS WERE REACHING FOR IT, BUT...
SWAPPTTT
... THE FROG WAS FASTER.
OH. UMM. I... LISTEN... I FORGOT TO SAY THAT AN EMBROIDERED BALL THAT HAS BEEN CAST BY A PRINCESS MAY BE CAUGHT ONLY BY A HUMAN HAND.
TOSS IT AGAIN!
OH, FATHER. YOU'RE SUCH A WRETCH!

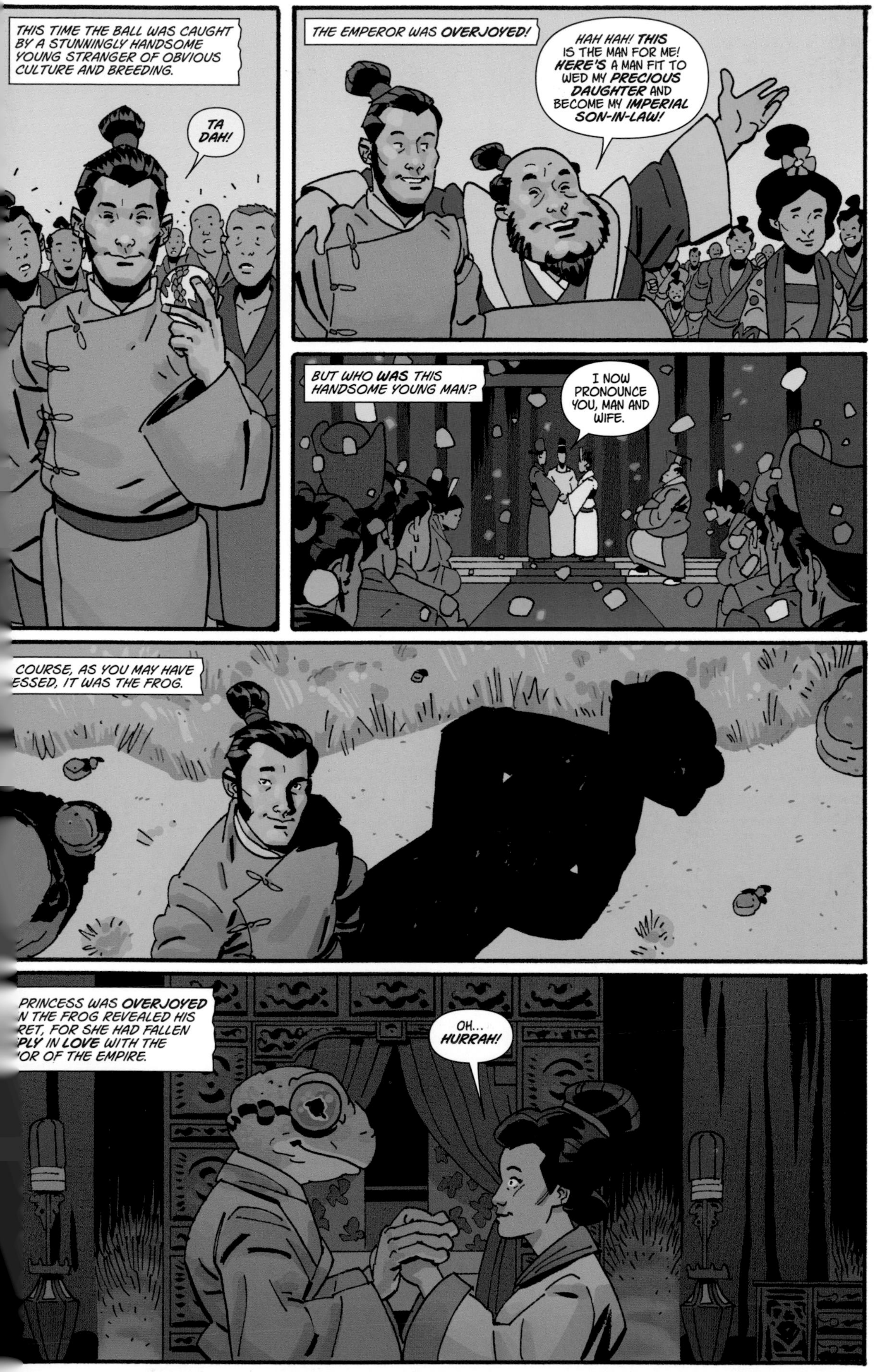
THIS TIME THE BALL WAS CAUGHT BY A STUNNINGLY HANDSOME YOUNG STRANGER OF OBVIOUS CULTURE AND BREEDING.
TA DAH!
THE EMPEROR WAS OVERJOYED!
HAH HAH! THIS IS THE MAN FOR ME! HERE'S A MAN FIT TO WED MY PRECIOUS DAUGHTER AND BECOME MY IMPERIAL SON-IN-LAW!
BUT WHO WAS THIS HANDSOME YOUNG MAN?
I NOW PRONOUNCE YOU, MAN AND WIFE.
COURSE, AS YOU MAY HAVE
ESSED, IT WAS THE FROG.
PRINCESS WAS OVERJOYED
N THE FROG REVEALED HIS
RET, FOR SHE HAD FALLEN
PLY IN LOVE WITH THE
OR OF THE EMPIRE.
OH... HURRAH!

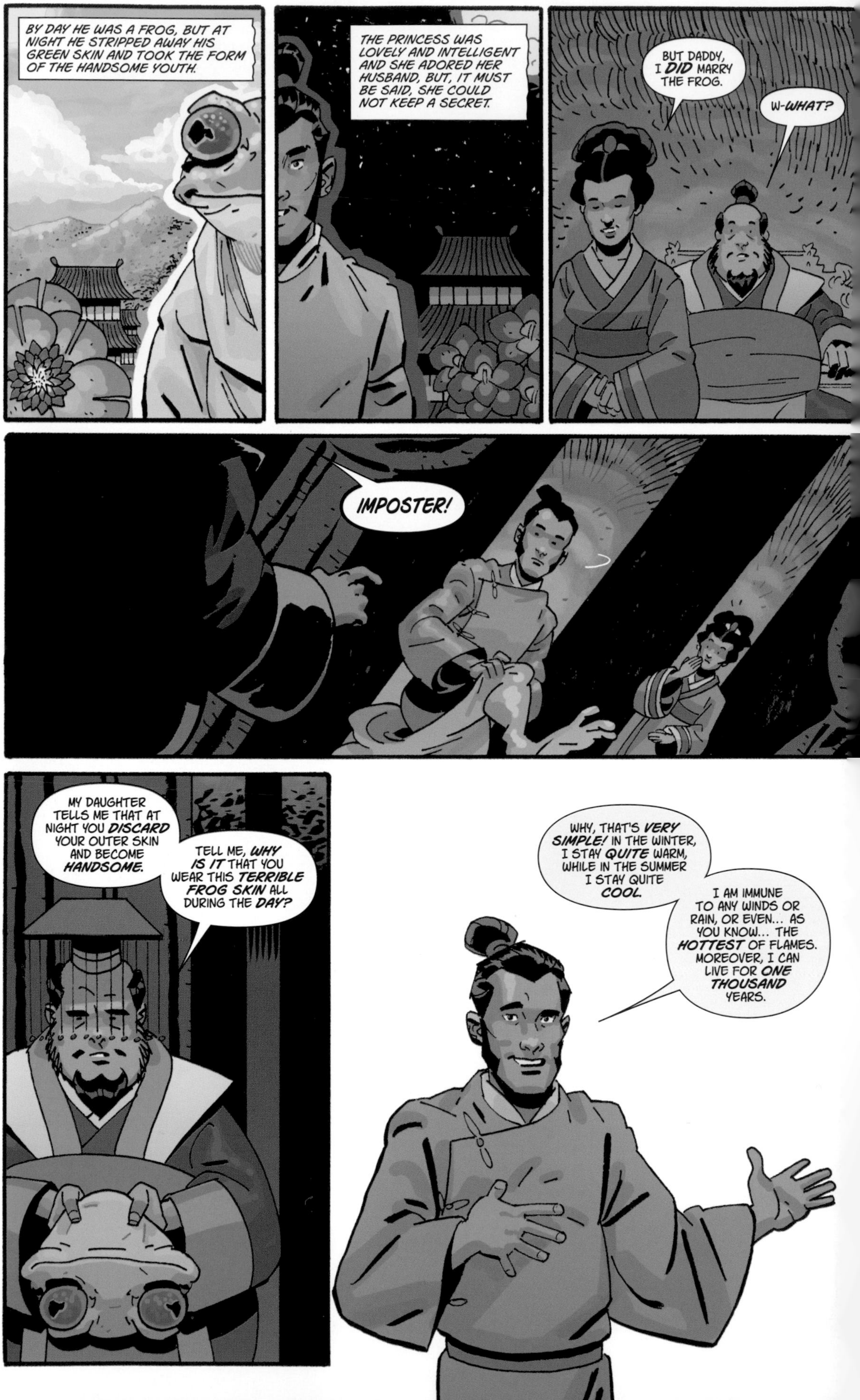
BY DAY HE WAS A FROG, BUT AT NIGHT HE STRIPPED AWAY HIS GREEN SKIN AND TOOK THE FORM OF THE HANDSOME YOUTH.
THE PRINCESS WAS LOVELY AND INTELLIGENT AND SHE ADORED HER HUSBAND, BUT, IT MUST BE SAID, SHE COULD NOT KEEP A SECRET.
BUT DADDY, I DID MARRY THE FROG.
W-WHAT?
IMPOSTER!
MY DAUGHTER TELLS ME THAT AT NIGHT YOU DISCARD YOUR OUTER SKIN AND BECOME HANDSOME.
TELL ME, WHY IS IT THAT YOU WEAR THIS TERRIBLE FROG SKIN ALL DURING THE DAY?
WHY, THAT'S VERY SIMPLE! IN THE WINTER, I STAY QUITE WARM, WHILE IN THE SUMMER I STAY QUITE COOL.
I AM IMMUNE TO ANY WINDS OR RAIN, OR EVEN... AS YOU KNOW... THE HOTTEST OF FLAMES. MOREOVER, I CAN LIVE FOR ONE THOUSAND YEARS.

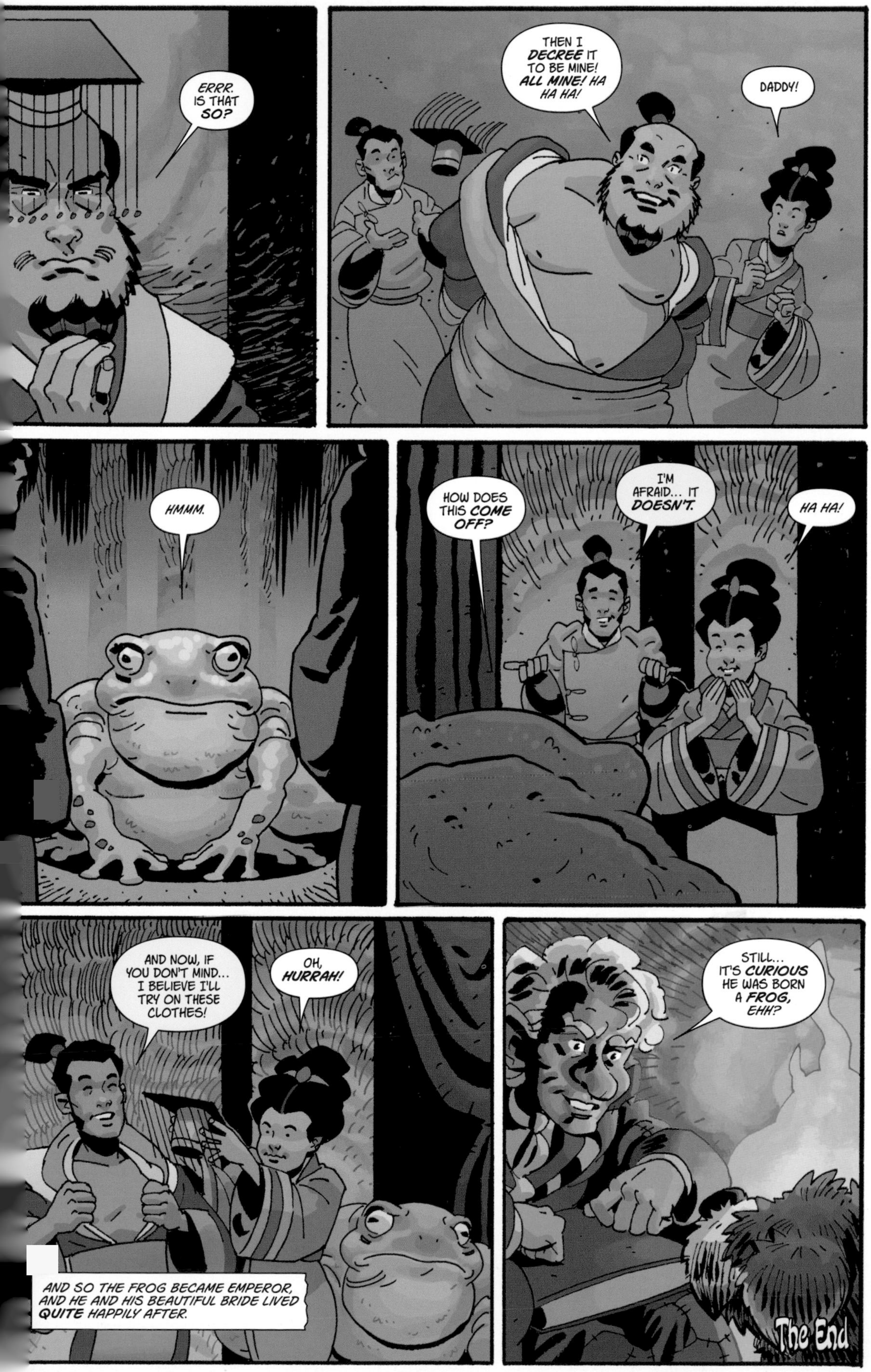
ERRR. IS THAT SO?
THEN I DECREE IT TO BE MINE! ALL MINE! HA HA HA!
DADDY!
HMMM.
HOW DOES THIS COME OFF?
I'M AFRAID... IT DOESN'T.
HA HA!
AND NOW, IF YOU DON'T MIND... I BELIEVE I'LL TRY ON THESE CLOTHES!
OH, HURRAH!
AND SO THE FROG BECAME EMPEROR, AND HE AND HIS BEAUTIFUL BRIDE LIVED QUITE HAPPILY AFTER.
STILL... IT'S CURIOUS HE WAS BORN A FROG, EHH?
The End

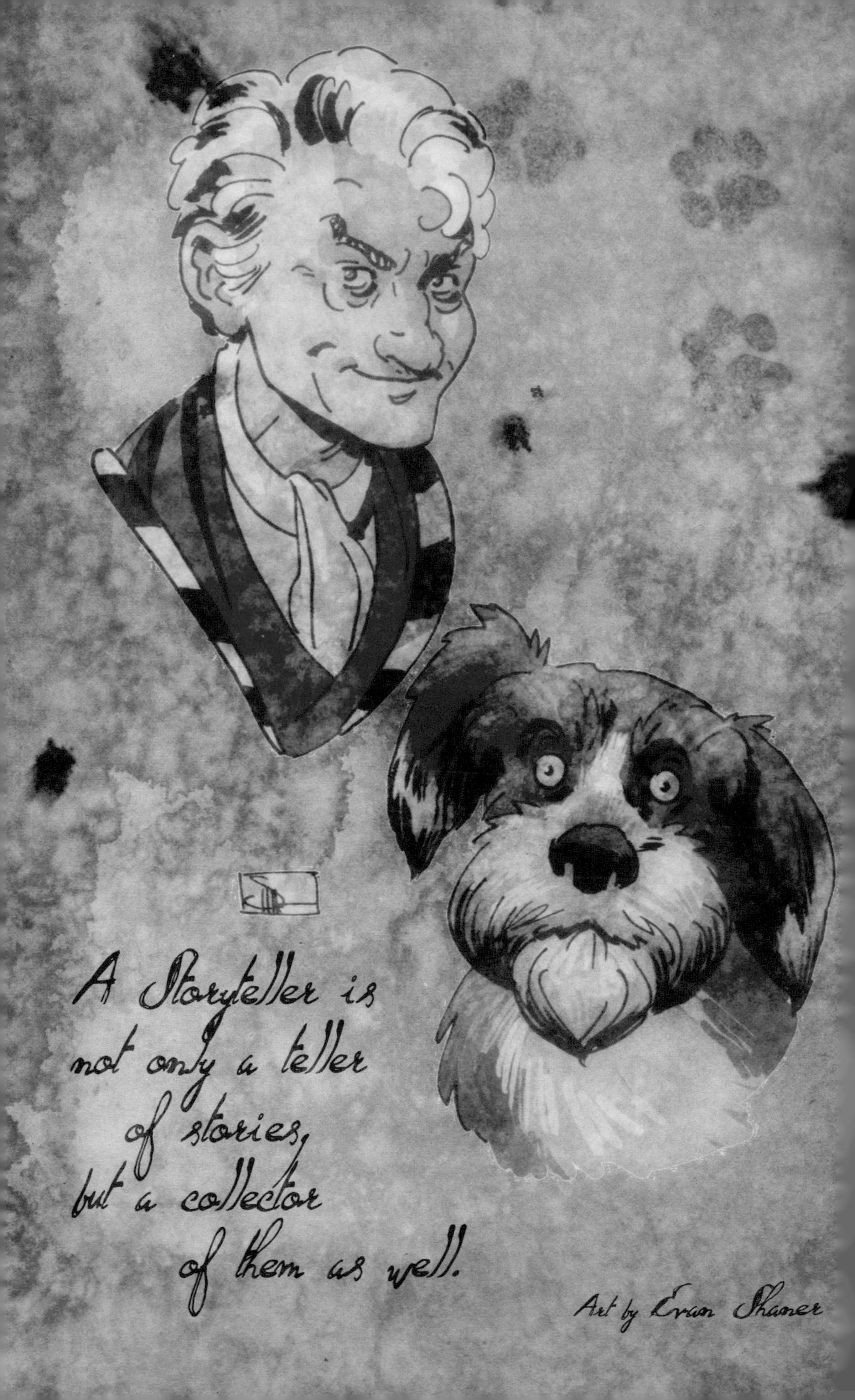

A Storyteller is
not only a teller
of stories,
but a collector
of them as well.

Art by Evan Shaner

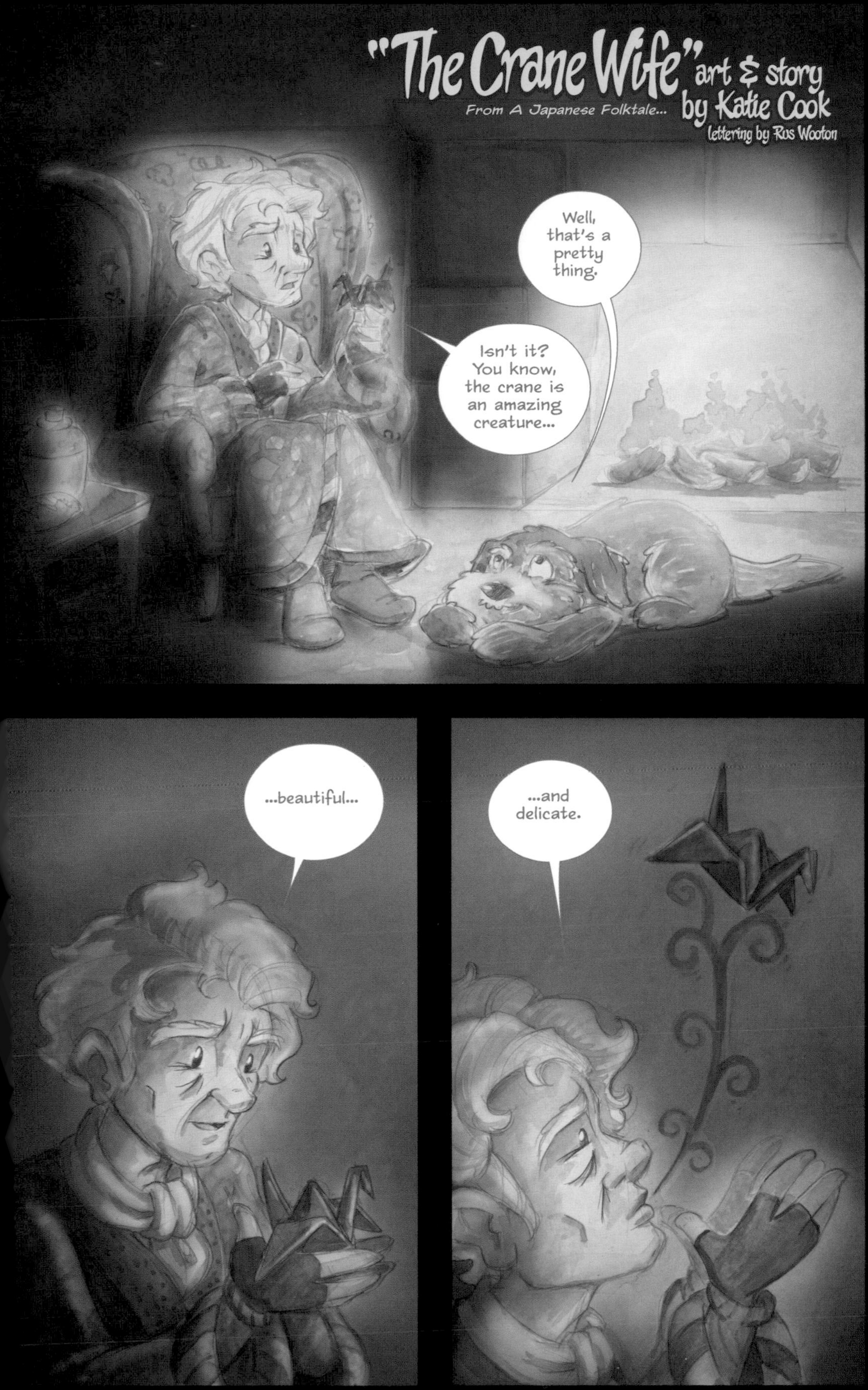
"The Crane Wife" art & story by Katie Cook
From A Japanese Folktale...
lettering by Ros Wooton
Well, that's a pretty thing.
Isn't it? You know, the crane is an amazing creature...
...beautiful...
...and delicate.

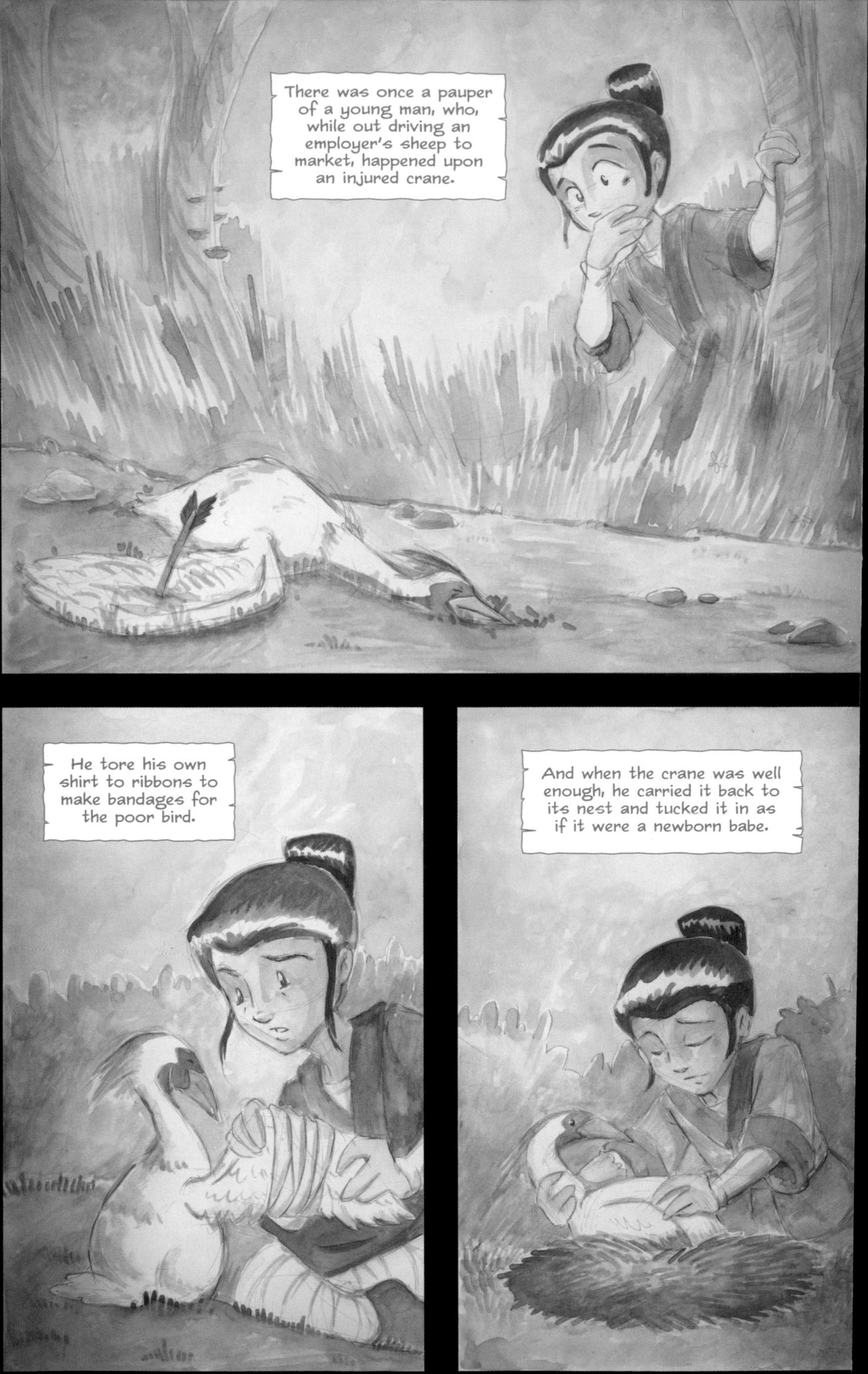
There was once a pauper of a young man, who, while out driving an employer's sheep to market, happened upon an injured crane.
He tore his own shirt to ribbons to make bandages for the poor bird.
And when the crane was well enough, he carried it back to its nest and tucked it in as if it were a newborn babe.

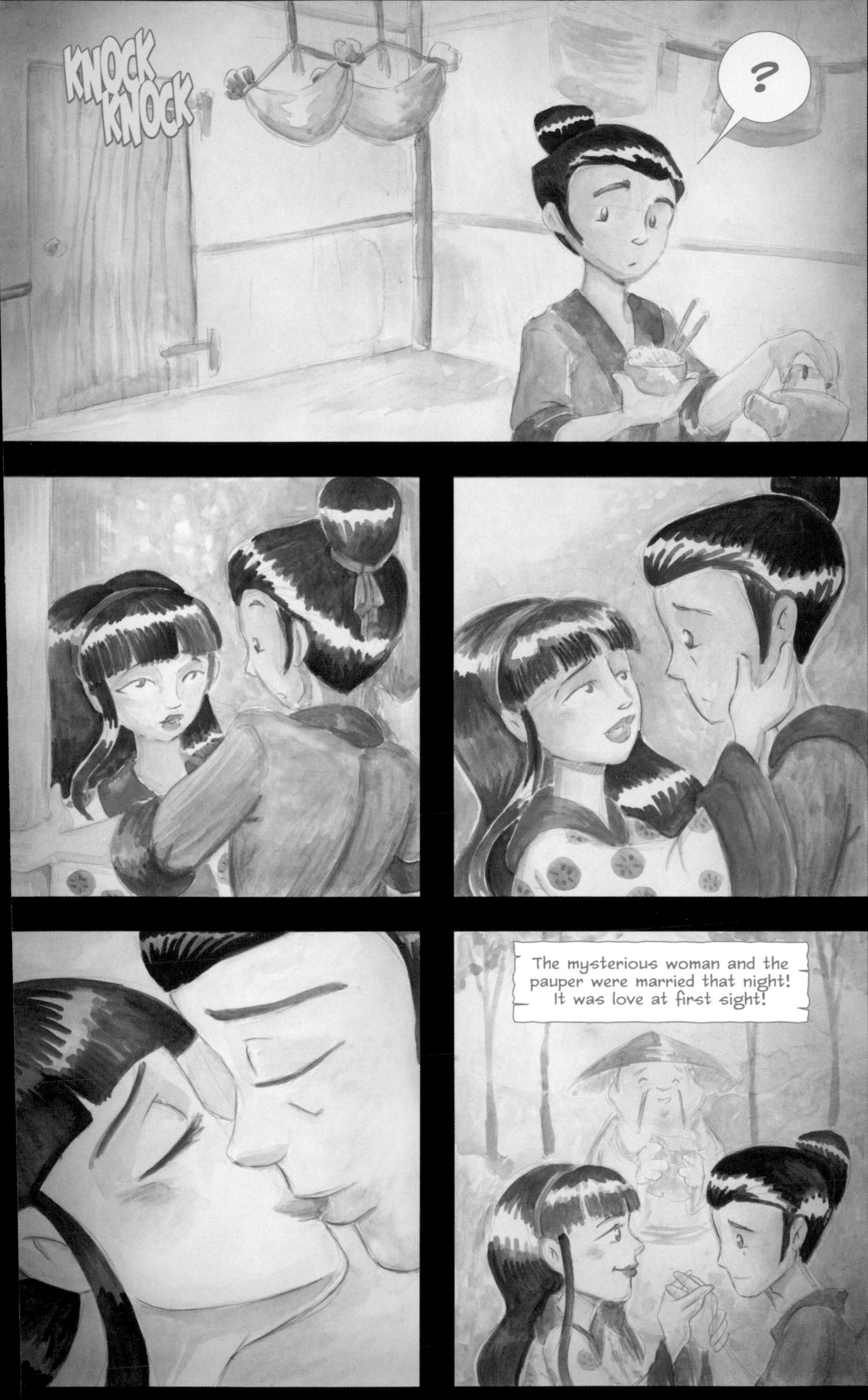
KNOCK KNOCK
?
The mysterious woman and the pauper were married that night! It was love at first sight!

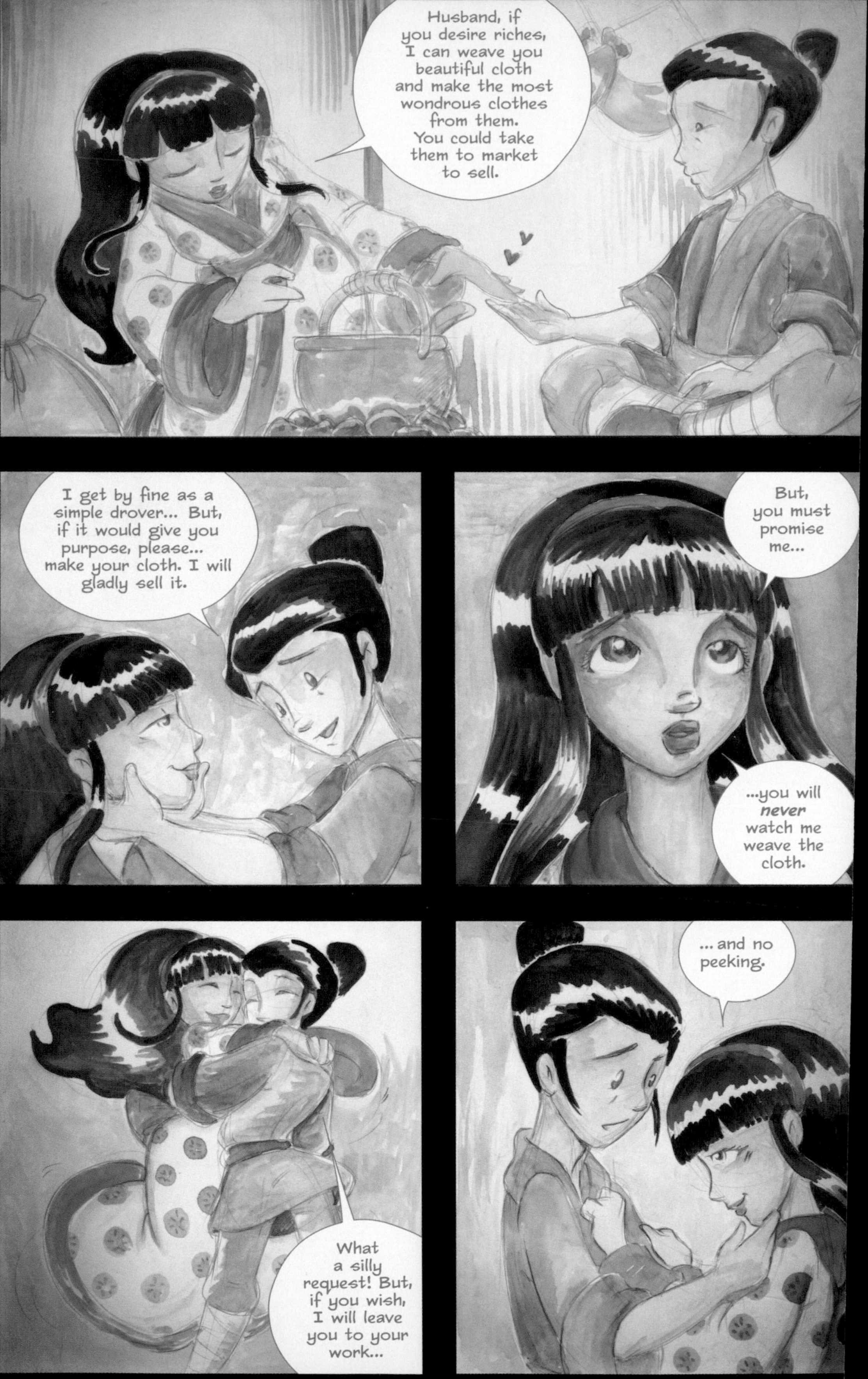
Husband, if you desire riches, I can weave you beautiful cloth and make the most wondrous clothes from them. You could take them to market to sell.
I get by fine as a simple drover... But, if it would give you purpose, please... make your cloth. I will gladly sell it.
But, you must promise me...
...you will *never* watch me weave the cloth.
What a silly request! But, if you wish, I will leave you to your work...
... and no peeking.

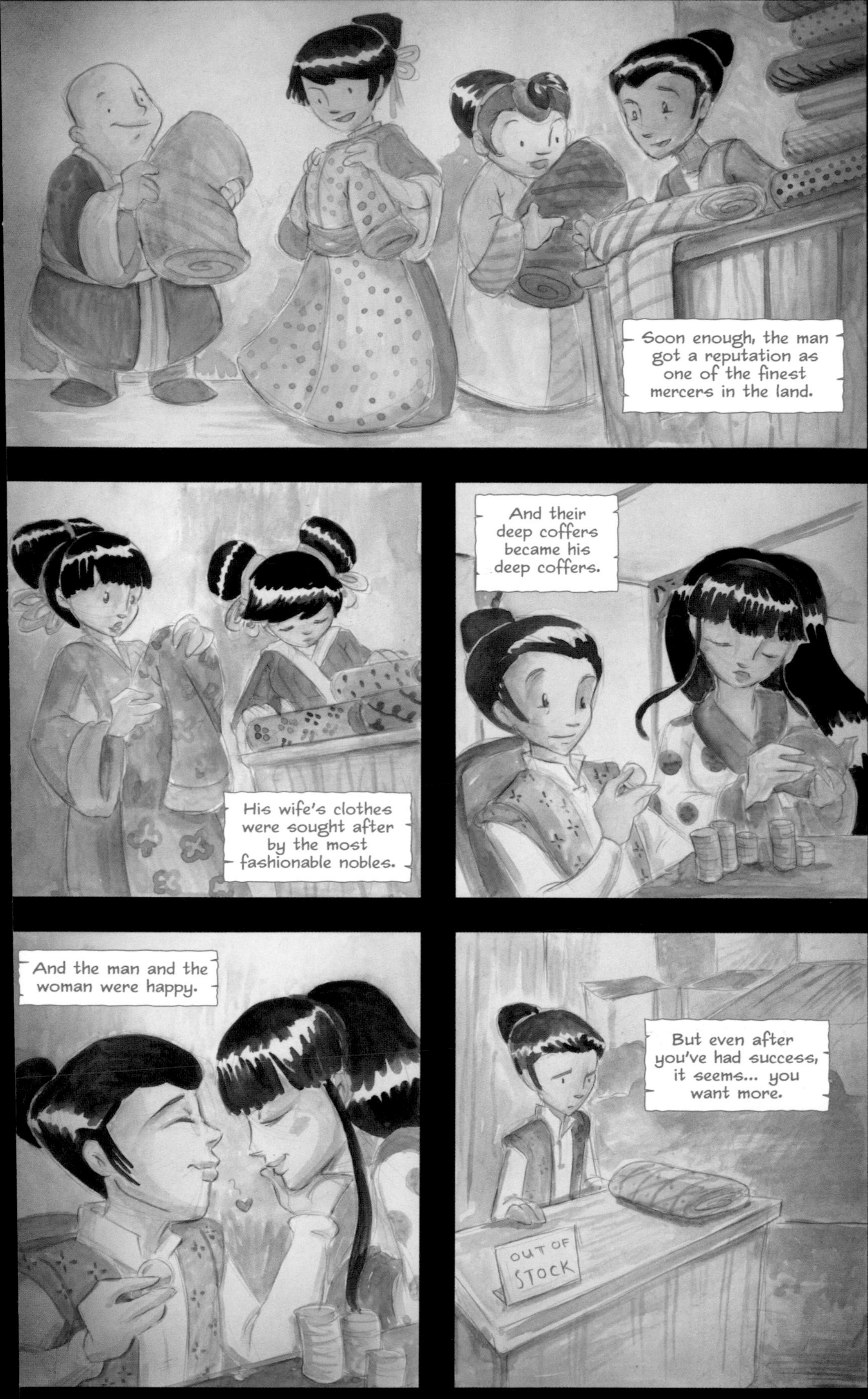

Soon enough, the man got a reputation as one of the finest mercers in the land.
His wife's clothes were sought after by the most fashionable nobles.
And their deep coffers became his deep coffers.
And the man and the woman were happy.
But even after you've had success, it seems... you want more.
OUT OF STOCK

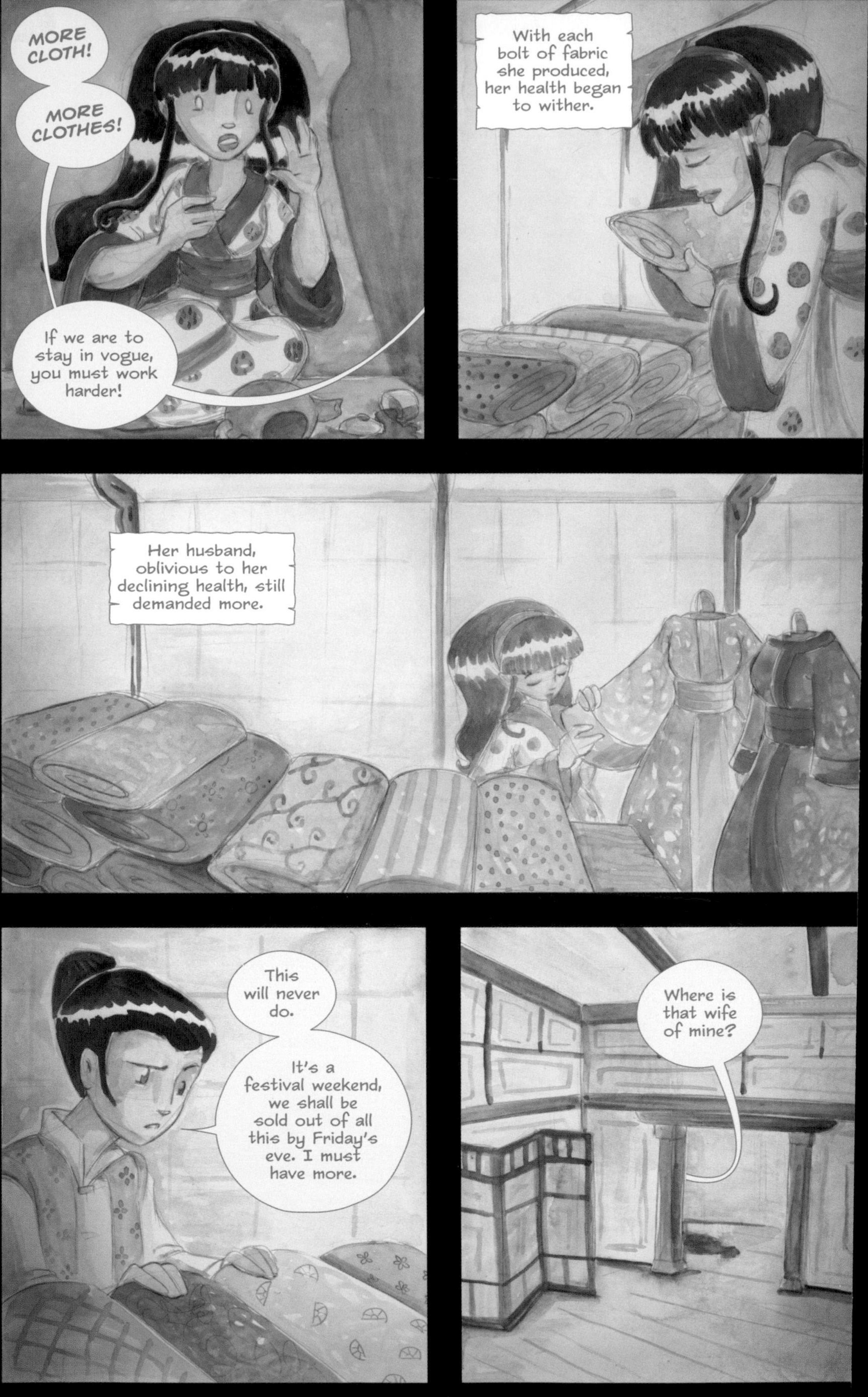
MORE CLOTH!
MORE CLOTHES!
If we are to stay in vogue, you must work harder!
With each bolt of fabric she produced, her health began to wither.
Her husband, oblivious to her declining health, still demanded more.
This will never do.
It's a festival weekend, we shall be sold out of all this by Friday's eve. I must have more.
Where is that wife of mine?

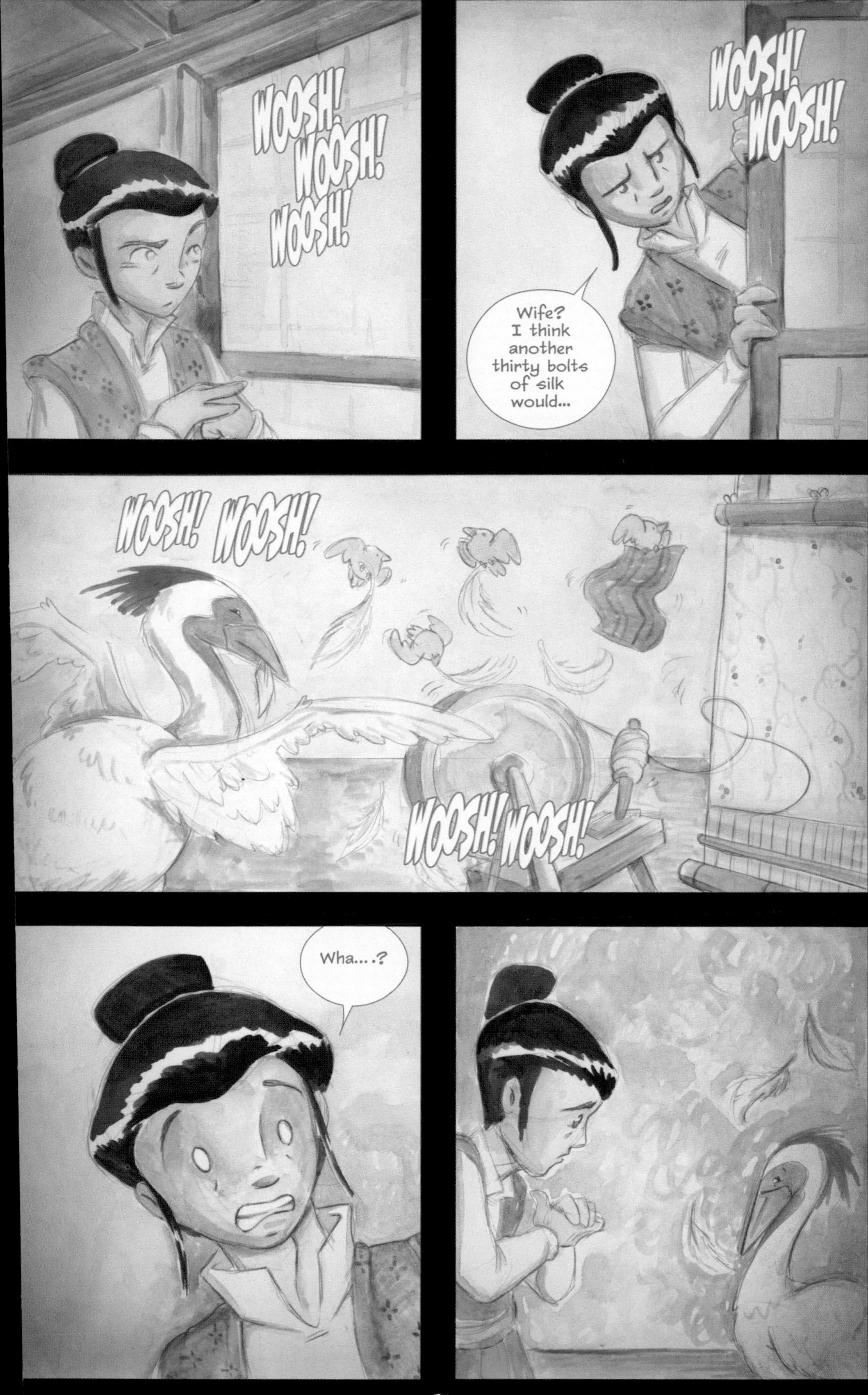
WOOSH! WOOSH! WOOSH!
WOOSH! WOOSH!
Wife? I think another thirty bolts of silk would...
WOOSH! WOOSH!
WOOSH! WOOSH!
Wha...?

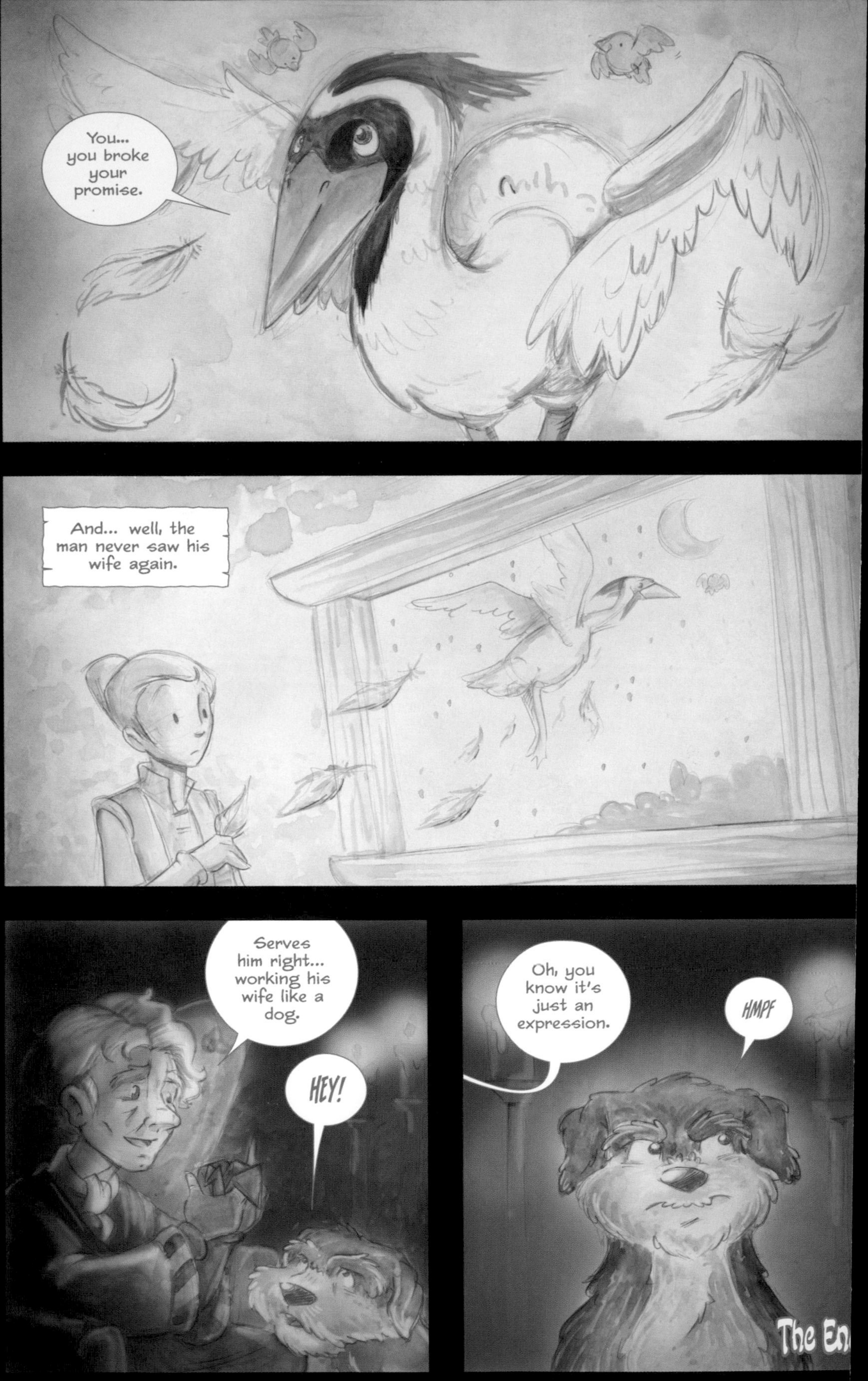
You... you broke your promise.
And... well, the man never saw his wife again.
Serves him right... working his wife like a dog.
HEY!
Oh, you know it's just an expression.
HMPF
The En

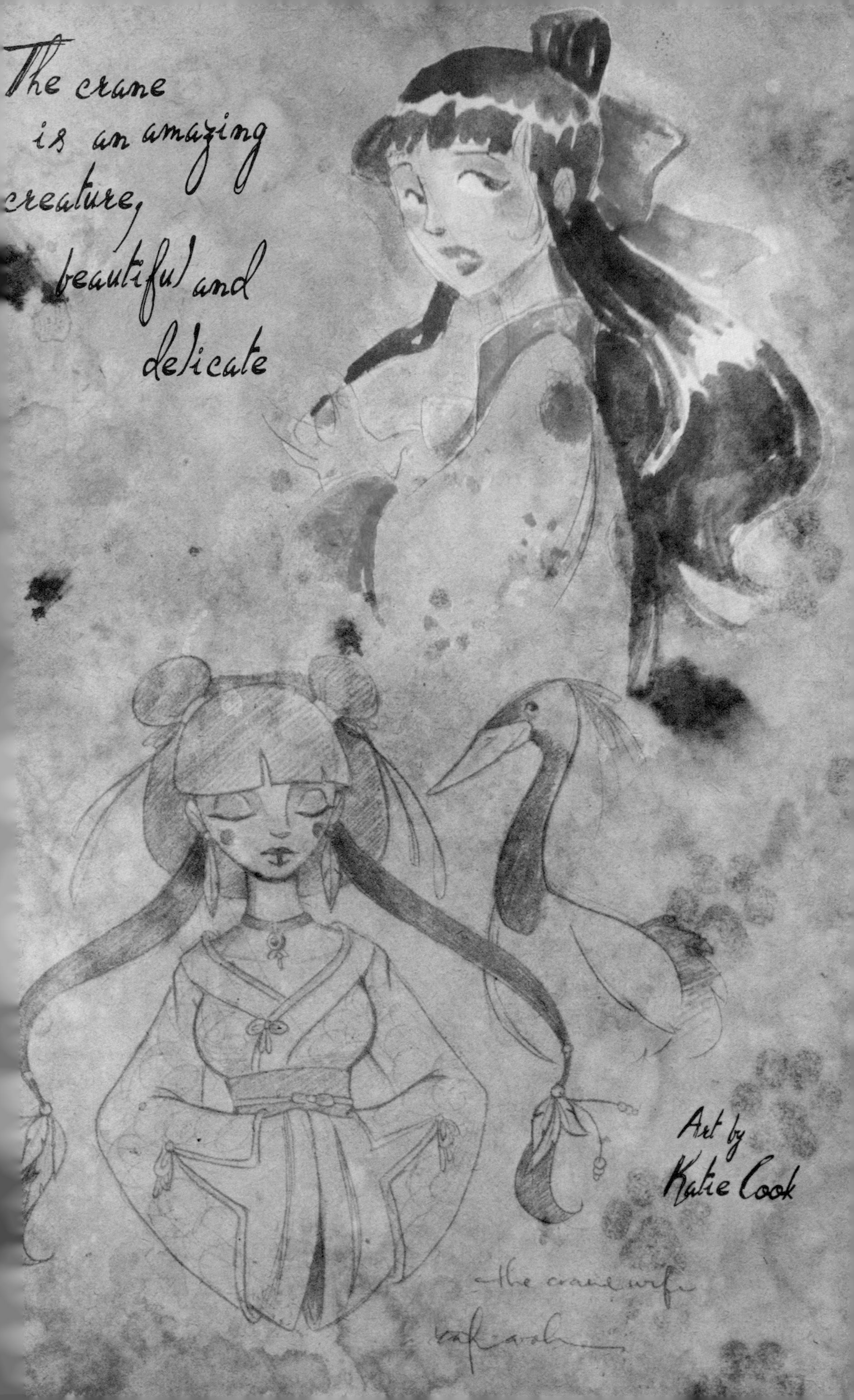
The crane
is an amazing
creature,
beautiful and
delicate
the crane wife
Art by
Katie Cook

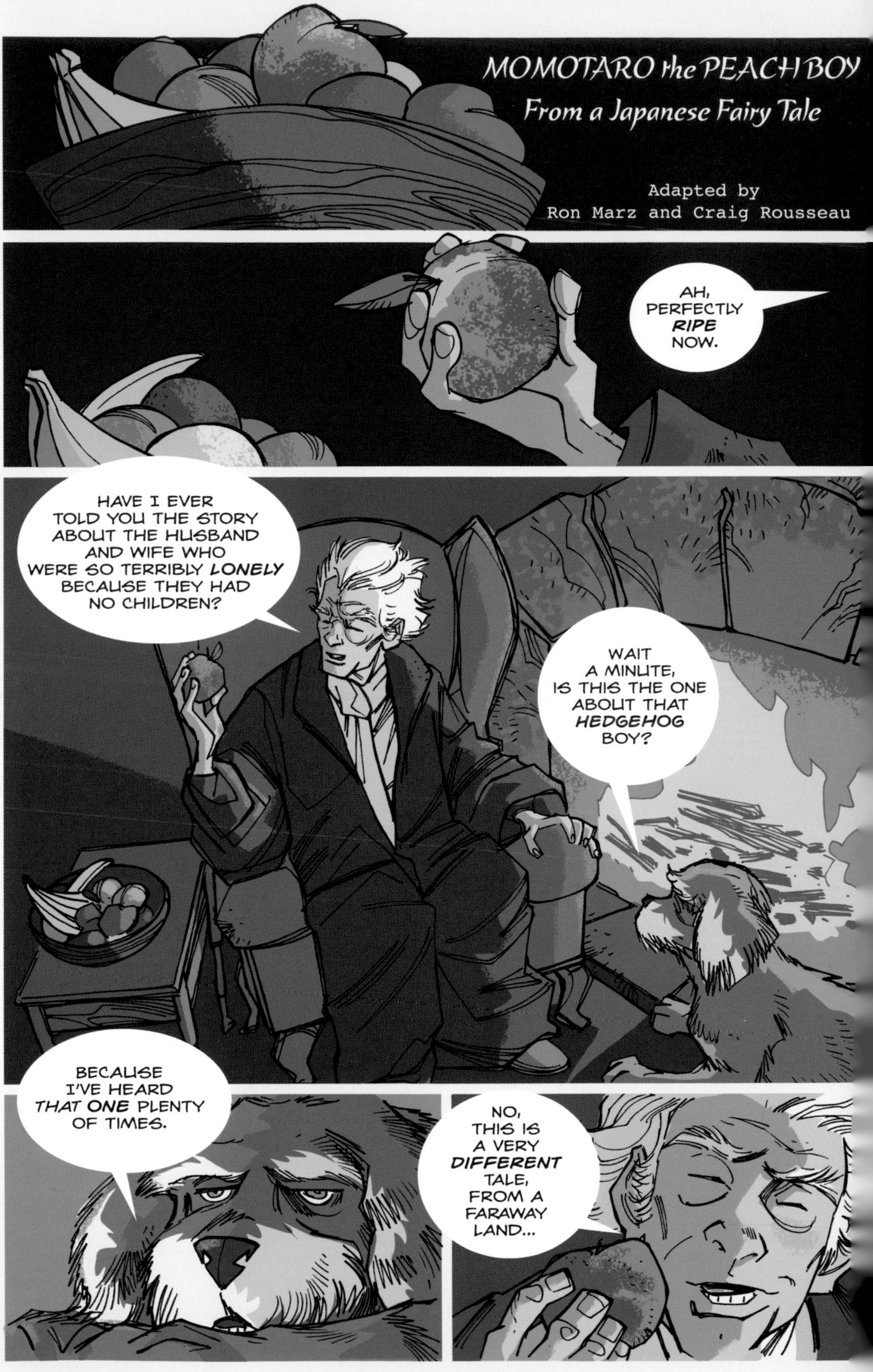
MOMOTARO the PEACH BOY
From a Japanese Fairy Tale
Adapted by
Ron Marz and Craig Rousseau
AH, PERFECTLY RIPE NOW.
HAVE I EVER TOLD YOU THE STORY ABOUT THE HUSBAND AND WIFE WHO WERE SO TERRIBLY LONELY BECAUSE THEY HAD NO CHILDREN?
WAIT A MINUTE, IS THIS THE ONE ABOUT THAT HEDGEHOG BOY?
BECAUSE I'VE HEARD THAT ONE PLENTY OF TIMES.
NO, THIS IS A VERY DIFFERENT TALE, FROM A FARAWAY LAND...

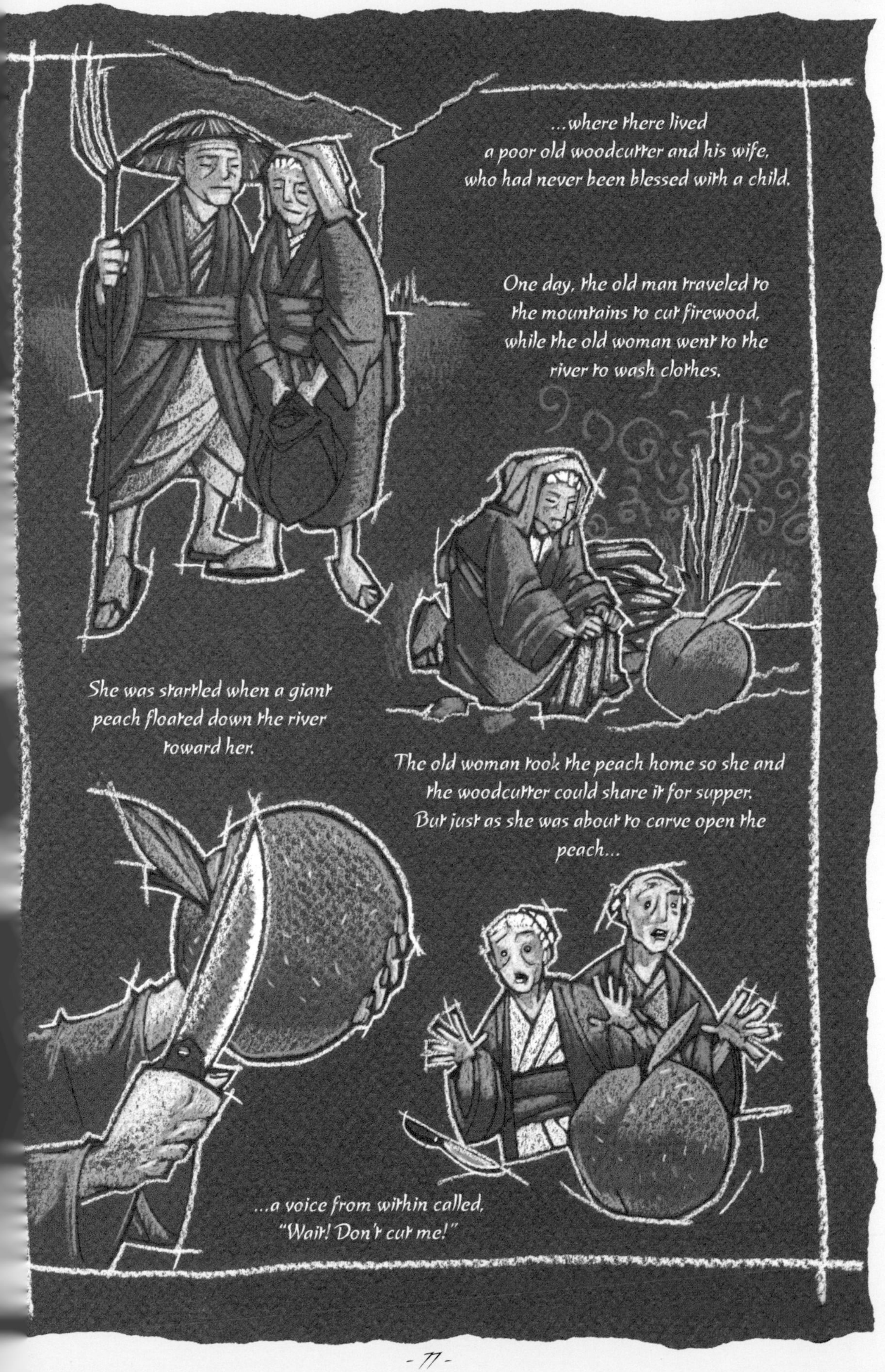
...where there lived
a poor old woodcutter and his wife,
who had never been blessed with a child.
One day, the old man traveled to
the mountains to cut firewood,
while the old woman went to the
river to wash clothes.
She was startled when a giant
peach floated down the river
toward her.
The old woman took the peach home so she and
the woodcutter could share it for supper.
But just as she was about to carve open the
peach...
...a voice from within called,
"Wait! Don't cut me!"

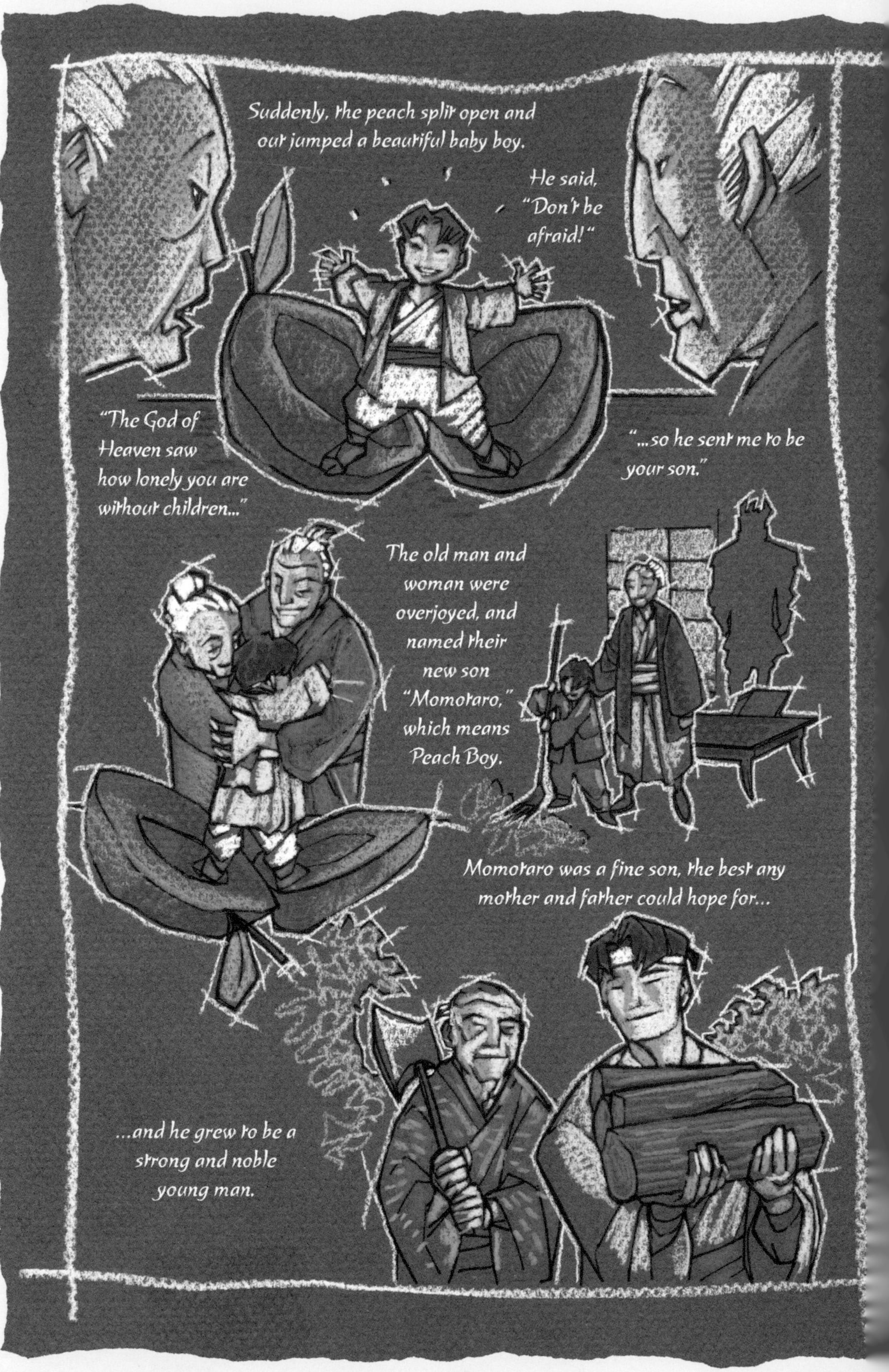
Suddenly, the peach split open and out jumped a beautiful baby boy.
He said, "Don't be afraid!"
"The God of Heaven saw how lonely you are without children..."
"...so he sent me to be your son."
The old man and woman were overjoyed, and named their new son "Momotaro," which means Peach Boy.
Momotaro was a fine son, the best any mother and father could hope for...
...and he grew to be a strong and noble young man.

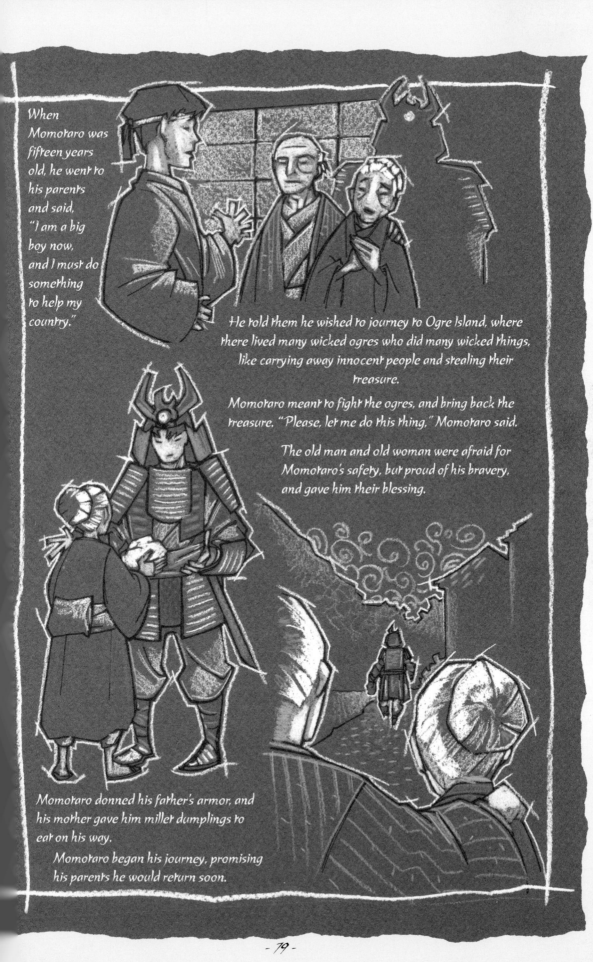

When Momotaro was fifteen years old, he went to his parents and said, "I am a big boy now, and I must do something to help my country."

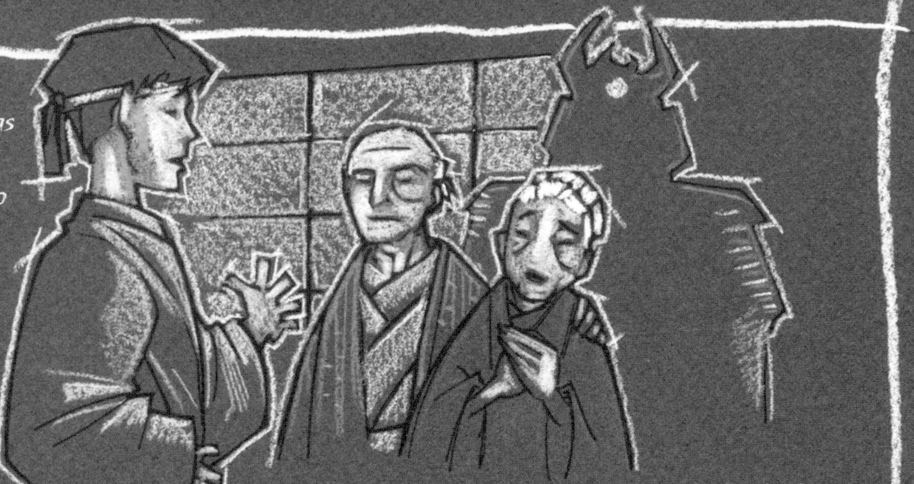

He told them he wished to journey to Ogre Island, where there lived many wicked ogres who did many wicked things, like carrying away innocent people and stealing their treasure.

Momotaro meant to fight the ogres, and bring back the treasure. "Please, let me do this thing," Momotaro said.

The old man and old woman were afraid for Momotaro's safety, but proud of his bravery, and gave him their blessing.

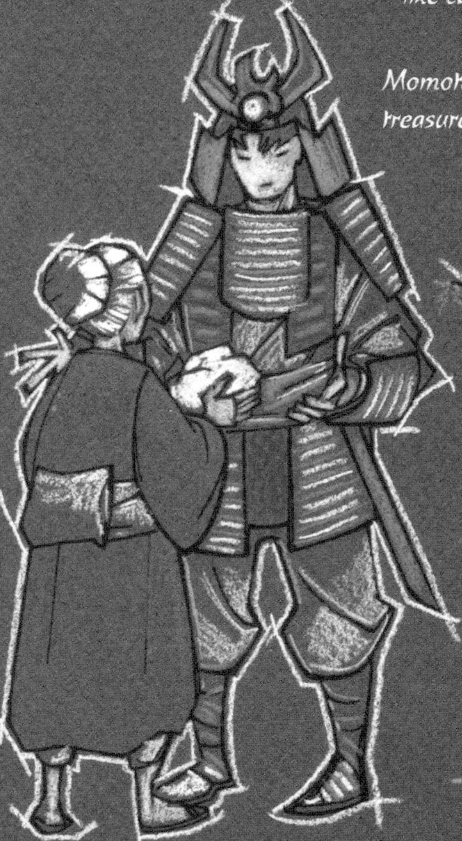

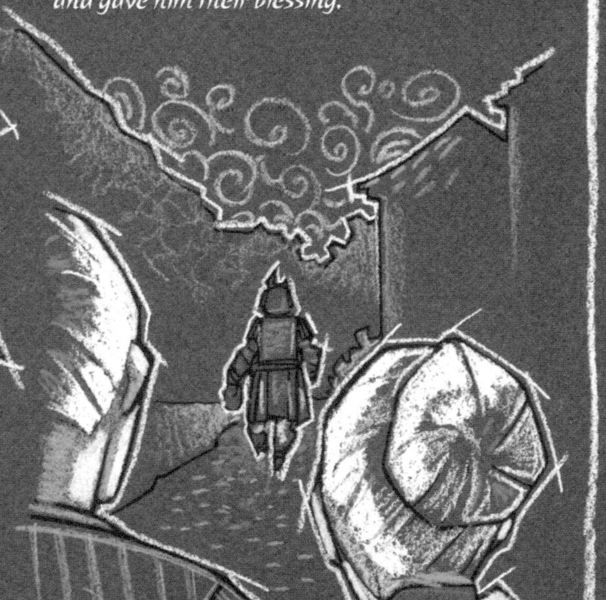

Momotaro donned his father's armor, and his mother gave him millet dumplings to eat on his way.

Momotaro began his journey, promising his parents he would return soon.

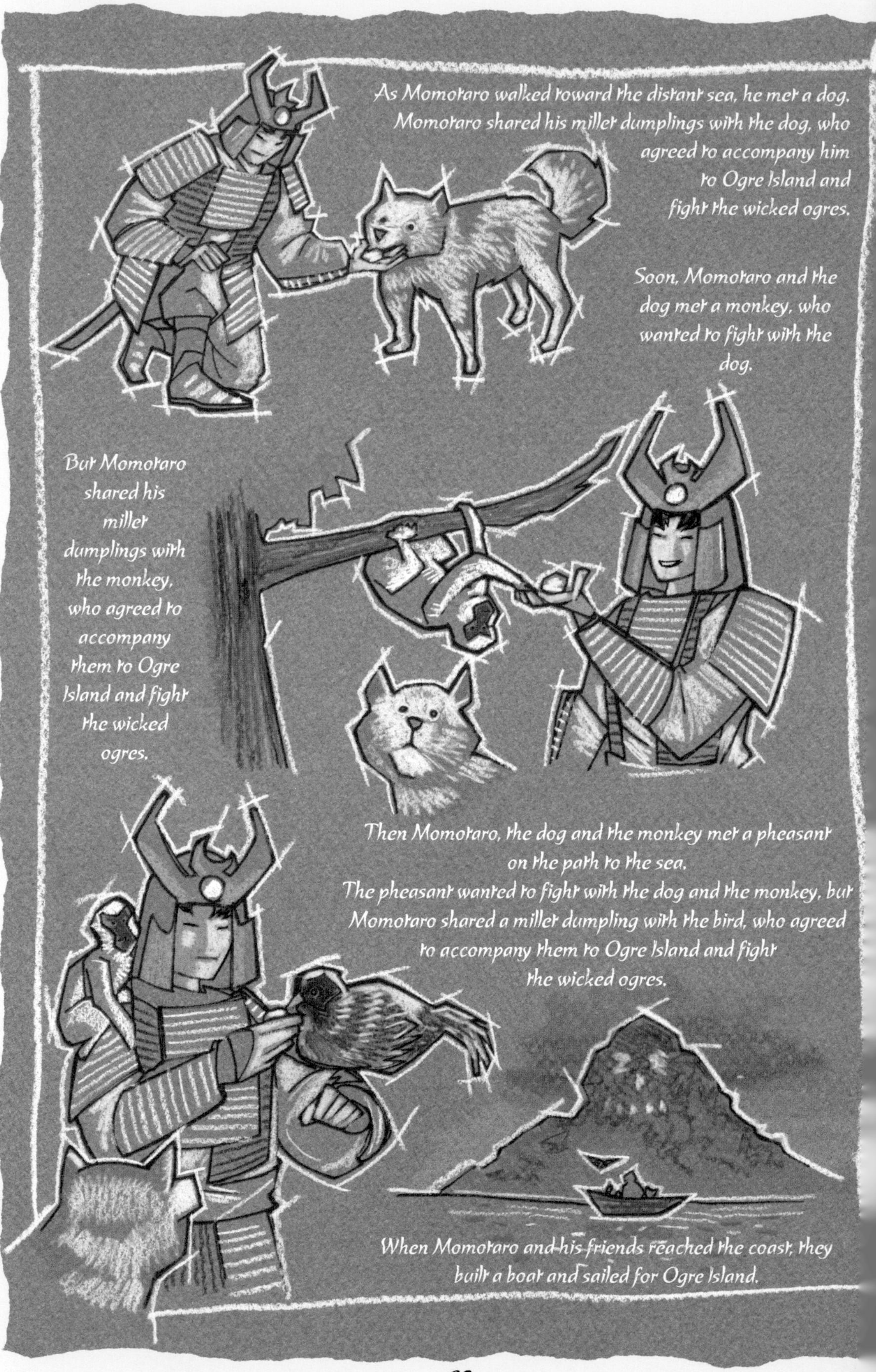
As Momotaro walked toward the distant sea, he met a dog. Momotaro shared his millet dumplings with the dog, who agreed to accompany him to Ogre Island and fight the wicked ogres.
Soon, Momotaro and the dog met a monkey, who wanted to fight with the dog.
But Momotaro shared his millet dumplings with the monkey, who agreed to accompany them to Ogre Island and fight the wicked ogres.
Then Momotaro, the dog and the monkey met a pheasant on the path to the sea.
The pheasant wanted to fight with the dog and the monkey, but Momotaro shared a millet dumpling with the bird, who agreed to accompany them to Ogre Island and fight the wicked ogres.
When Momotaro and his friends reached the coast, they built a boat and sailed for Ogre Island.

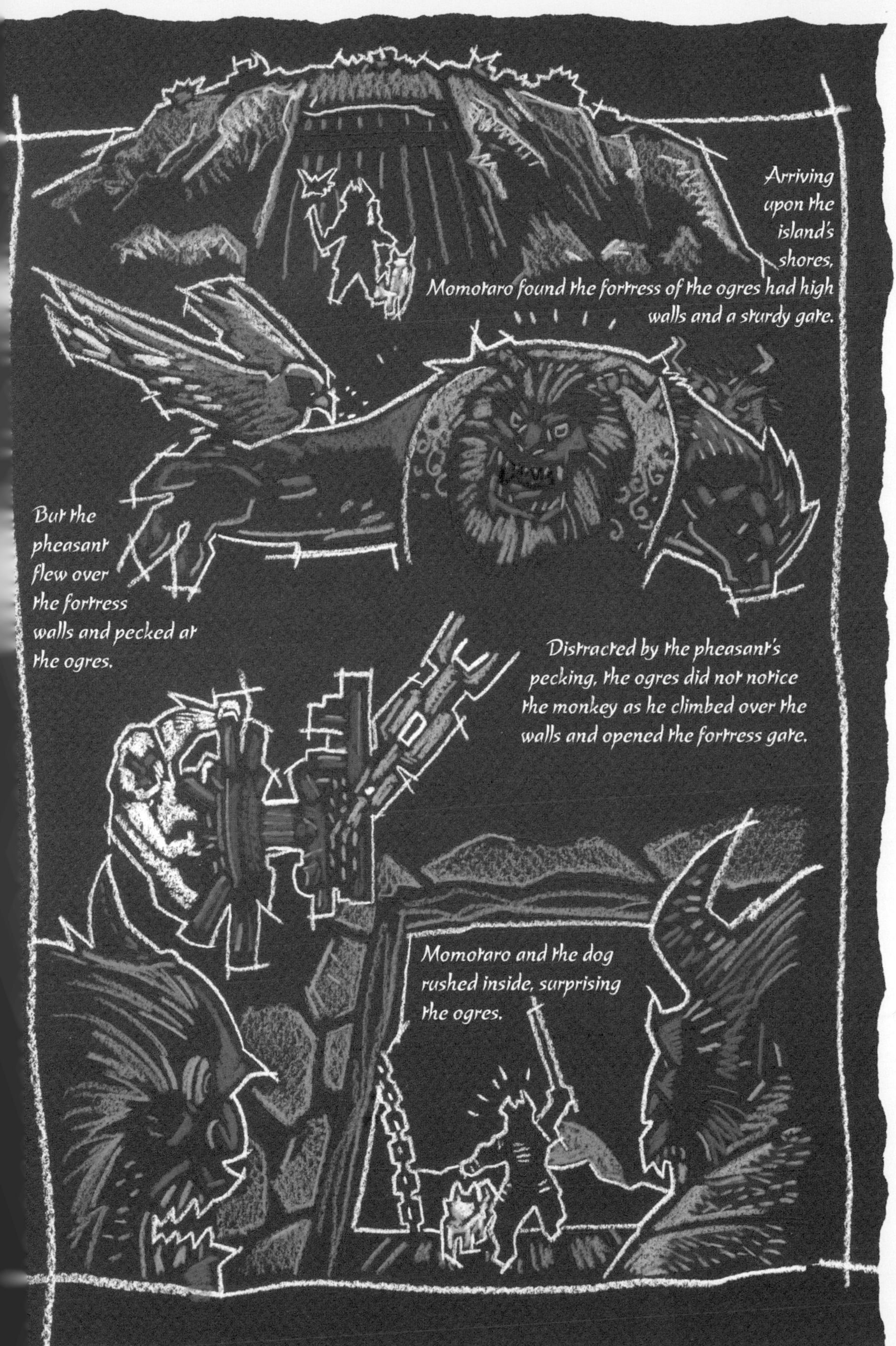

Arriving upon the island's shores, Momotaro found the fortress of the ogres had high walls and a sturdy gate.
But the pheasant flew over the fortress walls and pecked at the ogres.
Distracted by the pheasant's pecking, the ogres did not notice the monkey as he climbed over the walls and opened the fortress gate.
Momotaro and the dog rushed inside, surprising the ogres.

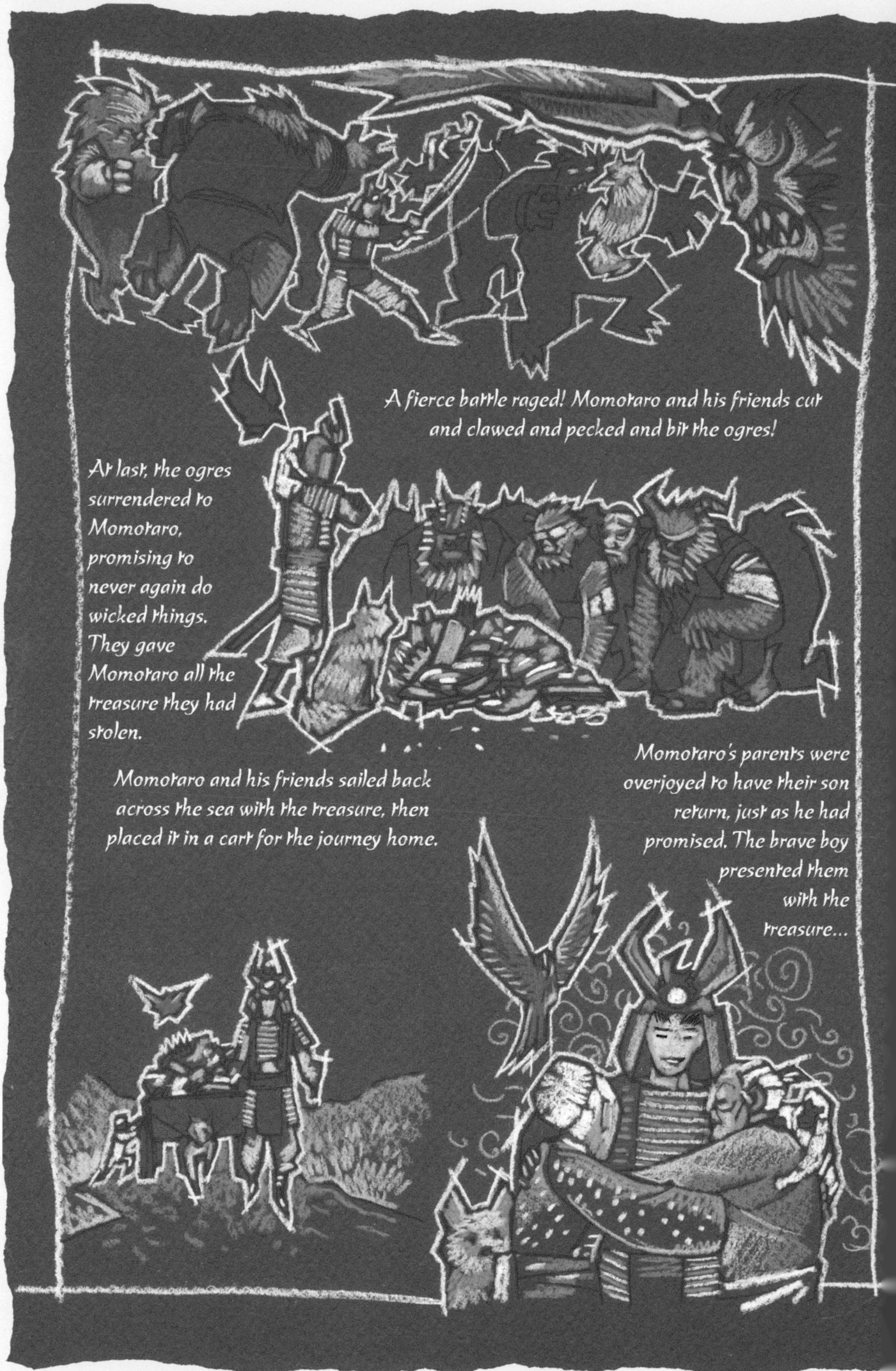
A fierce battle raged! Momotaro and his friends cut and clawed and pecked and bit the ogres!
At last, the ogres surrendered to Momotaro, promising to never again do wicked things. They gave Momotaro all the treasure they had stolen.
Momotaro and his friends sailed back across the sea with the treasure, then placed it in a cart for the journey home.
Momotaro's parents were overjoyed to have their son return, just as he had promised. The brave boy presented them with the treasure...

... AND THEY *ALL* LIVED HAPPILY TOGETHER FOR MANY YEARS TO COME.

THAT WAS A *NEW* ONE. I *LIKED* THAT ONE...

... ESPECIALLY THE PART ABOUT THE *DOG*. MOMOTARO *NEVER* WOULD HAVE DEFEATED THE OGRES WITHOUT *HIM*.

I SUPPOSE THAT'S SO.

I'LL BET *I* COULD DEFEAT OGRES.

WAG WAG WAG

GRRR GRRR

I'M SURE YOU COULD...

PAT PAT

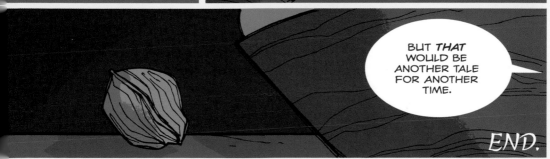

BUT *THAT* WOULD BE ANOTHER TALE FOR ANOTHER TIME.

END.

"The Witch Baby"
From An Early Russian Folk Tale

Based on the unproduced
Storyteller teleplay
written by Anthony Minghella,
Susan Kodieck & Anne Mountfield

Adapted by Nate Cosby
Art by Ronan Cliquet
Color by Adam Street
Lettering by Rus Wooton

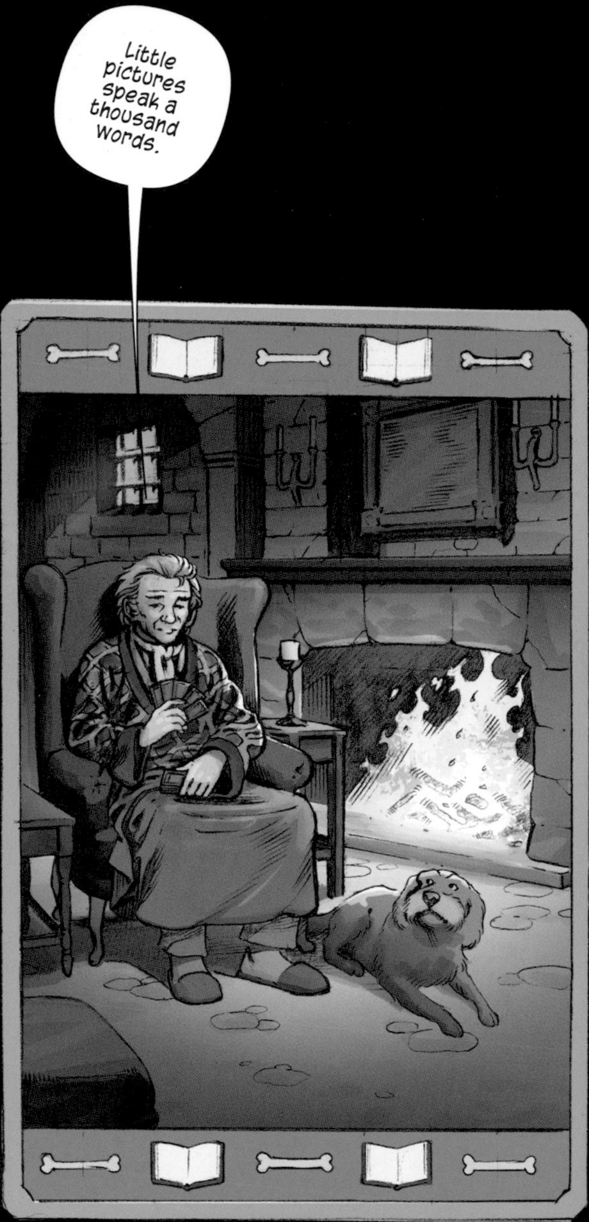
Little pictures speak a thousand words.

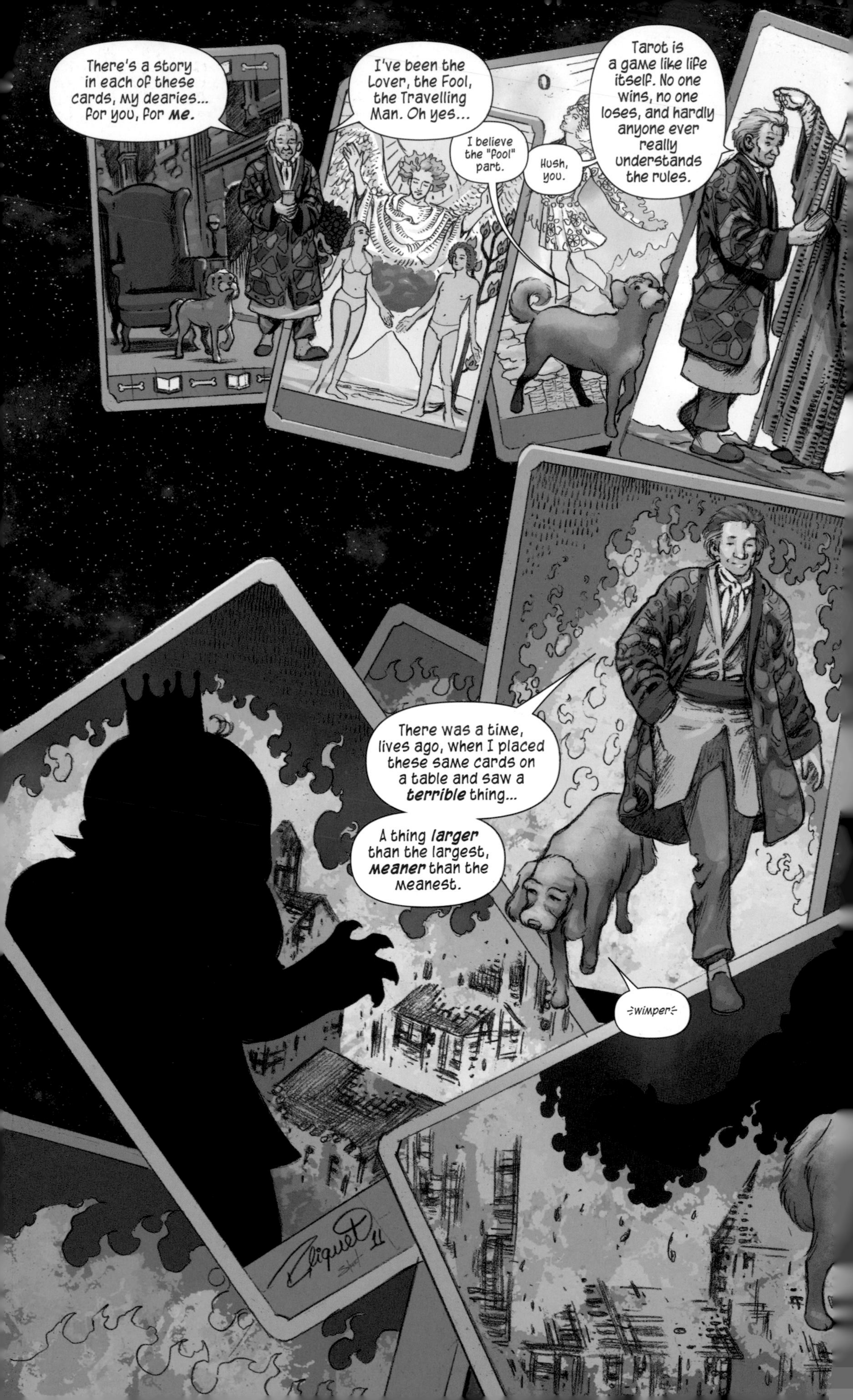
There's a story in each of these cards, my dearies... for you, for me.
I've been the Lover, the Fool, the Travelling Man. Oh yes...
I believe the "fool" part.
Hush, you.
Tarot is a game like life itself. No one wins, no one loses, and hardly anyone ever really understands the rules.
There was a time, lives ago, when I placed these same cards on a table and saw a terrible thing...
A thing larger than the largest, meaner than the meanest.
wimper

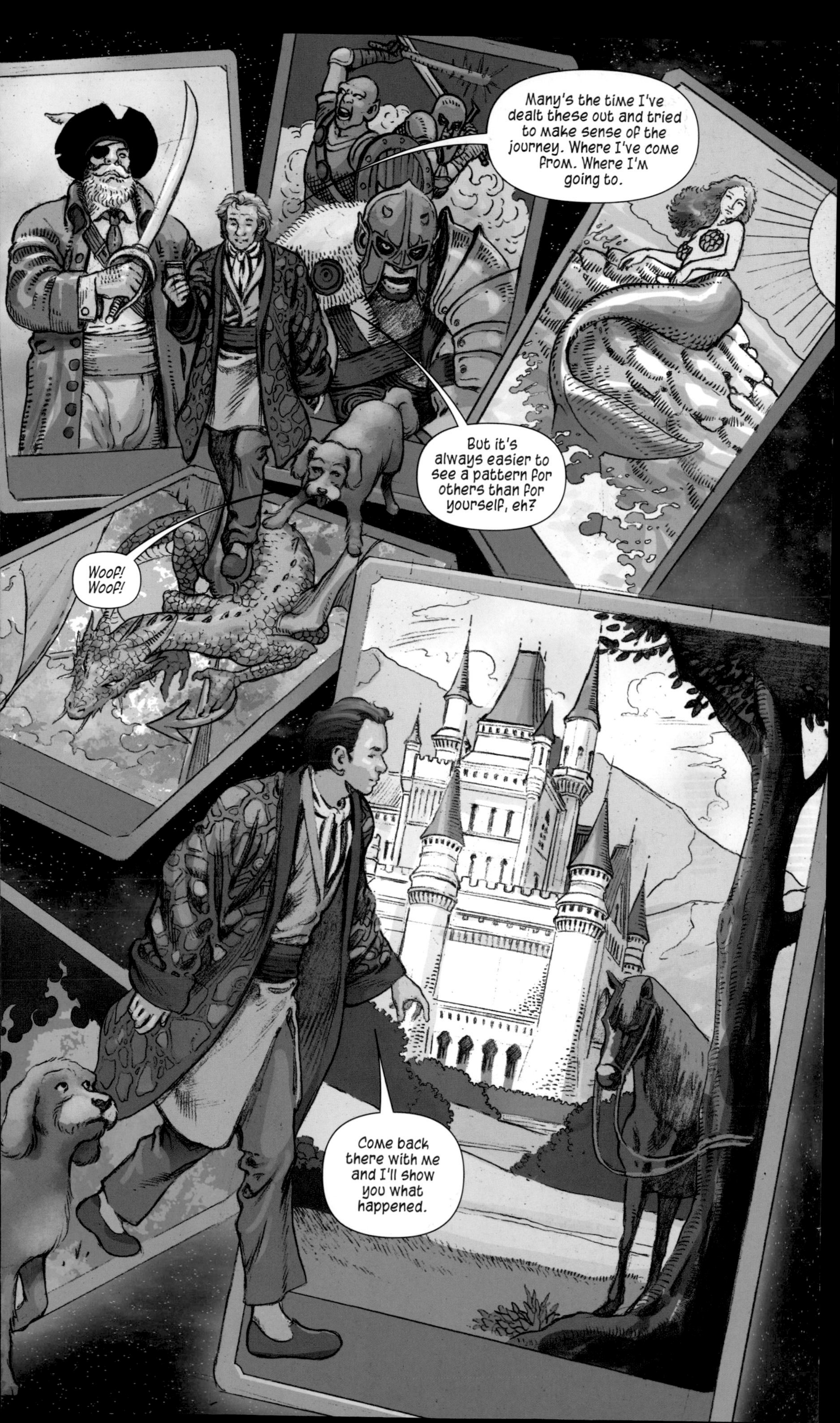
Many's the time I've dealt these out and tried to make sense of the journey. Where I've come from. Where I'm going to.
But it's always easier to see a pattern for others than for yourself, eh?
Woof! Woof!
Come back there with me and I'll show you what happened.

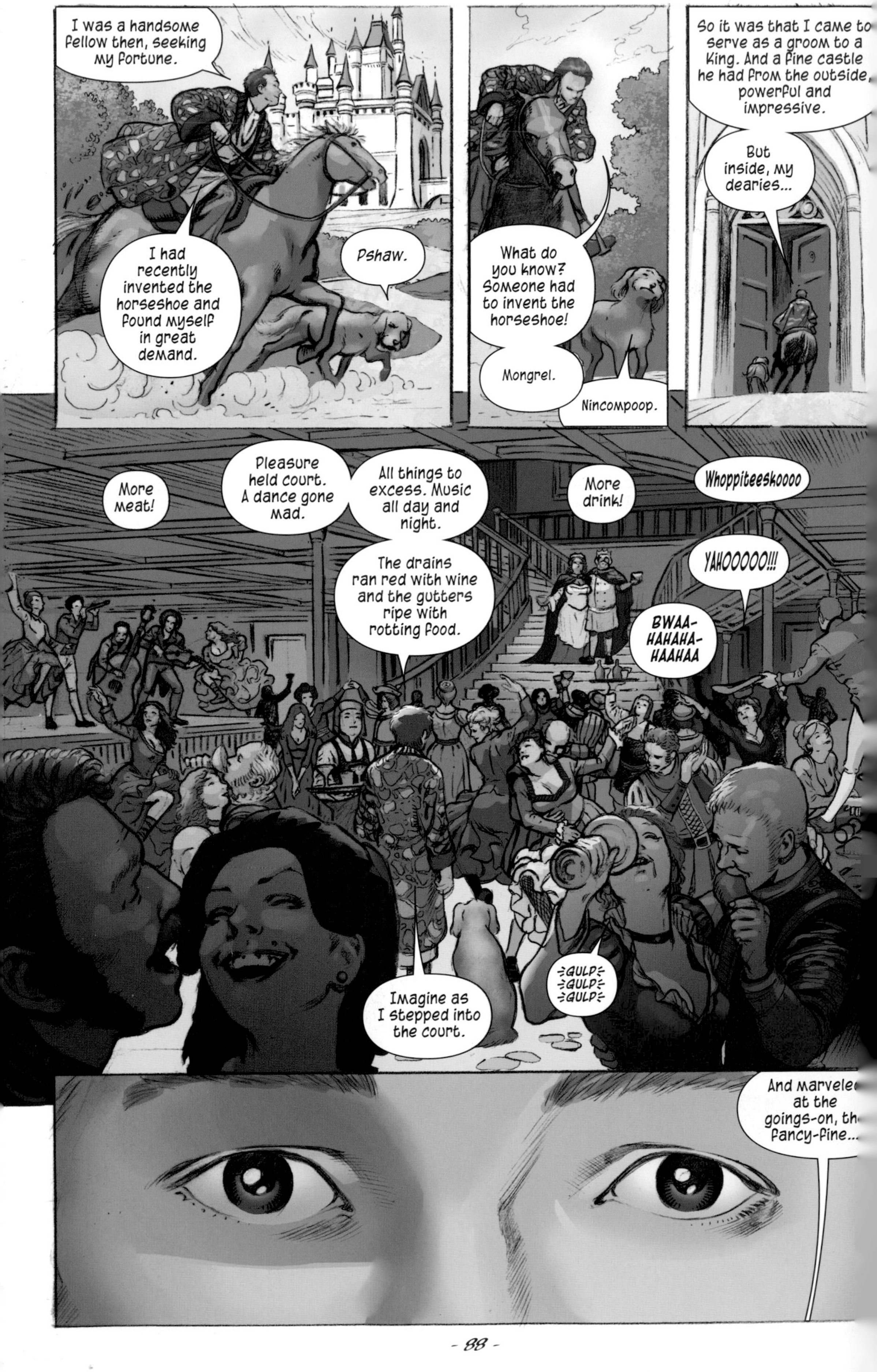

I was a handsome fellow then, seeking my fortune.
I had recently invented the horseshoe and found myself in great demand.
Pshaw.
What do you know? Someone had to invent the horseshoe!
Mongrel.
Nincompoop.
So it was that I came to serve as a groom to a King. And a fine castle he had from the outside, powerful and impressive.
But inside, my dearies...
More meat!
Pleasure held court. A dance gone mad.
All things to excess. Music all day and night.
More drink!
Whoppiteeskoooo
The drains ran red with wine and the gutters ripe with rotting food.
YAHOOOOO!!!
BWAA-HAHAHA-HAAHAA
GULP GULP GULP
Imagine as I stepped into the court.
And marvele at the goings-on, th fancy-fine...

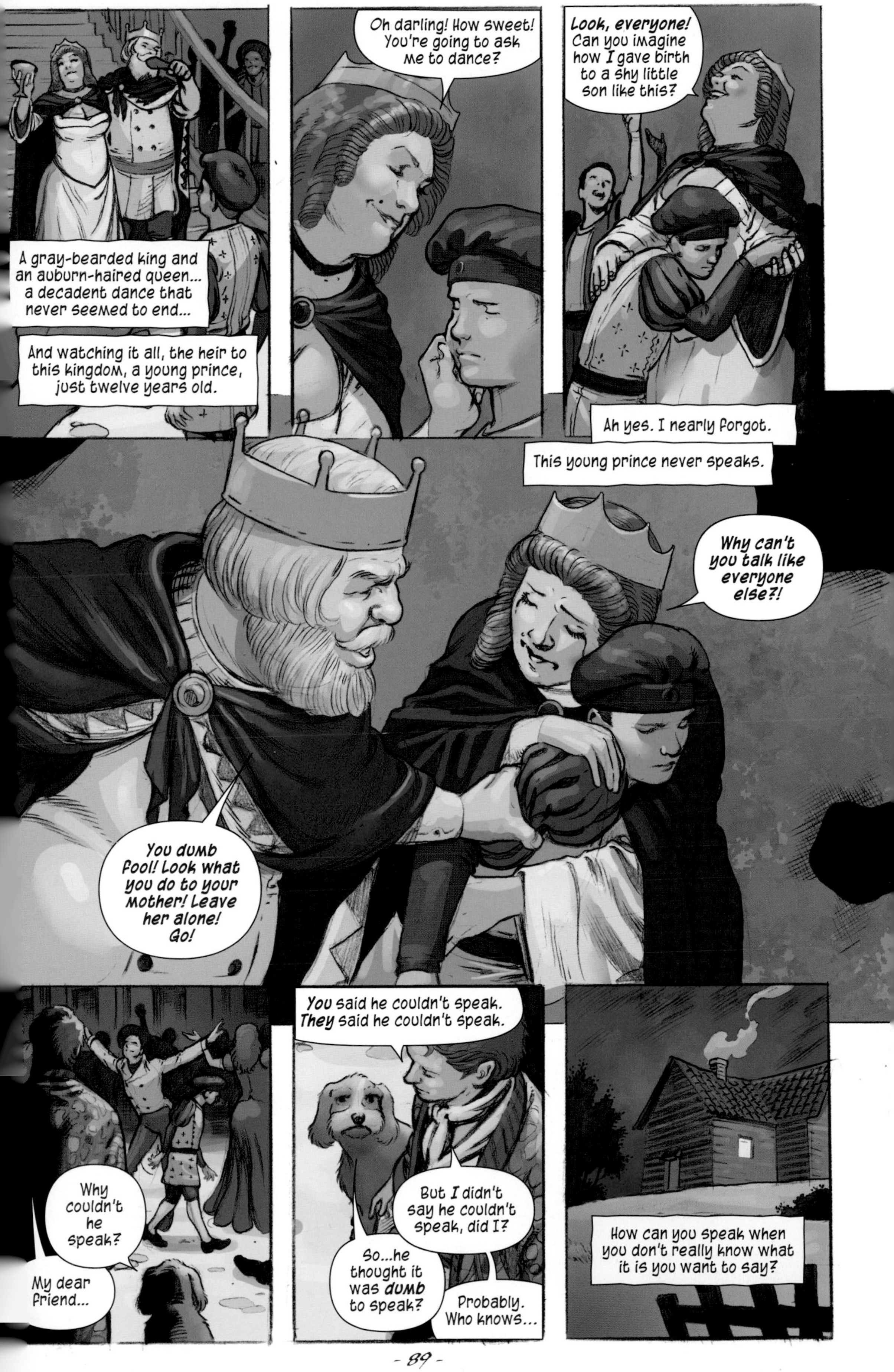
A gray-bearded king and an auburn-haired queen... a decadent dance that never seemed to end...
And watching it all, the heir to this kingdom, a young prince, just twelve years old.
Oh darling! How sweet! You're going to ask me to dance?
Look, everyone! Can you imagine how I gave birth to a shy little son like this?
Ah yes. I nearly forgot.
This young prince never speaks.
Why can't you talk like everyone else?!
You dumb fool! Look what you do to your mother! Leave her alone! Go!
Why couldn't he speak?
My dear friend...
You said he couldn't speak. They said he couldn't speak.
But I didn't say he couldn't speak, did I?
So...he thought it was dumb to speak?
Probably. Who knows...
How can you speak when you don't really know what it is you want to say?

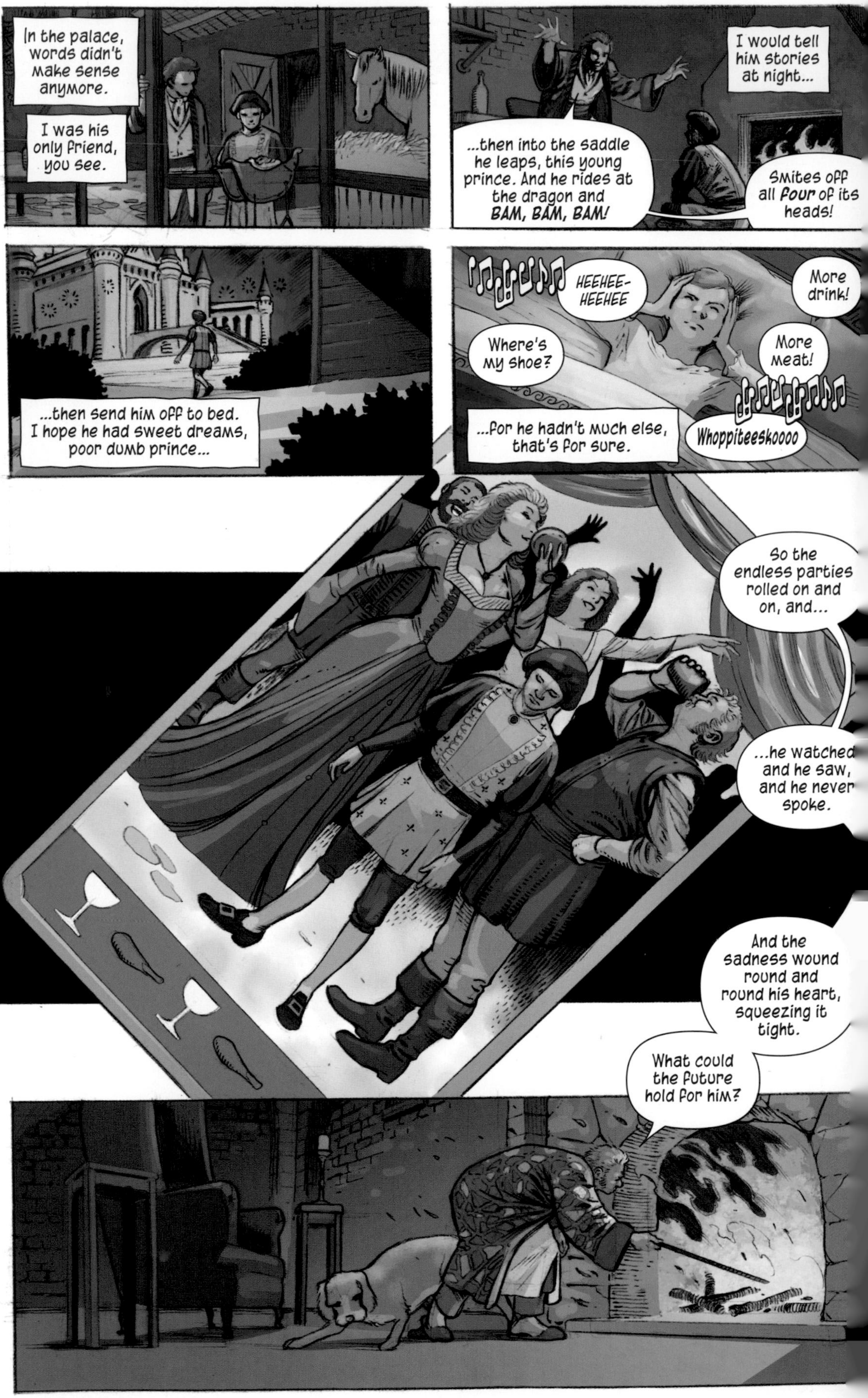
In the palace, words didn't make sense anymore.
I was his only friend, you see.
I would tell him stories at night...
...then into the saddle he leaps, this young prince. And he rides at the dragon and BAM, BAM, BAM!
Smites off all four of its heads!
...then send him off to bed. I hope he had sweet dreams, poor dumb prince...
HEEHEE-HEEHEE
More drink!
Where's my shoe?
More meat!
...for he hadn't much else, that's for sure.
Whoppiteeskoooo
So the endless parties rolled on and on, and...
...he watched and he saw, and he never spoke.
And the sadness wound round and round his heart, squeezing it tight.
What could the future hold for him?

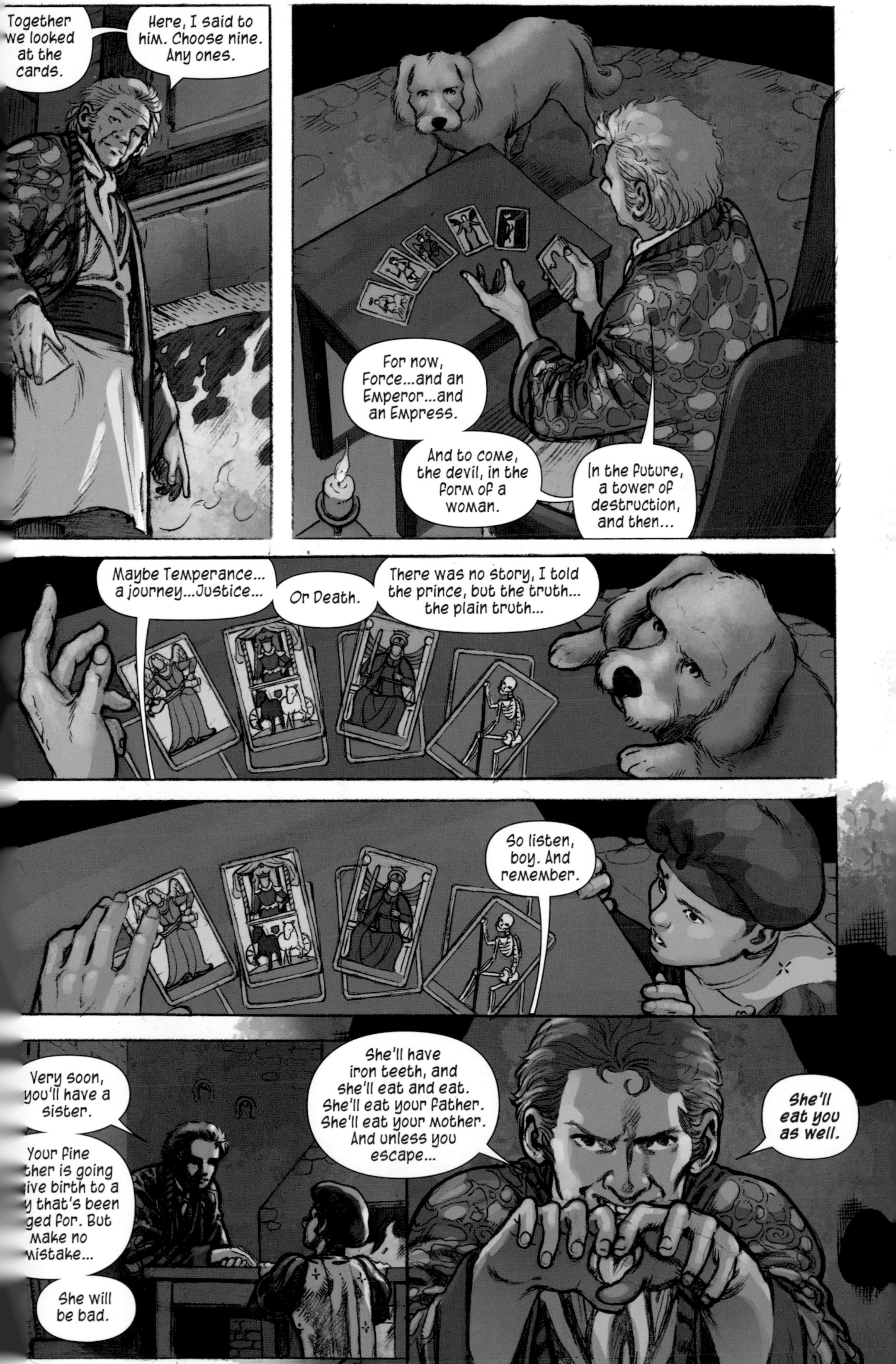
Together we looked at the cards.
Here, I said to him. Choose nine. Any ones.
For now, Force...and an Emperor...and an Empress.
And to come, the devil, in the form of a woman.
In the future, a tower of destruction, and then...
Maybe Temperance... a journey...Justice...
Or Death.
There was no story, I told the prince, but the truth... the plain truth...
So listen, boy. And remember.
Very soon, you'll have a sister.
Your fine
ther is going
ive birth to a
y that's been
ged for. But
make no
mistake...
She will be bad.
She'll have iron teeth, and she'll eat and eat. She'll eat your father. She'll eat your mother. And unless you escape...
She'll eat you as well.

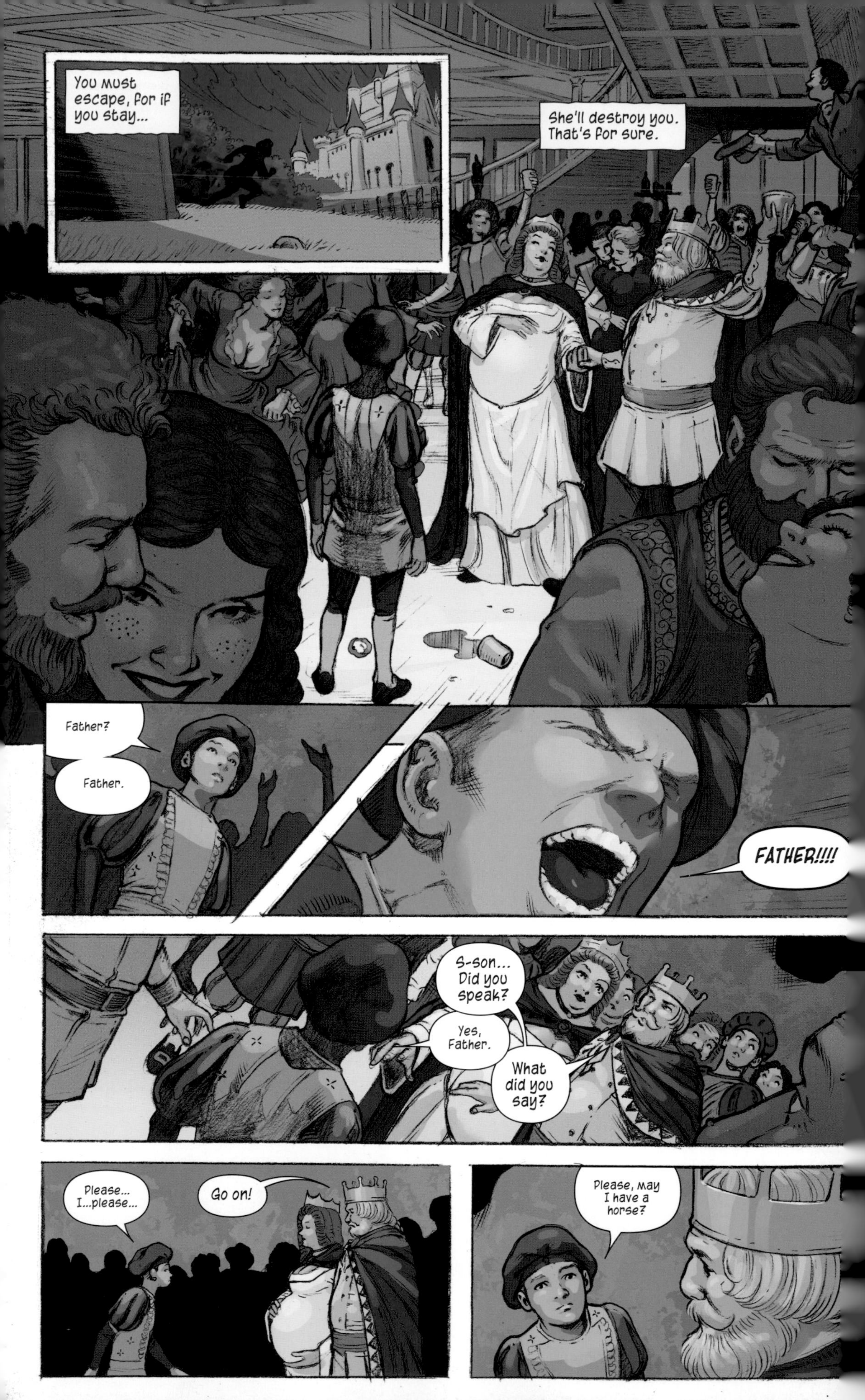

You must escape, for if you stay...
She'll destroy you. That's for sure.
Father?
Father.
FATHER!!!!
S-son... Did you speak?
Yes, Father.
What did you say?
Please... I...please...
Go on!
Please, may I have a horse?

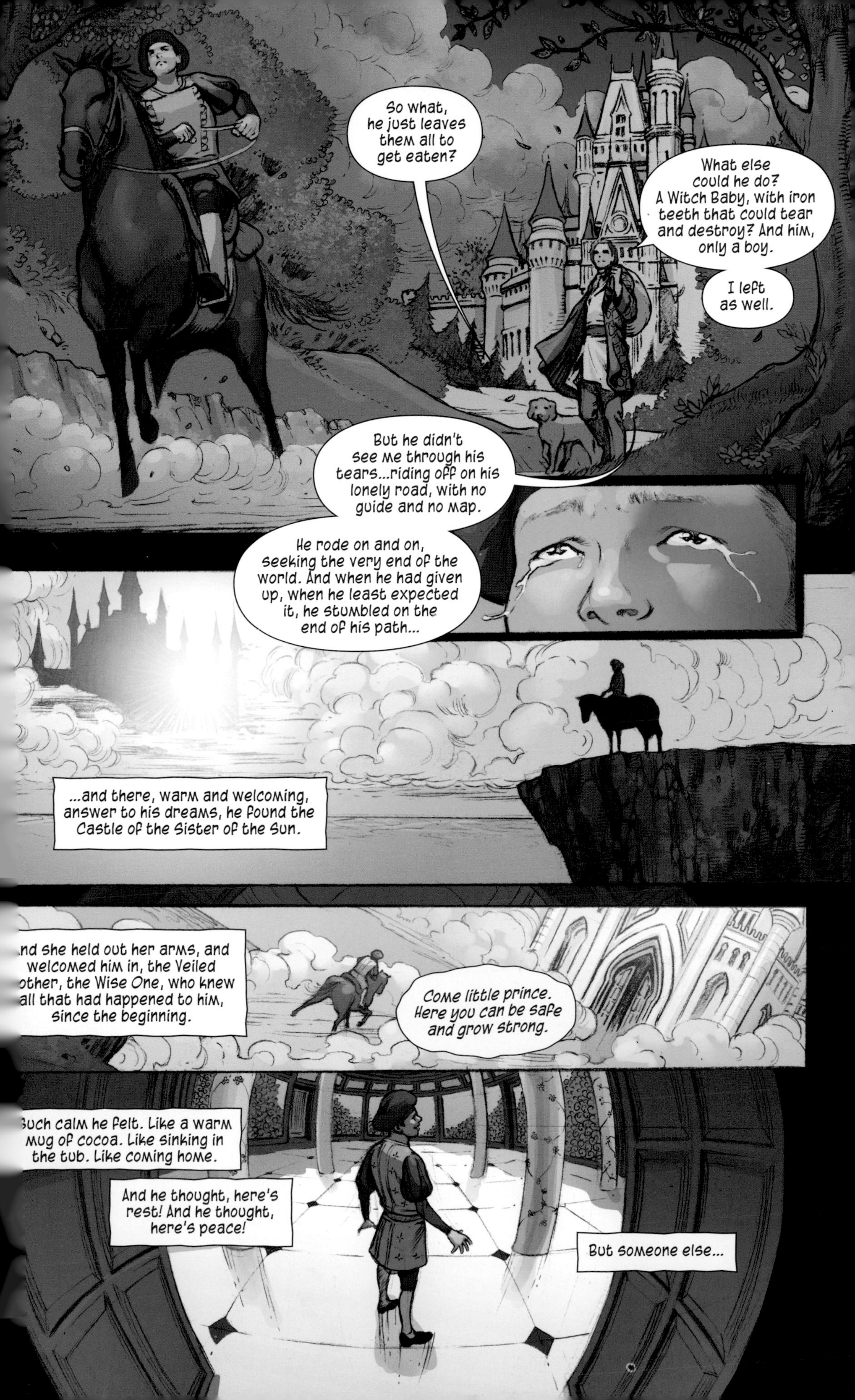
So what, he just leaves them all to get eaten?
What else could he do? A Witch Baby, with iron teeth that could tear and destroy? And him, only a boy.
I left as well.
But he didn't see me through his tears...riding off on his lonely road, with no guide and no map.
He rode on and on, seeking the very end of the world. And when he had given up, when he least expected it, he stumbled on the end of his path...
...and there, warm and welcoming, answer to his dreams, he found the Castle of the Sister of the Sun.
nd she held out her arms, and welcomed him in, the Veiled other, the Wise One, who knew all that had happened to him, since the beginning.
Come little prince. Here you can be safe and grow strong.
uch calm he felt. Like a warm mug of cocoa. Like sinking in the tub. Like coming home.
And he thought, here's rest! And he thought, here's peace!
But someone else...

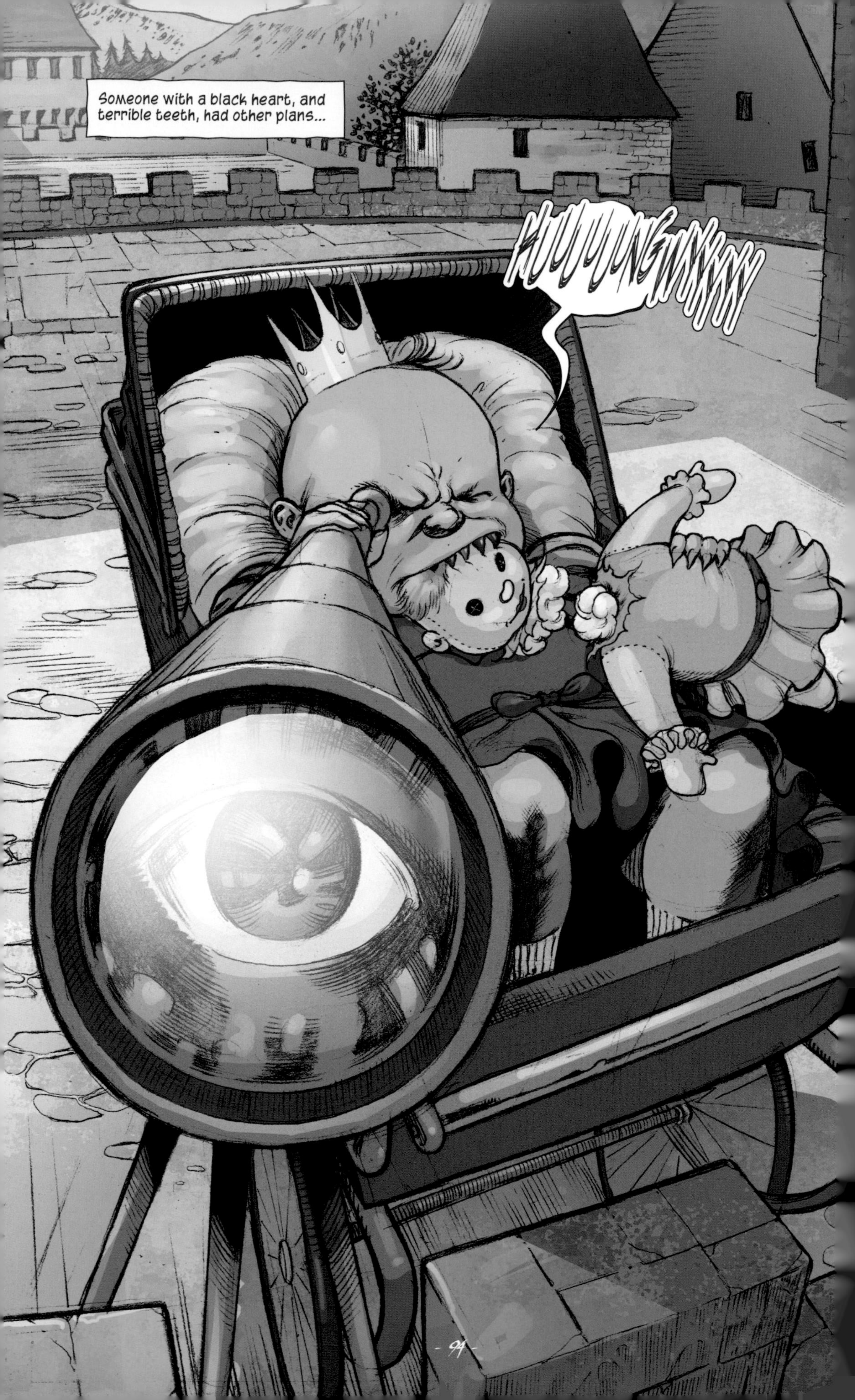
Someone with a black heart, and terrible teeth, had other plans...

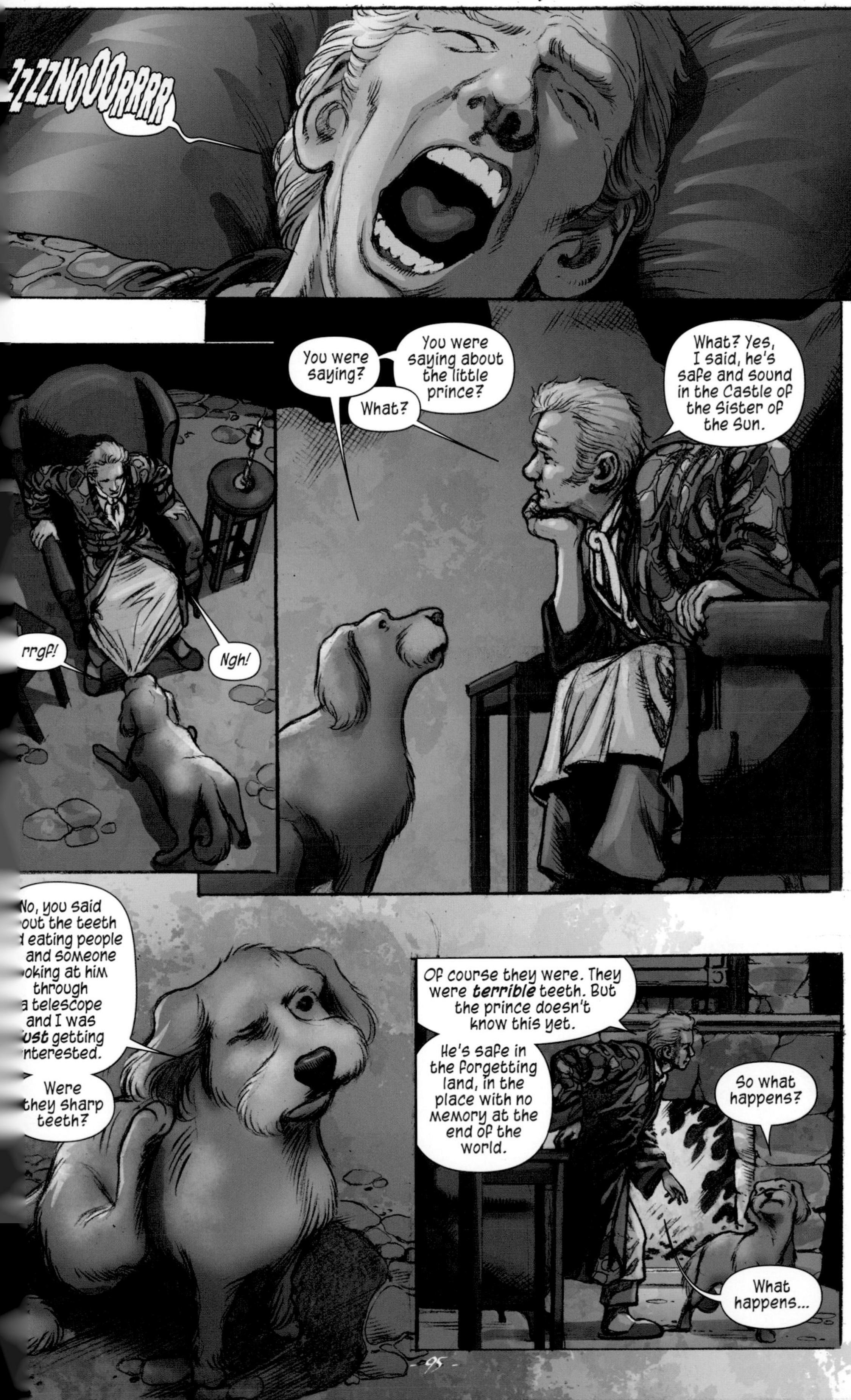
ZZZZNOOORRRR
You were saying?
You were saying about the little prince?
What?
What? Yes, I said, he's safe and sound in the Castle of the Sister of the Sun.
rrgf!
Ngh!
No, you said
out the teeth
eating people
and someone
oking at him
through
a telescope
and I was
ust getting
nterested.
Were
they sharp
teeth?
Of course they were. They were terrible teeth. But the prince doesn't know this yet.
He's safe in the forgetting land, in the place with no memory at the end of the world.
So what happens?
What happens...

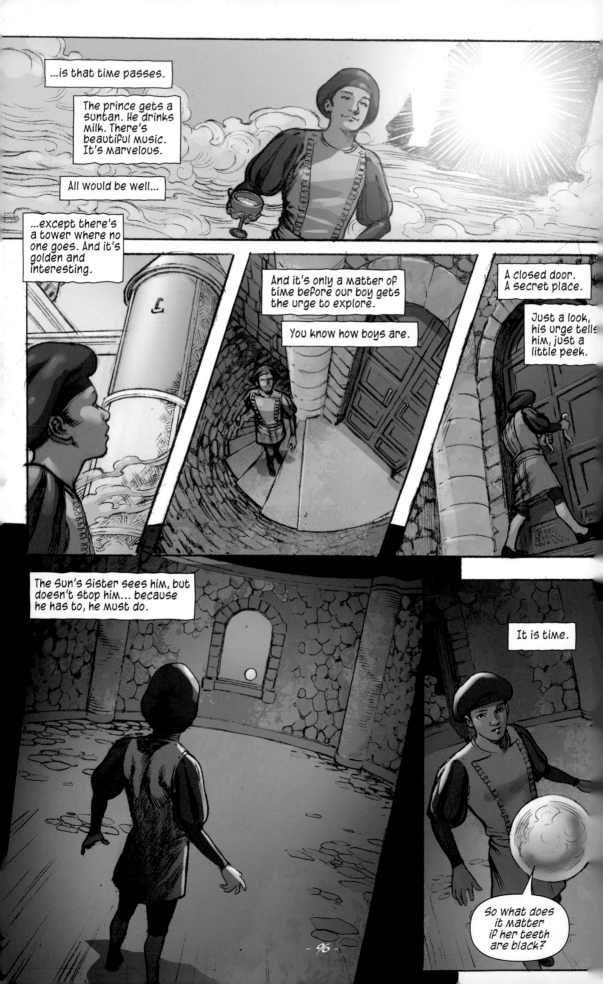

...is that time passes.

The prince gets a suntan. He drinks milk. There's beautiful music. It's marvelous.

All would be well...

...except there's a tower where no one goes. And it's golden and interesting.

And it's only a matter of time before our boy gets the urge to explore.

You know how boys are.

A closed door. A secret place.

Just a look, his urge tells him, just a little peek.

The Sun's Sister sees him, but doesn't stop him... because he has to, he must do.

It is time.

So what does it matter if her teeth are black?

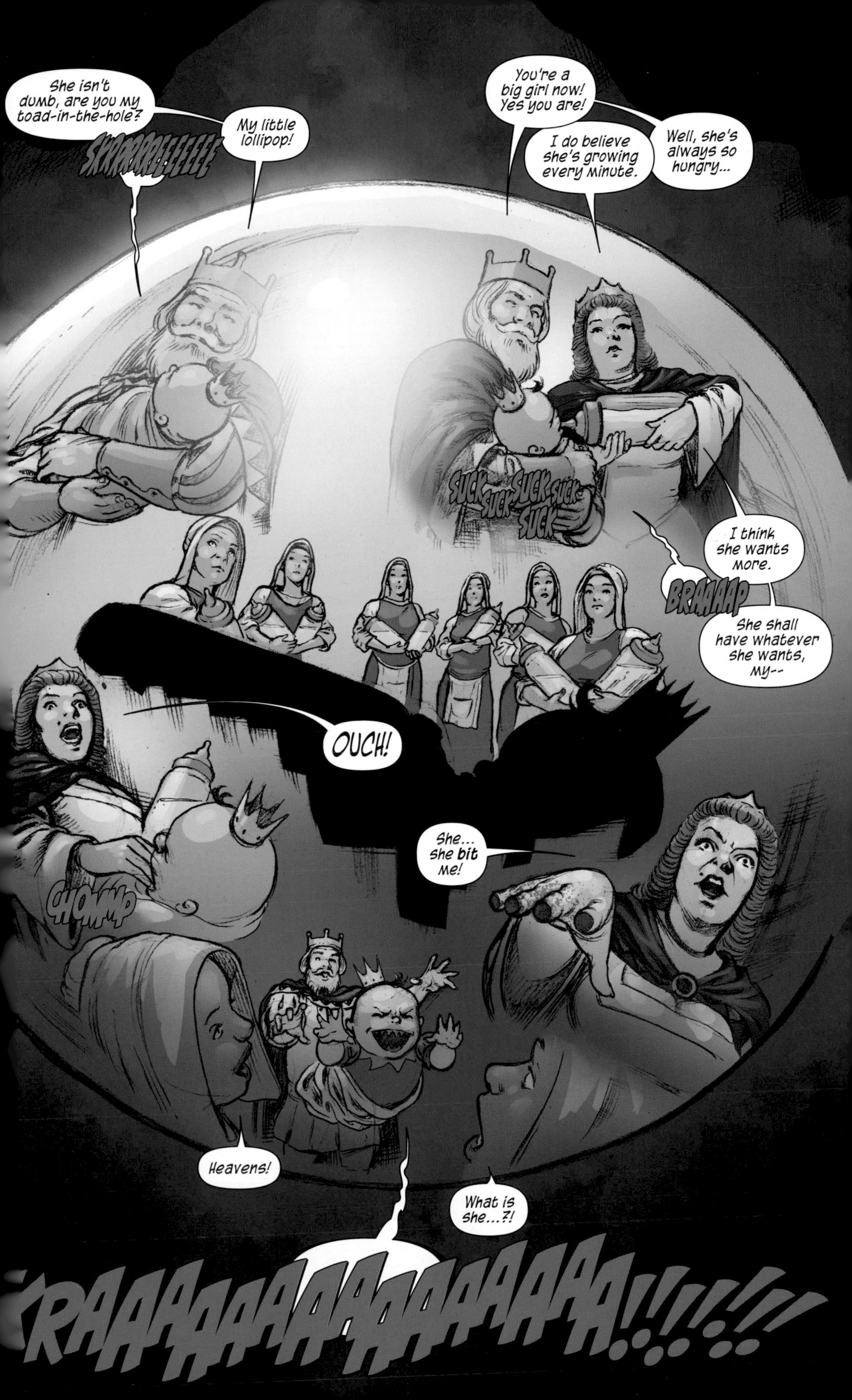
She isn't dumb, are you my toad-in-the-hole?
My little lollipop!
SKRRRREEEEEEEE
You're a big girl now! Yes you are!
I do believe she's growing every minute.
Well, she's always so hungry...
SUCK SUCK SUCK SUCK SUCK
I think she wants more.
BRAAAAP
She shall have whatever she wants, my--
OUCH!
She... she bit me!
CHOMMP
Heavens!
What is she...?!
RAAAAAAAAAAAAAAA!!!!!!

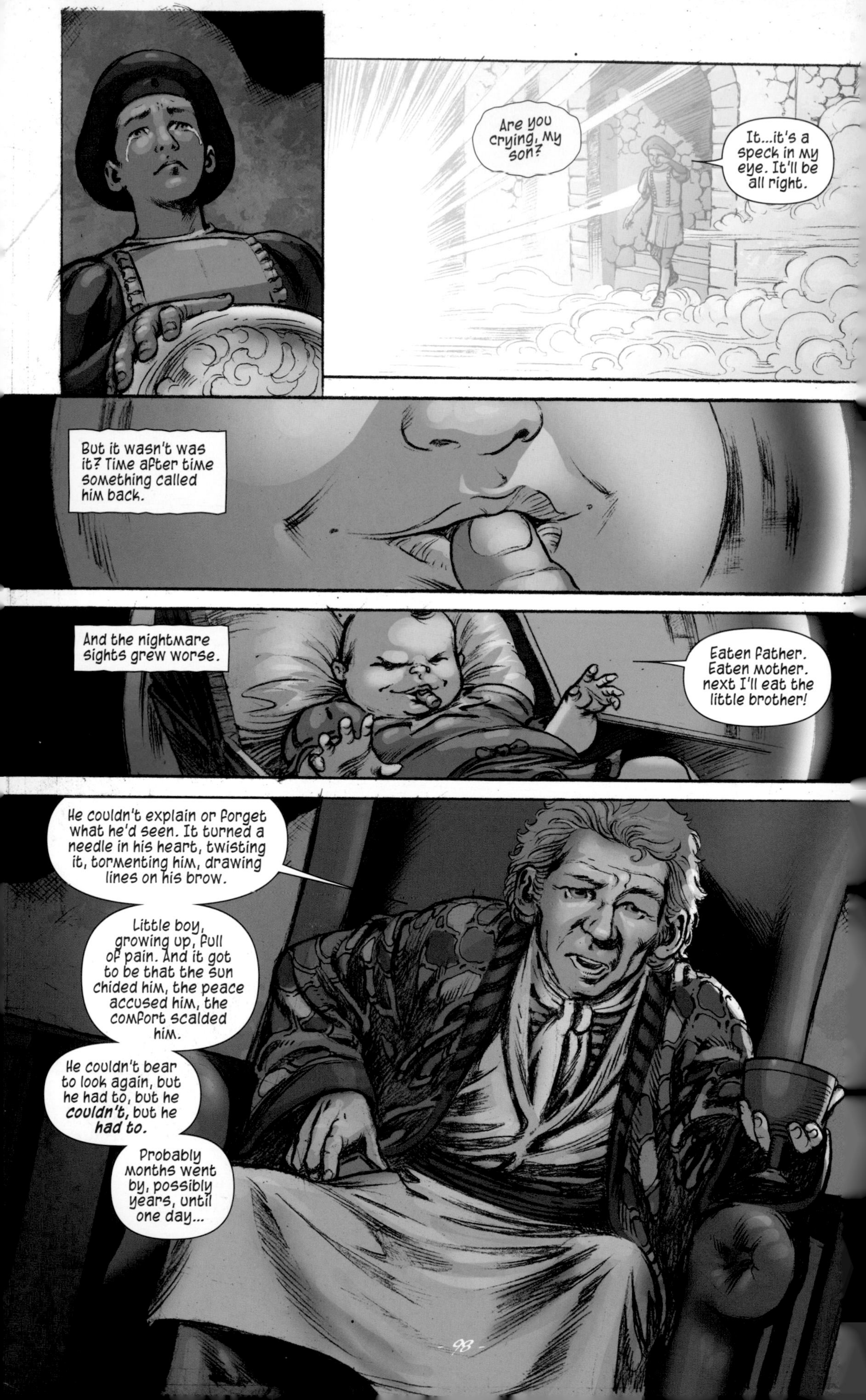
Are you crying, My son?
It...it's a speck in my eye. It'll be all right.
But it wasn't was it? Time after time something called him back.
And the nightmare sights grew worse.
Eaten father. Eaten mother. next I'll eat the little brother!
He couldn't explain or forget what he'd seen. It turned a needle in his heart, twisting it, tormenting him, drawing lines on his brow.
Little boy, growing up, full of pain. And it got to be that the sun chided him, the peace accused him, the comfort scalded him.
He couldn't bear to look again, but he had to, but he ***couldn't***, but he ***had to.***
Probably months went by, possibly years, until one day...

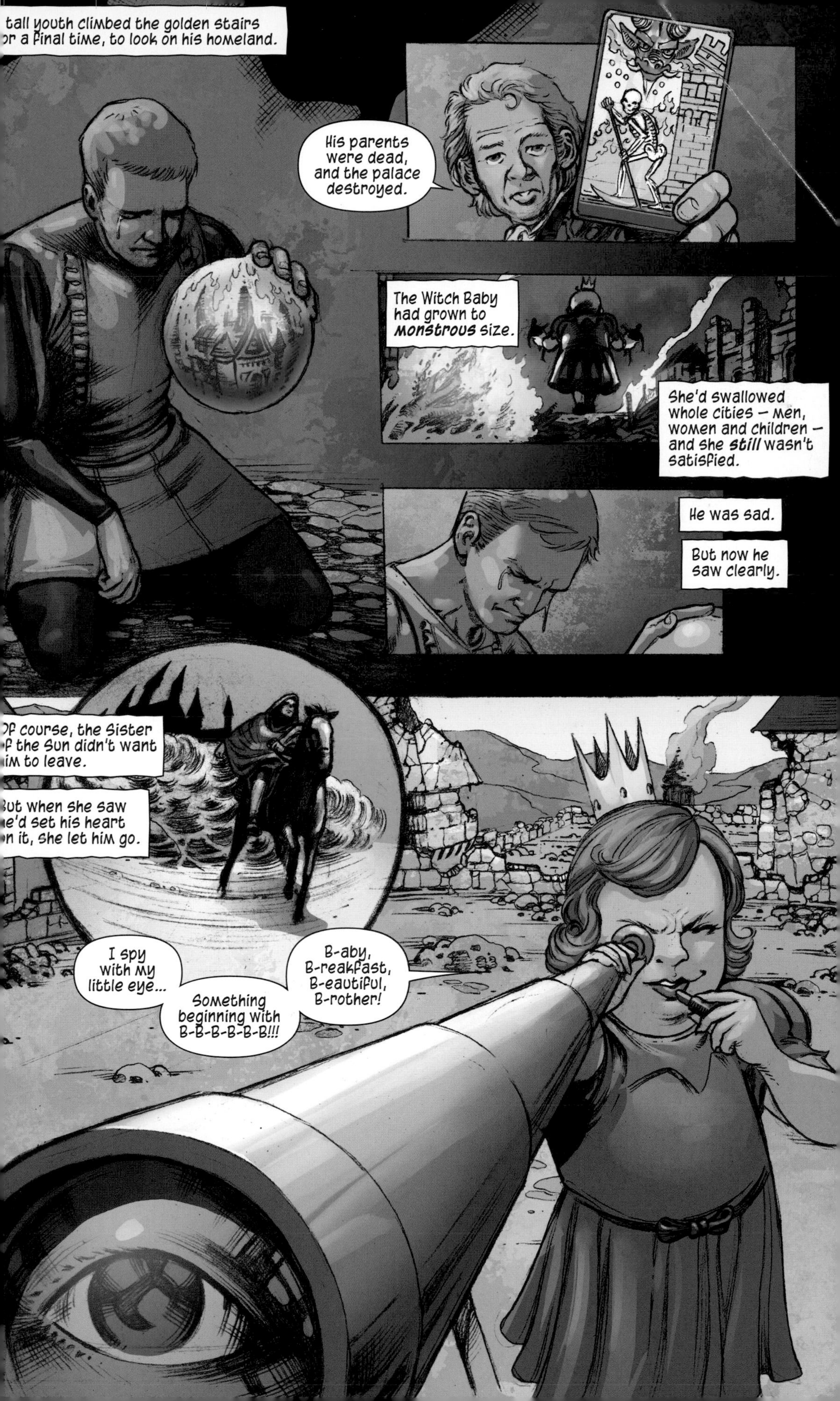

tall youth climbed the golden stairs
or a final time, to look on his homeland.
His parents were dead, and the palace destroyed.
The Witch Baby had grown to **monstrous** size.
She'd swallowed whole cities – men, women and children – and she ***still*** wasn't satisfied.
He was sad.
But now he saw clearly.
Of course, the Sister of the Sun didn't want him to leave.
But when she saw he'd set his heart on it, she let him go.
I spy with my little eye...
Something beginning with B-B-B-B-B-B!!!
B-aby, B-reakfast, B-eautiful, B-rother!

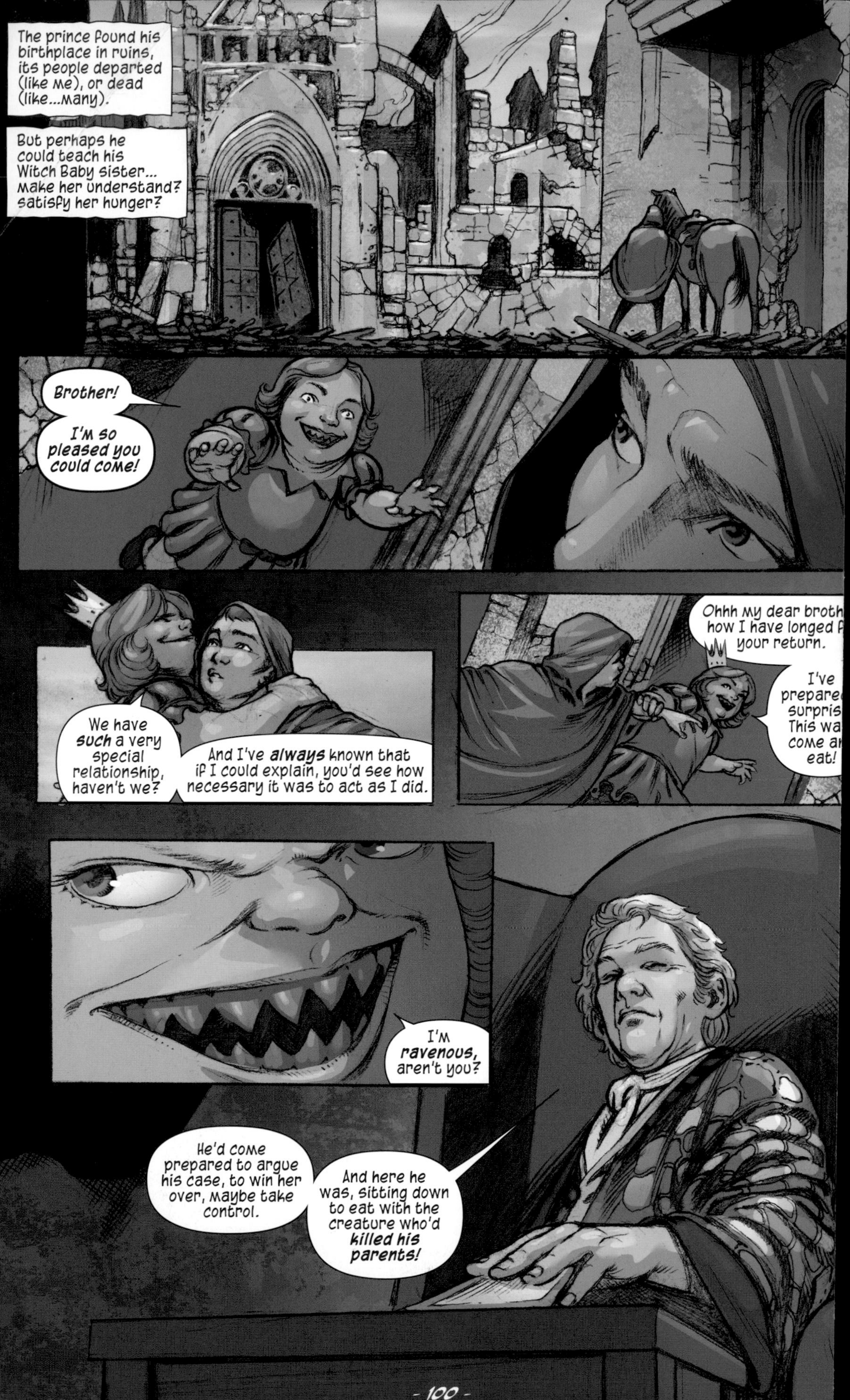

The prince found his birthplace in ruins, its people departed (like me), or dead (like...many).
But perhaps he could teach his Witch Baby sister... make her understand? satisfy her hunger?
Brother!
I'm so pleased you could come!
We have such a very special relationship, haven't we?
And I've always known that if I could explain, you'd see how necessary it was to act as I did.
Ohhh my dear broth how I have longed f your return.
I've prepare surpris This wa come a eat!
I'm ravenous, aren't you?
He'd come prepared to argue his case, to win her over, maybe take control.
And here he was, sitting down to eat with the creature who'd killed his parents!

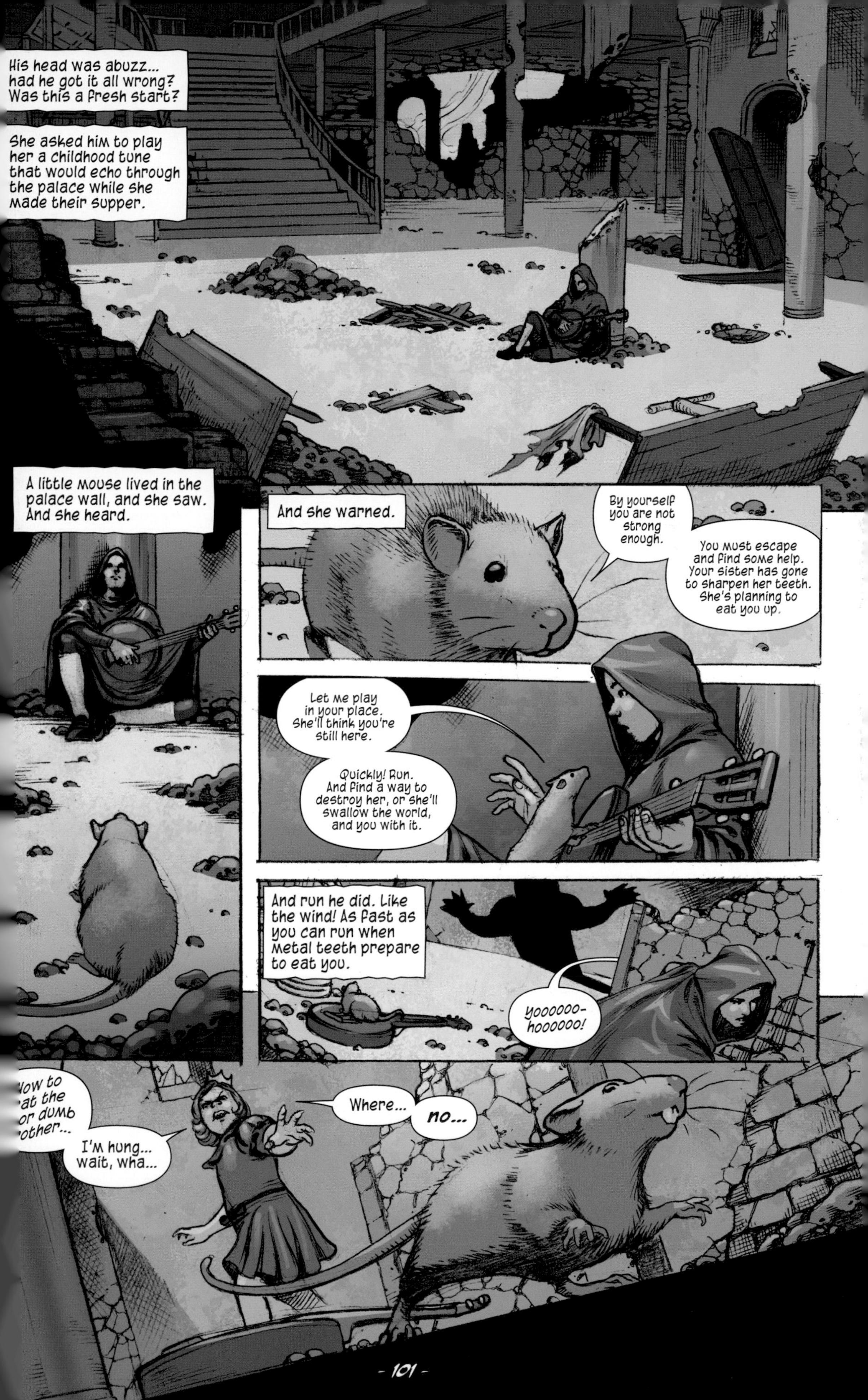

His head was abuzz... had he got it all wrong? Was this a fresh start?
She asked him to play her a childhood tune that would echo through the palace while she made their supper.
A little mouse lived in the palace wall, and she saw. And she heard.
And she warned.
By yourself you are not strong enough.
You must escape and find some help. Your sister has gone to sharpen her teeth. She's planning to eat you up.
Let me play in your place. She'll think you're still here.
Quickly! Run. And find a way to destroy her, or she'll swallow the world, and you with it.
And run he did. Like the wind! As fast as you can run when metal teeth prepare to eat you.
yoooooo-hoooooo!
I'm hung... wait, wha...
Where...
no...

GRRRAAAARGGHHHH...

SQUEEEAK

And the prince kept running.

His legs said stop, but he didn't.

Run! His heart said. Run and run! Until surely he was safe.

But looking back, he saw a thing, and listening--he heard a roar.

And he knew who it was, and he knew she came nearer, and he prayed for speed, and he prayed for help...

He saw the Witch Baby after him. Getting bigger.

And catching up.

The prince ran through forests, over rivers, up and down mountains. Faster than anyone had run before.

He thought the Witch Baby would never catch up.

But...

Did she?

C
Ye

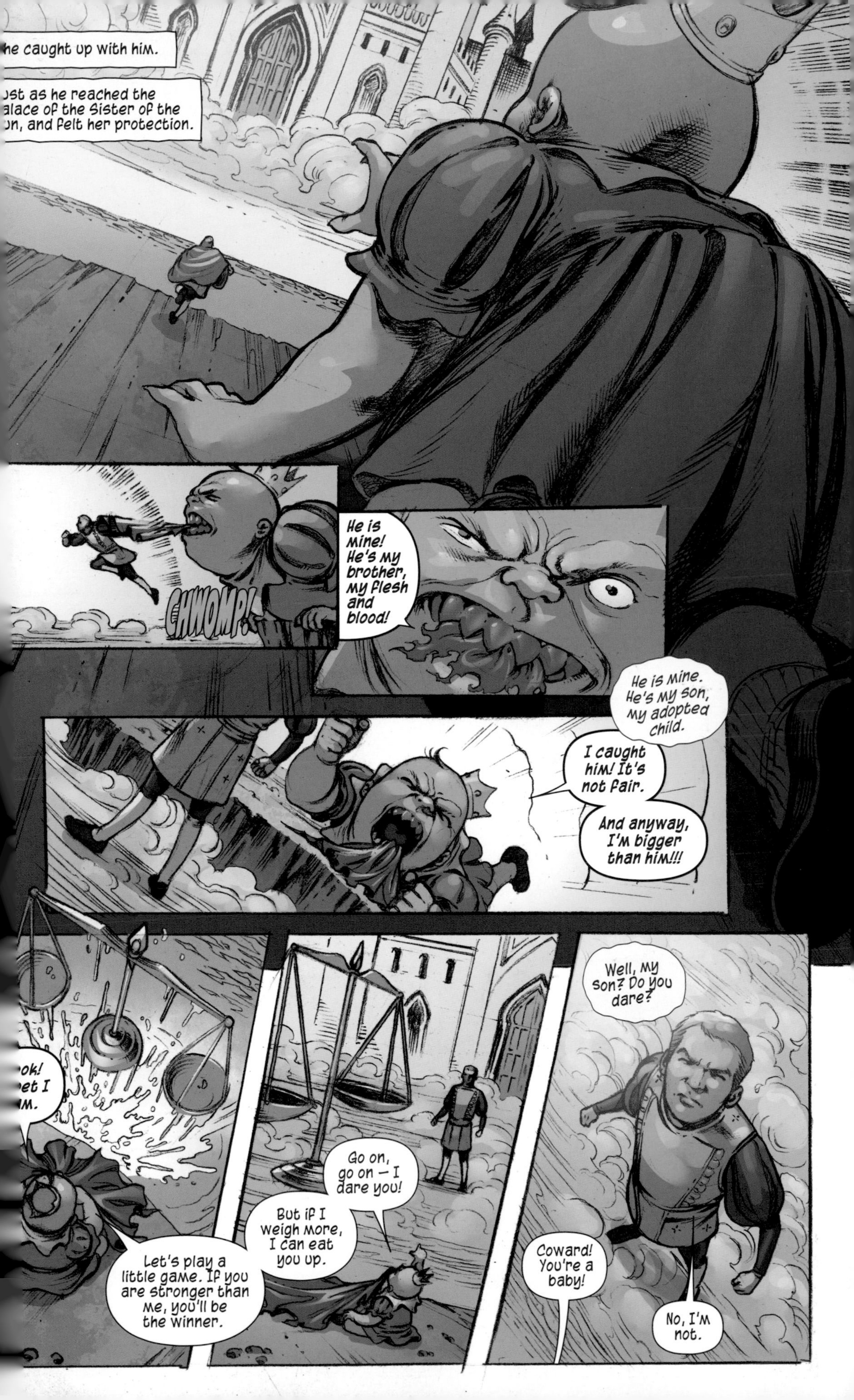
he caught up with him.
ust as he reached the alace of the Sister of the on, and felt her protection.
CHWOMP!
He is Mine! He's my brother, my flesh and blood!
He is Mine. He's my son, my adopted child.
I caught him! It's not fair.
And anyway, I'm bigger than him!!!
Let's play a little game. If you are stronger than me, you'll be the winner.
Go on, go on — I dare you!
But if I weigh more, I can eat you up.
Well, my son? Do you dare?
Coward! You're a baby!
No, I'm not.

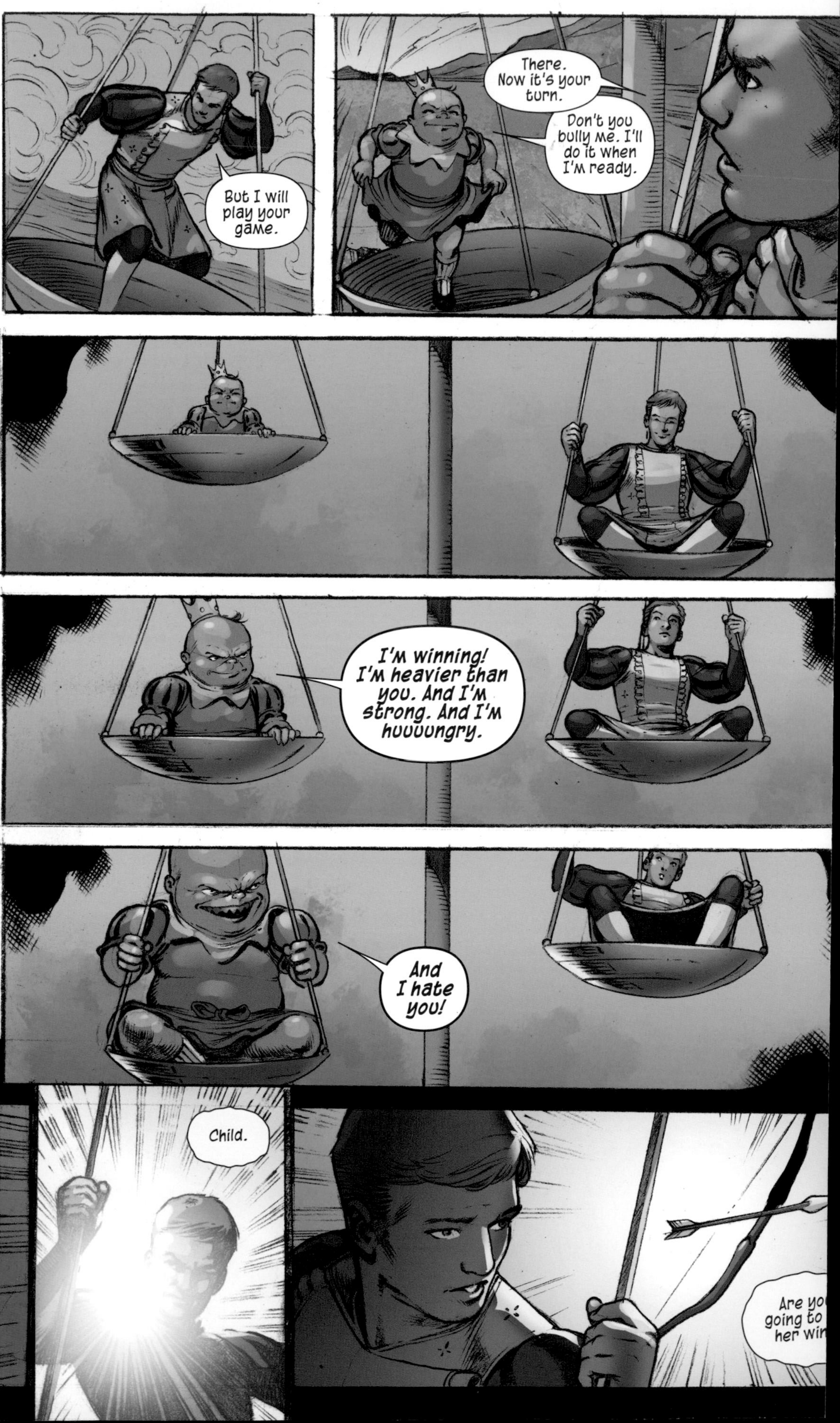
But I will play your game.
There. Now it's your turn.
Don't you bully me. I'll do it when I'm ready.
I'm winning! I'm heavier than you. And I'm strong. And I'm huuuungry.
And I hate you!
Child.

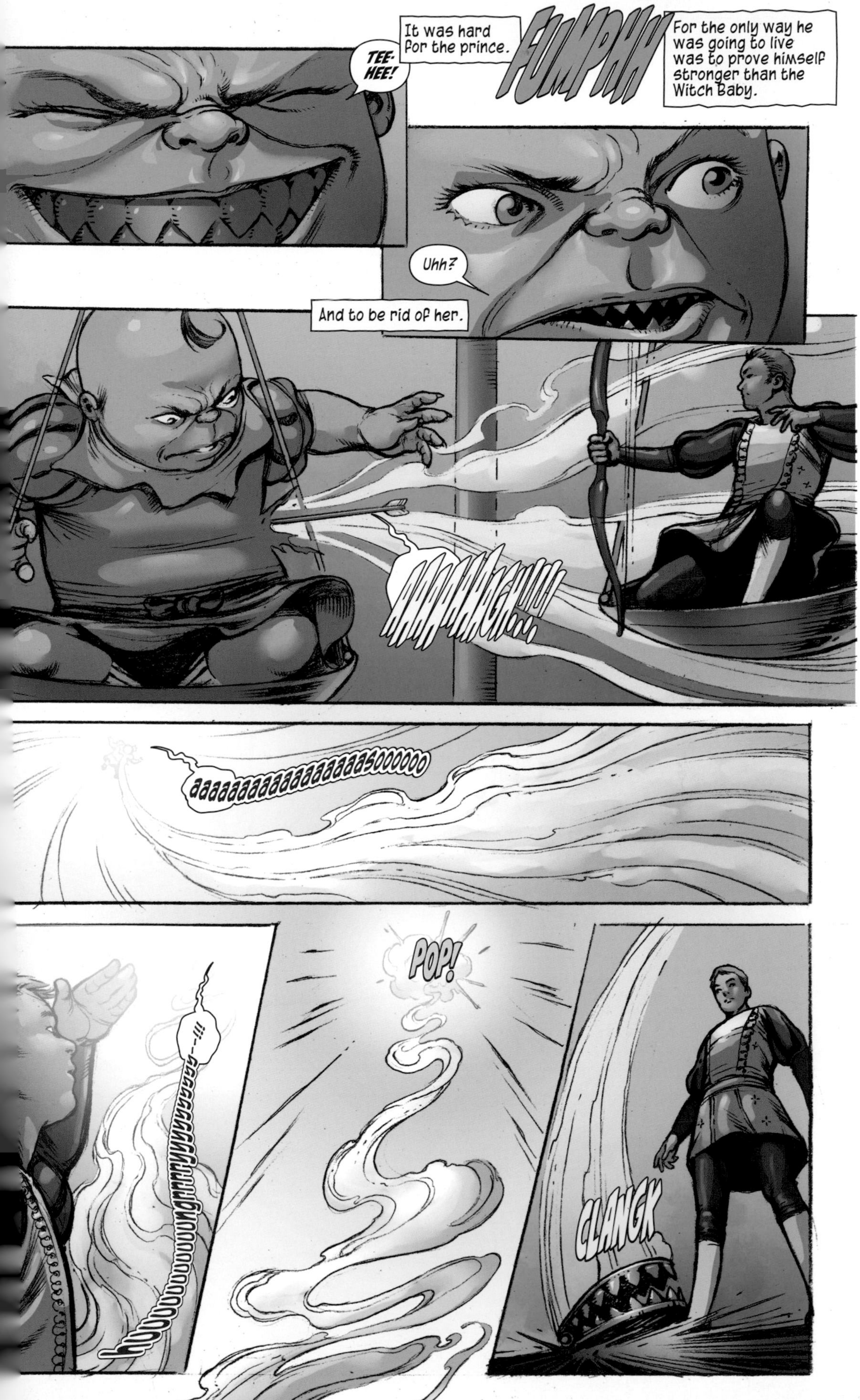
TEE-HEE!
It was hard for the prince.
FUMPHH
For the only way he was going to live was to prove himself stronger than the Witch Baby.
Uhh?
And to be rid of her.
AAAAAAAAGH!!!!
aaaaaaaaaaaaaaaaasoooooo
hoooooooooooouuuugghhhhhhAAAAAAAAAA--!!!
POP!
CLANGK

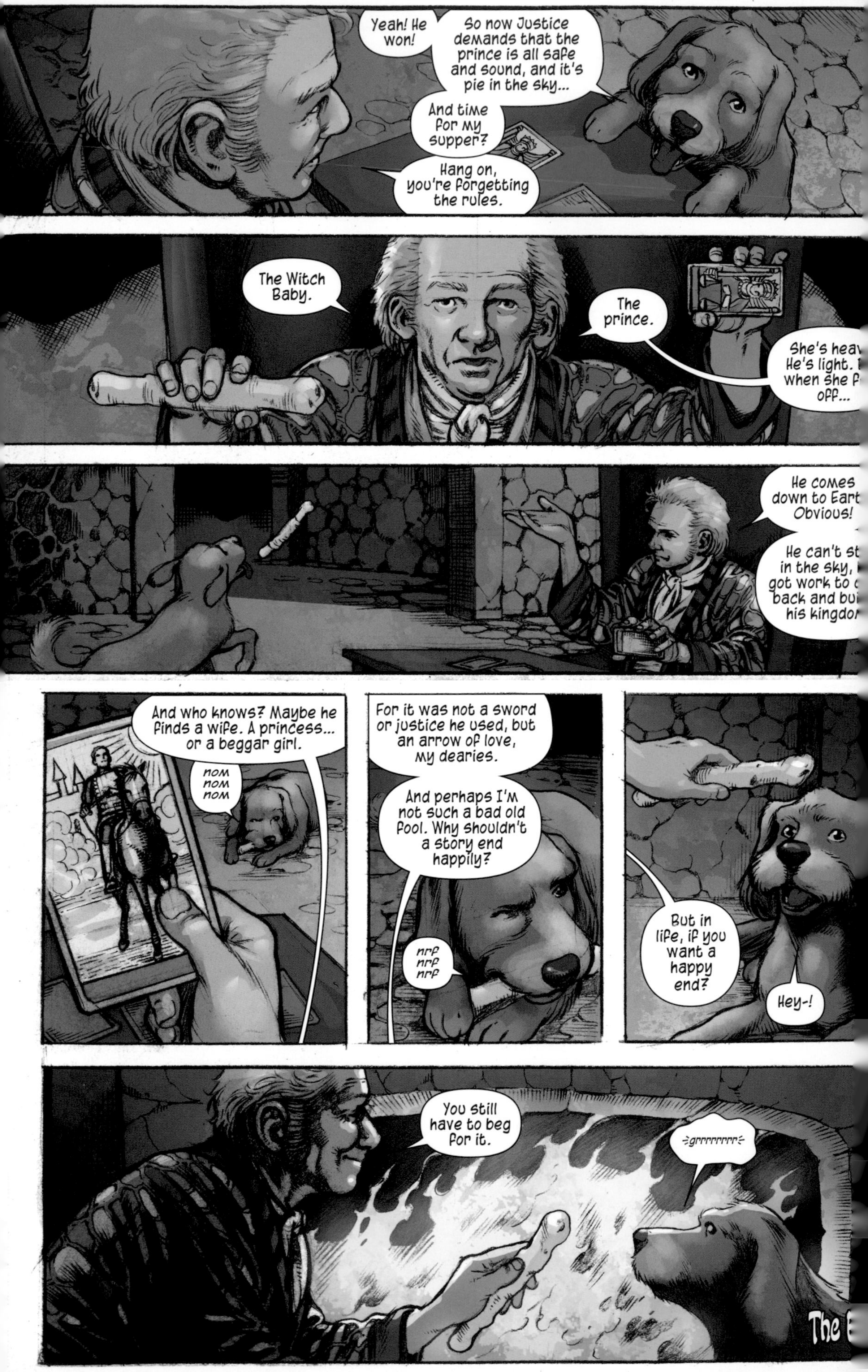
Yeah! He won!
So now Justice demands that the prince is all safe and sound, and it's pie in the sky...
And time for my supper?
Hang on, you're forgetting the rules.
The Witch Baby.
The prince.
She's heav He's light. when she f off...
He comes down to Eart Obvious!
He can't st in the sky, got work to back and bui his kingdo
And who knows? Maybe he finds a wife. A princess... or a beggar girl.
nom nom nom
For it was not a sword or justice he used, but an arrow of love, my dearies.
And perhaps I'm not such a bad old fool. Why shouldn't a story end happily?
nrf nrf nrf
But in life, if you want a happy end?
Hey-!
You still have to beg for it.
grrrrrrrr
The

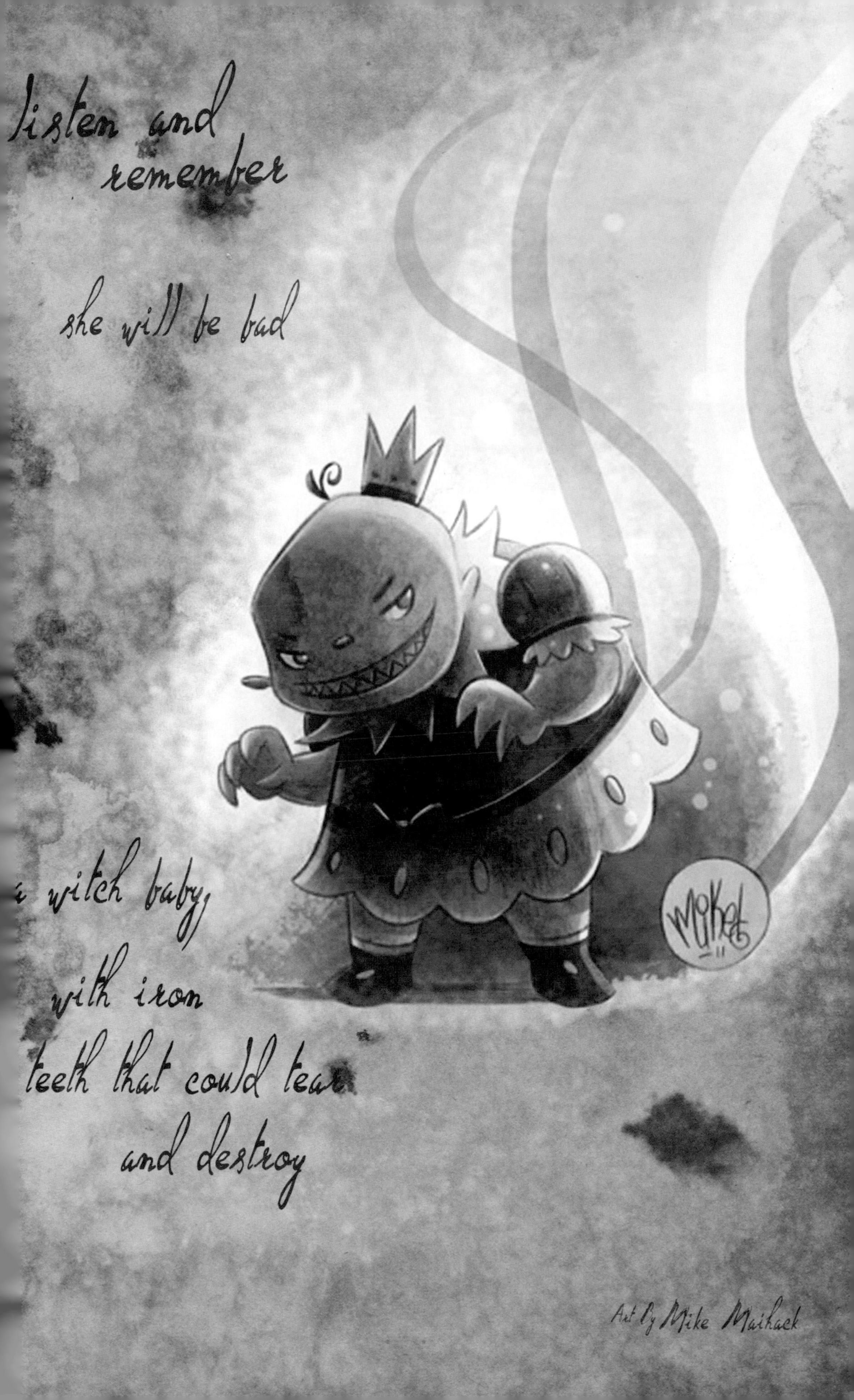
listen and remember
she will be bad
a witch baby,
with iron
teeth that could tear
and destroy
Art by Mike Maihack

A final few
wisps of
wisdom...

The sands of time slide through the hourglass, and with their passage comes new ways of telling stories, to those in front of your eyes or persons a world away! My time is not infinite, nor is yours. But our stories live on, long after we become the dust beneath the feet of our children's children's children's children's children's children's children. Tell your tales, keep adding chapters! And feel free to share the ones I've told to you. Don't worry, the stories are not mine. I'm just their teller.

The Storyteller

The StoryTellers...

Roger Langridge has been producing comics for over twenty years. Most recently, he has attracted critical attention for his work on Snarked!, the Harvey Award-winning *Muppet Show Comic Book* (both for Boom! Studios) and *Thor: The Mighty Avenger* (Marvel Comics); other works of note include Marvel's *Fin Fang Four*, Fantagraphics' *Zoot!* and *Art d'Ecco* (in collaboration with his brother Andrew), and the NCS, Ignatz, Eisner and Harvey Award-nominated comic book *Fred the Clown*. He currently lives in London with his wife Sylvie, their two children and a box of his own hair.

Colleen Coover is a comic book artist and illustrator living in Portland, Oregon. She is the creator of the adult comic *Small Favors,* and artist of the all-ages comedy *Banana Sunday,* the latter written by her husband Paul Tobin. The couple's most recent collaboration is the graphic novel *Gingerbread Girl,* published by Top Shelf Productions. She has worked for Marvel Comics, DC Comics, Dark Horse, Oni Press, Fantagraphics, and many others. She spends most of her time thinking up ways for comics to be more awesome.

Chris Eliopoulos started working in comics two weeks after he began his internship at Marvel. He began freelancing production work until he was hired on staff and worked all the way up to senior letterer before going freelance. He's lettered more books than he can even remember for Marvel, DC, Image and many other publishers and along the way wrote and drew *Franklin Richards: Son of a Genius* and wrote *Lockjaw and the Pet Avengers* for Marvel. Currently, he's co-creator with Nate Cosby on *Cow Boy*, a series being published for Archaia. Eliopoulos lives in New Jersey with his wife and twin boys.

Jeff Parker began his comics career as an artist for Malibu and DC Comics, and continued that path to animation on Sony's *The Big Guy and Rusty the Boy Robot.* After storyboarding for commercials and music videos, Jeff brought out his graphic novel adventure, *The Interman,* to much acclaim, and from there transitioned into writing. For Marvel he's written *X-Men First Class, Agents of Atlas, Hulk* and *Thunderbolts,* and created *Mysterius the Unfathomable* at Wildstorm. Parker lives in Portland, Oregon and is a member of Periscope Studio.

Cartoonist and illustrator **Tom Fowler** has worked in comics, advertising, and film and game design for such varied clients as Disney, Hasbro, MAD, DC Comics, and Marvel. He is best known for his work on the feature strip *Monroe* for *MAD Magazine*, and his critically acclaimed series *Mysterius the Unfathomable* with writer Jeff Parker. Most recently his work can be seen in the Marvel comic *Venom*. Tom lives and works in Ottawa, Canada with his wife Monique, their son Graham, and a dog named Zool. His wife named the dog. (For which he is very proud of her.)

Marjorie M. Liu is an attorney and New York Times bestselling author of paranormal romances and urban fantasy. In the world of comic books, she is also the writer of *NYX: No Way Home, Black Widow, X-23,* and *Dark Wolverine.* She lives in the American Midwest and Beijing, China. For more information, please visit her website at www.marjoriemliu.com or follow her on twitter @marjoriemliu.

Jennifer L. Meyer is an illustrator (& a fan of bunnies) working in the fantasy, children's, and product illustration markets. A young Chewbacca was the focus of her most recent comic work. You can find more about her work at www.jennifer-meyer.com and catch her on twitter @JenniferLMeyer.

Paul Tobin has been active in comics for almost two decades, writing a broad spectrum of material in genres from cyberpunk, to humor, to superheroes. Paul teamed with his wife, illustrator Colleen Coover, on *Banana Sunday,* which placed on YALSA's best graphic novels for teens, and has gone on to write hundreds of Marvel Comics starring Spider-Man, the Avengers, Hulk and many others. Paul is active with such media comics as Predators, and establishing comic book backstory for the *Falling Skies* television series. Paul lives in Portland, Oregon, where he likes to write in parks and is bald.

Evan Shaner is a prolific artist, constantly being commissioned to draw images of Captain Marvel. He has worked on Oni Press' *JAM! Tales from the World of Roller Derby* and is a member of the sketchgroup Comic Twart. He is the artist of the upcoming *Buddy Cops* for Dark Horse Presents. He lives in Denver, Colorado with his wife and daughter.

Katie Cook is a comic artist and writer. Katie is best known for her all-ages work in the Star Wars universe, but she's also done work for Marvel and *Fraggle Rock!* She also does her own weekly webcomic called *Gronk: A Monster's Story,* which she is told some people read on occasion. Her alignment is chaotic good and she lives in Ann Arbor, Michigan with her very tolerant husband, her daughter, her horde of cats (and a dog). Her delightful website is www.katiecandraw.com

Ron Marz has been writing comics for two decades, starting his career with a lengthy run on *Silver Surfer* for Marvel. Since then, he has worked for virtually every major publisher and compiled a long list of credits, including stints on *Green Lantern* for DC, *Star Wars* for Dark Horse, *Witchblade* for Top Cow, and as a staff writer for CrossGen Comics. His most recent work includes *Magdalena* and *Artifacts* for Top Cow, and *Voodoo* for the relaunch of the DC Universe. His creator-owned series include *Shinku* for Image; *Dragon Prince* for Top Cow; and *Samurai: Heaven and Earth*, and *Pantheon City* for Dark Horse. He lives in New York State, with his wife, three children, two dogs and four horses. But the horses live in the barn.

Craig Rousseau has been drawing comics for about 15 years. He's worked for DC (*Impulse, Batman Beyond*), Disney Adventures (*Kim Possible*), Image (Beckett's *The Cobler's Monster, Ronin Hood* and *47 Samurai*) Dark Horse (the creator-owned *The Perhapanauts,* currently at Image), Marvel (*Spider-Man Loves Mary Jane, Iron Man: The Armor Wars, HER-oes, Captain America: The Korvac Saga*) and is currently doing storybook work for Disney Press while enjoying the weather in New England.

Nate Cosby is a freelance writer/editor from Mississippi. He was an editor at Marvel Entertainment for six years, overseeing acclaimed series including the Eisner-Award winning *The Wonderful Wizard of Oz* and *The Marvelous Land of Oz,* as well as *Spider-Man, X-Men First Class, Thor the Mighty Avenger, Hulk,* and many others. Nate's a producer/writer for PBS' relaunched *The Electric Company,* where he's developed several animated properties (such as Captain Cluck). He's writing the upcoming *Cow Boy* for Archaia Entertainment, *Buddy Cops* for Dark Horse Entertainment, editing *Immortals: Gods & Heroes* (based on the upcoming film from Relativity Media) for Archaia and co-writes *Pigs* with Ben McCool for Image Comics. Nate lives in Colorado and needs more coffee. Follow him on Twitter @NateCosBOOM.

Ronan Cliquet was born in 1989 in Brazil. He started work in the US Comics Market when he was 17 years old, and the book in question was *Friendly Neighborhood Spider-Man Annual* #1 for Marvel Comics. From that point on Ronan did a myriad of titles for Marvel such as *Marvel Adventures Fantastic Four, Wolverine First Class,* and many issues of *Marvel Adventures Super Heroes.* Ronan lives in São Paulo, Brazil, where he also teaches art at Quanta Academia de Artes.

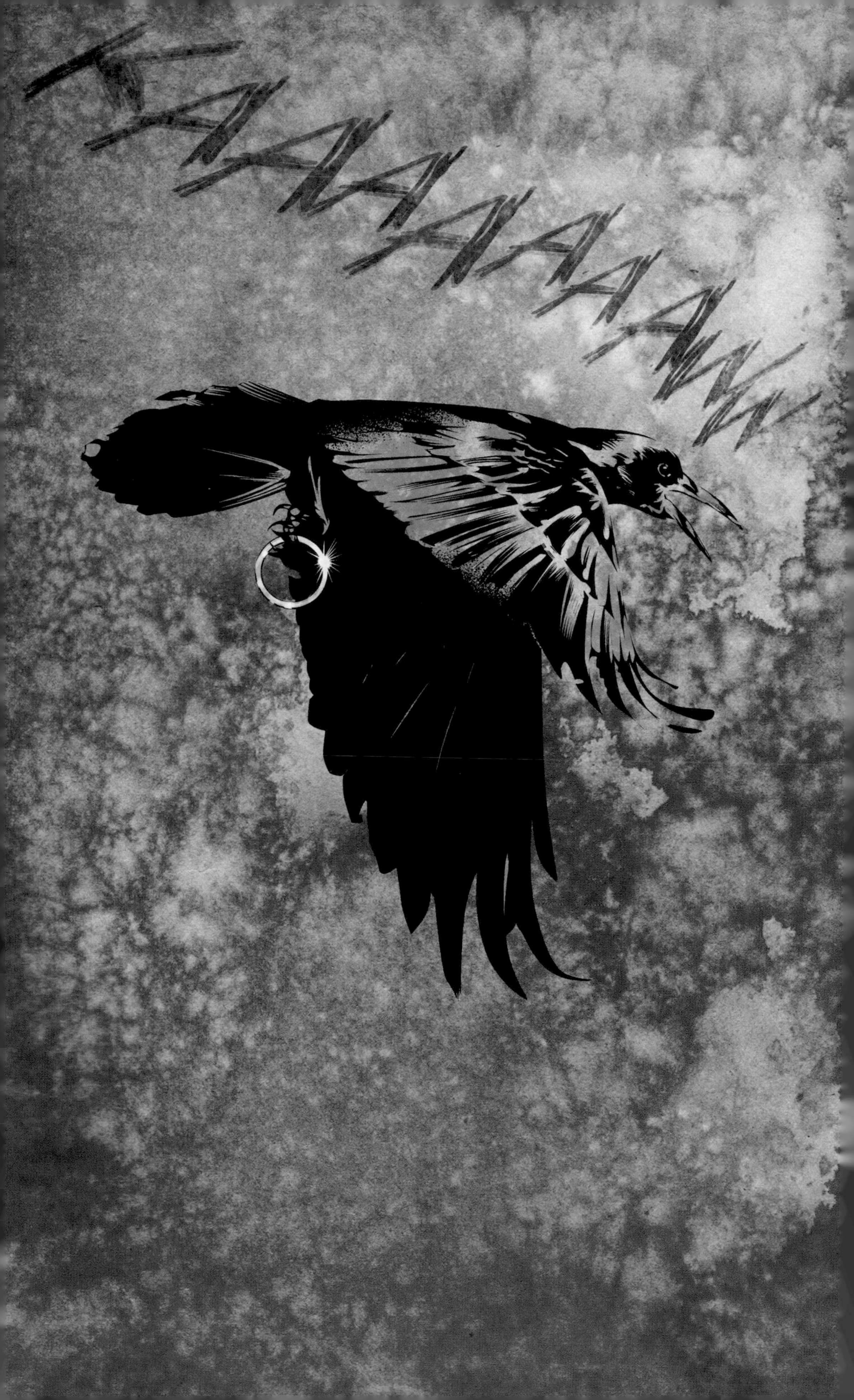
KAAAAAAAWW

When people told
themselves their past
with stories, explained
their present with stories,
foretold the future with
stories, The best place
by the fire was kept for...

THE STORYTELLER ™

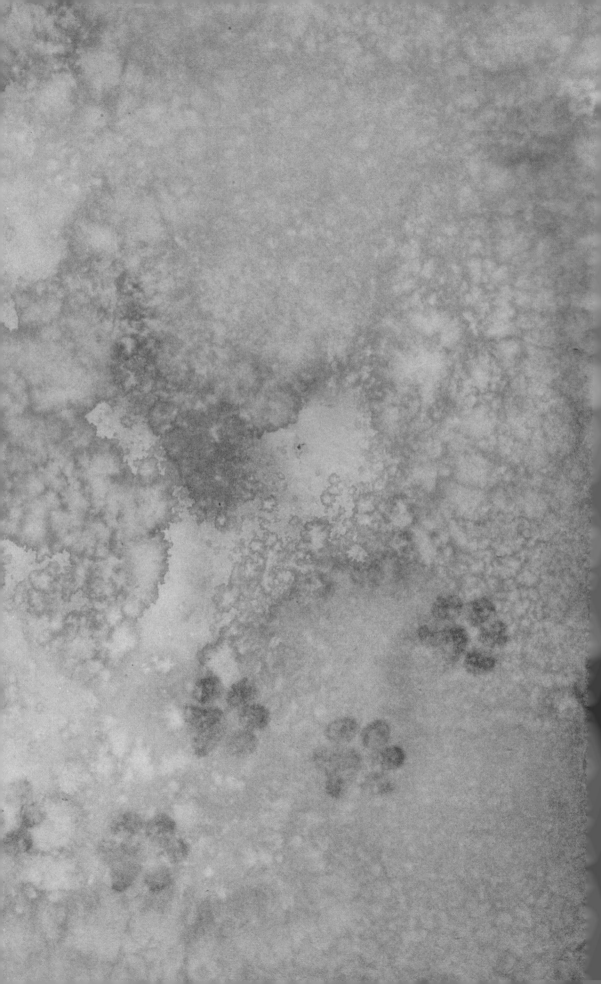